A LIFE
CONSIDERED

A LIFE
CONSIDERED

CRAIG BRESTRUP

Camino Bay Books
Gualala, CA 95445

Book design and publishing services:
Constance King Design

Back cover, author photo:
Merri Lu Park

Other books by Craig Brestrup

Reverence for Existence: A Way of Knowing
Disposable Animals: The Harms We Inflict & How We Stop

Camino Bay Books
Box 9
Gualala, CA 95445
info@caminobaybooks.com
800-463-8181

ISBN: 978-0-9657285-2-2
Printed in USA

*I went to the woods because I wished to live
deliberately, to front only the essential facts of life,
and see if I could not learn what it had to teach,
and not, when I came to die, discover that
I had not lived. I did not wish to live what was
not life, living is so dear...*

Thoreau, *Walden*

*So if you compliment me on being wise—and I
wish I were worthy of that estimate...—in this way
alone do I deserve it: I follow nature as the best
guide and obey her like a god. Since she has carefully planned the other parts of the drama of life,
it's unlikely that she would be a bad
playwright and neglect the final act.*

Cicero, *How to Grow Old*

CONTENTS

A SHORT LIFE STORY

ESSAYS

NATURE'S WAYS

ETHICS PERSPECTIVES

AMERICA'S WAYS

A
SHORT
LIFE
STORY

How the
Story Began

AS I BEGIN TO WRITE, I've just turned seventy-three—not enough years to qualify as *old,* says my wife, but certainly drifting into its territory, says my body. I was recently diagnosed with atrial fibrillation, a heart condition that may or may not reduce my life expectancy or life quality but will affect aspects of how I live during the years to come. I mention this only to help place myself at this present stage of life. I have no interest in writing an inspirational piece about illness or dying. It wouldn't be appropriate, since, although aging, I'm neither sick nor dying, and I would lack interest in such a project even if I were. The heart dysfunction is a fact of life, unwelcome but not a tragedy, and of no relevance to what I have to say. My age is not a preoccupying concern in itself. It is relevant as an indicator of the duration of my existence, the time I've had to observe and reflect on a longish life and the times and country I have inhabited.

My mother is ninety-five years old. I speak with her of aging as progress toward graduation. This term seems to console her because she is a Christian lady, so death and promotion to heaven are much on her mind. On only one occasion have I ever heard her reflect on her life. It was recent and brief, like a thought that had escaped its corral. She was saddened by something and feeling her years and wondering if she would have had more fun had she worried less about saving for a secure old age. It was so uncharacteristic of her that it took me aback. I responded that she might be right, it was worth thinking about, but she said no more. The moment passed and was never repeated. I come from a family that keeps things close to the chest, so much so that I sometimes wondered if there was anything there to be kept close. Had the prospective subjects of self-reflection withered from lack of attention? It seems to me that anyone in life's homestretch who lacks interest in surveying the years of their presence on this good Earth will thereby miss much of value during their last chapter, the time above all for review, interpretation, and appreciation. Not reviewing for the first time, surely (if it were it would not likely happen, the fate I fear for my family), but the culmi-nating time, the time that encompasses all the others. And not merely a survey of *their* years but the years that history may note, events they enjoyed or endured, the highlights and lowlights of their nation and culture, as well as those of other nations and cultures. Neglecting this review would be like taking a world tour without reflecting on the expe-rience or writing notes home or keeping a journal. Could it have been so tedious and uninteresting? Was the traveler not fully there? Or did the traveler lack personal investment in the journey?

These thoughts arose over recent days as I camped alone in the desert with plenty of time for contemplation—of interior matters as well as of this striking landscape. I've spent considerable time over the last thirty years hiking deserts and getting to know their ways, but I've never felt sated. It seems an environment made for reflection along with the satisfactions I receive simply from being pres-ent. The desert is also an effective teacher, as it punishes lack of foresight: There is no water near camp, an excellent lesson for those who tend to take essentials for granted—a lesson I learned the hard way the first time I came many years ago. I have come with water enough for a week, if I'm careful with it.

I am a heavy reader of magazines—both paper versions, which I favor, and online publications. A few days ago I received one of my periodic general delivery "care" packages from my wife, containing mail, books, and periodicals. (They used to include homemade cookies, but the rigors of transit too often turned them to kibble.) After picking it up from the post office I diverted to a coffee shop to download the last week's assortment of e-mails, e-newsletters, -magazines, and -newspapers. Returning to camp and settling inside the camper, since high wind turned the outside aversive, I worked my way through the e-stuff (not that I could follow links in the absence of Wi-Fi, but the headlines and the few descriptive sentences that came with each were enough to get the drift) and then the paper materials, and uncharacteristically found myself bored and skipping over a great deal. Because I have valued information about politics and society for as long as I can remember, this was odd and felt serious. I took it as an inner advisory: Break this habit, it said. There's not much new to be found in the news and a whole lot that will break the spell of my presence in this desert. It is time to attend more to the firmament and to monzogranite (which composes the great rock piles that are distinctive here), Joshua tree and creosote bush, and less to worldly hullabaloo.

It's still new, but I believe I've "graduated" from the news, at least mostly. I will continue to receive online the *New York Times*, *Los Angeles Times*, *New Yorker*, *The Atlantic*, and *New York*. All the rest—the aggregating political commentary sites, the advocacy/fundraising messages, and the other attention-seeking missives—I will unsubscribe. It isn't exactly cold turkey, but headed the right direction, and my inbox will be greatly relieved. (I've never succumbed to [anti]social media, so there's nothing there to reject.) I will let several of my printed magazine subscriptions lapse. I will also be more selective about what is worth reading in the remaining publications. In place of all that, with the time and attentive capacities saved, I should have more space for contemplation as well as for indulging the pleasures of less disturbing reading (anything but the news) along with writing and time uncommitted. I feel better already. I had considered doing this for quite a while and found reasons to put it off, but now—facing so intensely the contrast between desert peace and societal cacophony of desire, fear, and conflict—this time the change feels mandatory if I am to have any chance of maintaining the equanimity and perspective I value so highly.

Why this change at this time? Aging tends to favor greater selectivity and reflection. That is surely part of it, probably the main part, although the human drama reported in the news is not, on the whole, attractive. My life has been what I call a good one, and my health remains mostly intact, so on those dimensions I have no reason for personal lamentation, regret, or anxieties that might have turned me inward or bitter. Rather, as when a job is nearly done or a book nearly finished or a life nearing completion, I want to pause and consider where I am and how I got there. Alongside these elements, there is this: Here, in 2018, my country is not doing well. Along with that, owing to climate change and other factors, much of the world also seems to have fallen into an incipient, secular "slough of despond" that disappoints and surprises me. Wasn't progress in the saddle? Hadn't the "end of history" arrived as the Cold War departed? Or was our vision of true progress too narrow, as, for example, what General Electric had in mind when in the early sixties it paid Ronald Reagan to proclaim, "Progress is our most important product."

Perhaps real progress is not merely a *thing* but many actions—practicing new ways of living, loving, and relating to the great mysteries. We borrow this concept when we speak of "progress in our spiritual quest," but that just means we're moving closer to something ultimate, something more metaphor than measure. Progress in the conventional sense is a material thing, as when our devices become more functional in one way or another or when science expands its understanding and technology becomes more adept at manipulating things, building things, and currently, eviscerating our privacy. Scientific knowledge, I hope, will go forward wisely and forever. As for all the other dimensions of what's called progress, many are objectionable or problematic; to my knowledge, no one has suggested when enough would be enough. Progress without a valuable goal or an ultimate purpose strikes me as absurd, especially when we neglect so much of importance that falls outside its limited purview and is often its victim.

I know this may sound like typical old-guy disgruntlement, but I deny the value typically accorded such progress. I see no lost golden age, no "In my day, we..." nonsense. Although I am fairly certain that in my college days, during the 1960s, we actually were more alive, optimistic, and high-minded, it clearly wasn't sustainable: It faded or was co-opted by that omnivorous demon, capitalism, and its equally demonic enabler, getting ahead. Whatever the past amounted to comparatively and wherever my own life is headed currently have nothing to do with my generalized assessment of the present; objectively speaking, the times feel ominous. Consider the political realm and its corruption and dysfunction: the economic realm, which is geared toward endless growth despite the costs and futility and with most of its poisoned fruits accruing to the upper 10 percent; the stark, almost apocalyptic, divisions within this country; endless war- making and ever-growing expenditures to keep the bombs falling; the serene neglect of the two most significant threats we face, anthropogenic climate disruption and the prospect of nuclear holocaust. Who, outside the progress cult, could argue that *ominous* is not the proper adjective?

There are still people, thank goodness, who see

where we're headed. They offer radical, transformational responses that are, I think, necessary to turn the tide, but they lack the power to do so. I have mild hope that more frequent and intense climate disasters will offer sobering slaps to the face that might have salutary effects on human behavior, but that's a hell of a way to go about making change, and there is no guarantee it would work or happen soon enough. We could as easily allow our ruling oligarchs to rule ever more autocratically as handmaidens to the autocrat himself. Out of extreme anxiety, a majority of citizens might be soothed by the reassurance the autocrat would claim to provide. This scenario would be much like the present state of affairs but fortunately not yet for a majority.

I have wondered if my consternation is what prompts me toward reflection and writing and have decided that I would have responded similarly if the times were very different, say, cheerful, spirited, and inspiring. Extremes provoke us the most; either pole would stimulate inquiry. Saying that, I realize that although extremes might be more provocative, even humdrum undramatic times would be worth reflection. It isn't just the nature of specific external affairs that matters but a person's response to those affairs and the nature of that participation. Besides, the times would be strange indeed if they didn't occasionally touch most points along the continuum.

So the somewhat dismal cultural present and the dismal future that may flow from it are the contemporaneous provocations that have turned me, not inward exactly, but away from that segment of the outer world that's become grim and over which I have no control. This is a big and rather sorrowful change of attitude. I don't let it depress me, for I have learned from study and practice the virtues of acceptance, nonattachment, and equanimity, but it does disconcert me. I wonder, "Why couldn't we humans do better?" That's part of why I write: to see if I can understand my life's currents, the historical period when they evolved, and my development in relation to that history. If I am human, and if humanity has failed in important ways, then I feel obliged to understand my participation, my share of the responsibility, my part in the play.

The question of why humans haven't done better has preoccupied me for years. An answer seems vital if humanity turns out to have time for reconsideration and new directions. It is altogether possible that during the first 95 percent of its existence, *Homo sapiens* did in fact do better in many ways. So say many who have delved into those early times; not that they were idyllic but in terms of relations with known others and Nature, in their spiritual experience and maybe even their *joie de vivre*. I agree with them—but those days are remote from us, and we may have changed too much to access fully what our species knew then or to learn from it. I'm not a conventionally religious person, but it is sometimes hard not to wonder if we suffer from a late-arriving, metaphorical "original sin." Perhaps this sin arose and left us stricken and flawed over the most recent five percent of our time on earth. Such a sin perhaps might be inherent to large settlements, burgeoning numbers, and dominance of material measures of value, followed closely by yearnings for power over Nature and power over others. Its biological counterpart, what has been called the possibly lethal mutation of our form of intelligence (lethal in its preponderant short-sighted cleverness compared to vision and wisdom), may be a parallel and complicit story. Both stories are informative and implicitly invite us to take them into account; the effects of both may tend to constrict the awareness that could usefully do so. It may also be that we are like many other species in that we will expand to fill all available space until something irresistibly limits us. For example, in the absence of predators, white-tailed deer populations eventually encounter starvation as they exceed the carrying capacity of their habitat. In various forms, this type of fate is thought to have finished off a variety of hapless civilizations along the way. Since humans became apex predators, limitation via predation won't happen unless it comes as, say, an infectious disease pandemic or something that dramatically afflicts our fecundity (maybe via the chemicals we discharge into the air, water, and soil). If it's true that we're just acting naturally, and since it's clear that we don't do well at societal self-restraint, then the only other prospects would seem to be self-destruction through thermonuclear means or, more gradually but just as effectively, human-caused climate disruption. Oh, what a beatific gift it would have been had we received capacities for wisdom and humility equal to those for egoistic self-delusion and -gratification. But we didn't, and the point I raised above remains: If we manage to avoid extinction, will we have learned what it takes to survive in a better way, and more to the point, to flourish?

I am clear that my self-understanding and the cultural perspectives I've arrived at have been greatly influenced by my time in places like this desert—not necessarily like it in topography and climate, or plants and animals, but in Nature's unique, always fascinating manifestations. The ways I respond to these places—to their expressions of physicality and beauty and the spirituality so evidently inherent in them—is equally important. I see now that when I set out in this direction in the 1980s, I was unconsciously journeying toward a new home, in the deep, old sense of a place where souls gather and affection abides. This new home was far less concerned with human affairs than with the natural world that provided the wherewithal for those affairs to arise and sustain themselves. Reading and a beginner's experience had prepared the soil. Seeds aplenty took root as I acquainted myself with mountain and desert and eventually became intimate with them. Nearly halfway through my probable lifespan at the time,

I turned, changed, and found where I needed to be. I could not forget, however, that by then I had lived four decades during which, unknown to me, many different influences had prepared a way for the later ones I cherish.

Do we ever really understand what calls us to love? Of a woman or man, a place, an activity or endeavor, a calling—to commitments of any kind? Only partially, I think. An affinity of one with the other, a mutual responsiveness, a sense received of durable fullness, rightness, completion, the conviction that if I allow this to happen, my life will be meaningful in ways that it wouldn't be without it. When I found myself opening to Nature without having consciously asked for it, these elements were a large part of the change.

Even so, throughout my life both before and after turning to Nature, I have been deeply attentive to surrounding sociopolitical events. Whether I could influence them or not, and I never had high expectations about that (even though I was naively hopeful in my youthful years), I wanted to understand them. The intellectual responses to many of these happenings came in tandem with the emotional ones. How could they not when the information pertained variously to napalmed villages, racial confrontations, and the unending prospect of nuclear war? But from now on, thanks to the revelation when I returned to my desert campsite, I want to be less comprehensively attentive to contemporary events and more attentive to living meaningfully and preparing for the death that time is bringing my way at its own indeterminate pace. Toward concurrent external history I will try to maintain the detached attitude of an anthropologist observing the customs and practices of an unfamiliar culture.

Over the forty-five years of my professional work, all of it in what are sometimes called "helping" professions, my aim was always (no self-righteousness here, just the facts) to add a little good to the world, subtract a little suffering.

Making a living as an economic vehicle and aspiration was never primary. I began as a clinical social worker doing therapy in nonprofit counseling clinics, then moved into the position of executive director; together these occupied twenty-one years. During the latter part of this period I gravitated toward an animal-rights philosophy, vegetarianism, and a view of the natural world (all the world, really) as essentially sacred. I left mental health and social services to work as the executive director of animal-protection organizations. During the most recent part of this period, I moved into part-time work, helping my wife with fundraising and administration for the wildlife rehabilitation center and animal sanctuary she founded in the mid-1970s and still leads. I also aimed toward increased retirement from the work world, which now is close to complete.

After all those years, all those human and nonhuman animals, it's a serious question how much good I did. I'll never know for sure, but certainly it was worth the effort, even if the results fell short of expectations. Doing the right thing does not depend on success for it to have been the right thing to do.

I vaguely remember reading a few years ago a piece about a philosopher who wrestled with a question: What difference would it make to the lives we lead if we knew that in, say, ten years, the world would end and there was absolutely nothing that could prevent it? What if scientists could foresee something such as an asteroid collision? Would I cease worrying over the dismal state of our society, which has been so much on my mind? Perhaps many of us would consider what could make those final ten years, and by extension would have made our time on into the future if we still had one, valuable. The philosopher's point was that a large measure of what makes endeavor important to us is seeing it as part of an endless cultural flow into a future to which we want our efforts to contribute and from which we want our successors to benefit. With that gone, so too goes much of the personal significance of our efforts. I'm not sure how seriously to take this proposition, but it does seem that many of us care about how the world, and our nation's part in it, goes, and we care in more than a passing way. Rather, we care in a way that carries a sense of obligation to bring such honor and good intention as we can into our projects and outcomes. The things that matter most, those that pertain to doing things well, to the intrinsic worth and meaning of an activity, that respond to the needs of others: these sorts of endeavors would continue being valuable in themselves, whether for a day or a decade. The awakened knowledge of that value might just be enough to make the final decade a uniquely good one, especially if enough others joined us.[1]

What would efforts characterized by honor and good intention look like? My first thought is exactly that missing thing whose absence helps make the present so dismal: hope might appear, even if sobered. There is so much wrong and seemingly so many who are invested in its continuing wrong that I can't find it in me anymore to hope for better, or more accurately, to expect what's better. During those 1960s I proposed earlier as superior to the present, hope was abundant. I imagined that every demonstration, sit-in, strike, and petition was part of a surge that would inevitably sweep away American injustices and replace them with enlightened, merciful practices. Even after the sit-ins, demonstrations, and so forth abated, hope remained. In areas such as civil rights there really was progress, even though bigotry remains a perhaps indelible blot on the nation's conscience.

Along with hope, I would add fraternity, solidarity, egalitarianism, morality, and compassion as essential

---

1. After writing this I went in search of the philosopher and his book mentioned above. He is Samuel Scheffler and the book is *Death & the Afterlife,* which I read and discovered that my recounting of his assertions was basically accurate. His "afterlife, by the way, is not Heaven; it is the time and events that follow the end of our individual lives.

to honorable intention. I could add more, but these are crucial. I don't write merely to lament what's missing. I'm more interested in placing my personal years in the context of the impersonal ones in which mine have been embedded—personal history as lived within and shaped by national history. What has been the relation between them? How have I responded to the weight, the challenges and opportunities, that history during this time laid before me? History flowed along before I was cast into its currents as if in a small boat. Since then I have worked to steady my boat's course, link it to other boats, and occasionally bring it to shore, navigating toward a goal until such time that the boat sinks and I am cast out of history forever.

The most characteristic aspect of living consciously as part of history, I believe, is this: Time and events and sheer existence arrive as an unceasing series of confrontations, offerings, and queries. Our job is to pay attention, respond properly, and never forget the great mystery from which it all emerged. The responses we give carry the ethical gravitas that is definitive for the authenticity and goodness of our transit down that flowing historical stream. I hope I have paid sufficient attention. I want my life to mean something.

Since I have found the journey to be of great interest, I will write what I call a quasi-autobiographical tour through post–World War II history, with emphasis on what I see now as its formative effects on my development and perhaps that of others in my early-baby-boom cohort. I want to think critically about American society since 1945, apart from my presence within it, and insofar as possible to understand how my membership was shaped. Although I know my story is to some degree representative of others that could be told about this period, in many ways I know it to be quite unrepresentative in the manner of its eventual spooling out. I would enjoy hearing from those who traveled this time and have other stories to tell.

Chapter 1

Formation: Early Years

I ESTIMATE MY MAIN FORMATIVE years lasted until I was about twenty-eight, which sounds late but in recollection feels true to the facts. Compared with the growth of other mammals, that is not merely slow but embarrassingly so. It seems strange that over one third of my years so far were formative, but that may be an overly literal and limited way to imagine what it means for a human to form and be formed. Personal and professional development may be analogous in that an early period of rapid learning is followed by a longer and slower one in which refinement and depth are progressively achieved but never finalized. Once one has made one's way through childhood and adolescence and formally entered early adulthood via college, a vocational program, or direct entry into a workplace, each way composing first venturings into a career, some part of their twenties will have passed. In my case the process was delayed by choosing and rejecting three or four post-BA educational career paths and dropping out of graduate schools twice before one stuck. Throw in a brief, failed marriage and a confrontation with my draft board over their invitation to join the gathering in Vietnam, and you've about finished a busy post-adolescent decade.

But even with the divorce and other events, I maintain it was entry into a career at age twenty-eight that really marked the end of this period, even if not totally. Like most people, I was still in a formative stage for many years to come—and still am, albeit less noticeably and with very different goals. Individual development, as I picture it, is something like building a wall across variable terrain, one stone at a time, sometimes several per day, sometimes fewer. The wall just keeps going, but with an increasingly secure and predictable foundation and with smaller, more slowly added stones until it turns the corner and the final one drops into place. If well built, the wall will stand for a while longer as a legacy, an honorable one if the right stones are chosen and properly fitted and placed.

This discussion of an initial development period reminds me of Erik Erikson's work during the twenty-five or so years after 1950, which I studied for my first professional work. He proposed eight stages of psychosocial development. Like any model of this sort, it has its limitations and critics, but in my view it captures much that is important in one's personal evolution. Erikson describes each stage as a period of conflict whose resolution greatly affects the following stages and so one's ultimate psychological health and competence. Not surprisingly, most of the stages—five, as it happens—play out before adulthood is supposed to kick in at around age eighteen. One hopes by then to have formed, through experience and practice, trust, autonomy, initiative, industry (i.e., proficiency), and identity. With reasonable success at meeting the challenges of each stage, one is prepared for the final three: intimacy, generativity, and integrity. Speaking generally, this perspective on human development can be illuminating so long as you don't overdo stage sequencing and demarcation. I write now from the stage of integrity, which means that, as I reflect on my life, I am mostly satisfied and certainly a long way from the alternative of despair, in which one feels their life was wasted or largely failed. As my narrative rolls out, I hope to achieve a balance between the psychosocial nature of Erickson's focus and the socio-political sphere, since both are crucial.

I was launched into history's flow only days after the bombs fell on Hiroshima and Nagasaki. With thematic consistency, my birth came within the confines of a military hospital on an army base in Texas while my father piloted a bomber somewhere over the Pacific.[1] Mother was from Texas, Father from Minnesota: a marriage made by World War II, since without it they surely would never have met and, come to think of it, I would not be here.

We lived in Texas for a couple of years after the war's end, then in Minnesota for three or four. I have only two more or less coherent memories of the time in Minnesota, when I was pre-school age, before moving to Texas. Both express a sense of affliction. In one I am in the basement of our home, smashing plastic or wooden dolls with a hammer and feeling angry with my father, who must have punished me for something. In the other I have been mandated to walk to the home of our elderly babysitter, who had reported misbehavior on my part, and to apologize. (The events may have been connected; I don't know.) In fairness, I also have fragments of other memories that are more positive, mostly involving time with grandparents. The rest is blank.

If I were the therapist of someone who reported the doll memory, I would undoubtedly wear it out with discussion and interpretation. Lacking that, and reclaiming the memory for myself, I will say only what seems obvious—I had a troubled relationship with my parents. All kids of that age have occasions of anger toward their parents, but breaking of the dolls gives my memory a more poignant and pregnant aspect, especially now as I put it into the context of all that happened afterward. Who knows whose

---

1. Despite the context of my birth, I eventually became a pacifist, largely in reaction to a later war, but who knows what vibes of this one I incorporated.

dolls they were or how they got in that basement? There were no girls in the family: Gosh! Could some early antagonist of stereotypically gendered roles have given them to me? Very doubtful, but with a punitive father, I risked punishment for breaking them. Did the dolls represent a family? How did I manage to disappear the smashed remains and avoid facing the music? And why was I so angry with my father? I assume it must have been he, since my mother more often conciliated. I must have been punished for something, but what? Why has it remained so vivid?

As a current memory, I mark this as the beginning of my father's and my alienation. Only now have I arrived at that conclusion; I haves no evidence to support it—there couldn't be any—but it seems to fit. I suspect he always objected to me—my mere presence? his having to be a father? who knows?—as much as I eventually did to him. It would be interesting to know what, at that age, I represented for him to reject. I'll never know, but he was young, freshly back from the war, and suddenly a father, so it could have been associated with these circumstances. His eternal silence about his family history and his feelings about his place in the postwar world was complete; eventually I lost interest. As he aged he grew bombastic, reactionary, and overtly racist, qualities that completed the alienation. Sixty-five years after my destruction of the dolls, I stood with mother and one of their friends at his hospital bedside and witnessed his dying without a glimmer of loss or sadness. I was there to support mother.

I will say that I am reasonably sure I satisfactorily resolved my alienated feelings toward my father, meaning that I consciously considered rather than repressed them and mostly emptied them of force. But I always feel a twinge of envy when I see men enjoying their fathers or I read about their missing of, or their admiration for, them. To my mind, good parents and the good families they build are among the most admirable forms of human expression. It follows that the pleasure one feels in one's relations with parents, even when both generations are old, is one of the higher pleasures. I wish I had had it.

When the 1950s began, as I picture it, Mother won the geographic argument, and the family, now with a second son, moved to the Texas Panhandle, nearer her parents and siblings. I suspect that even at the age of five, I must have felt the culture shock between Minneapolis and a tiny, dusty settlement in the South with fewer than fifty people, surrounded by cotton fields. From a desk job in the city to driving a truck servicing farmers' fuel needs—that was Dad's transition. I never knew what he thought about it because we never talked, about that or anything else memorable. Soon a third son arrived and until I left for college the family lived in that dusty little place on the margin of the lower middle class. As the oldest, I was the prime bearer of parental hopes, mostly Mother's, I presume, since only she spoke of them. I was a good student, moderately shy but not friendless, and when the time came, happy to leave for the university at eighteen.

Childhood feels, in retrospect, dull and uneventful insofar as anything of much interest remains in my conscious memory; dull or not, however, I know that many events are still eventful in the sense of leaving an ill-defined penumbra of inner effects. I lived for twelve years in that little farming village; today it has faded to practically nothing. It used to have two small general stores, a tiny post office (only about fifteen feet square, but in its own structure), a one-chair beauty shop (ladies only), a blacksmith, and—when the mechanic was sober enough to open—a garage. It also had two cotton gins, a butane/propane outlet where my father worked, a Baptist church, a Church of Christ, and until I was in third grade, a school with six grade levels, two to a classroom. Maybe a dozen homes, a main thoroughfare (speaking grandly) passing through that wasn't paved until we'd been there several years, and a single parallel dirt road constituted the main residential area. Migrant workers doubled the population for a few months every year, living in the barracks adjacent to one of the gins. As I now think of it, that had to have been a noisy place to make a home, with bad air into the bargain. As far as I could tell, the resident Anglos didn't much concern themselves with migrant welfare. (This sounds familiar, since apparently the ethnic dynamic is little changed in this country.) One full-time Mexican American family had a dozen children, which made for a disproportionate impact on the numbers and ethnicity of the settlement. (They also had an unexplained affinity for the letter *R*—all twelve of the kids' names began with it.) Once a tornado dropped in and took out one of the gins. The Baptist preacher across the road from us refused to go to the storm cellar, saying he put his fate in the Lord's hands. He survived. The wife of one of the general store proprietors was said to be a hussy and, when her husband was off to market, to adulter with various area farmers. (There didn't seem an equivalent pejorative for them.) She appeared exotic to me, and maybe the shenanigans spoken of were true.

Robust hypocrisy did well in our little town. I learned this unequivocally while in high school and working for the U.S. Department of Agriculture during summers. My job was to measure the acreage planted in various crops to ensure that farmers were abiding by their agreements with the government; it was an effort to regulate how much of each crop was produced and was intended to prevent excess or deficiency and maintain price stability. Slipping in a few extra acres of more lucrative crops would increase a farm's profit while defeating the intent of the regulations, even if it was to the advantage of anyone who could get away with it. More than once men whom I had met in church would encourage me to adapt my measures to their desires—that is, to deceive. Although I had drifted away from the church, the morality it had helped form precluded my collusion, which would have been ironic knowledge for anyone who recognized it.

Until high school I was a faithful member of the little town's Southern Baptist church, which had a membership always well under seventy-five and sometimes not half that. Last time I drove through, it had been put on a truck and hauled away section by section, toward what use in its new locale I never heard. Because of the enthusiasm, if not the quality, of my gospel singing, I was made song leader when my predecessor abandoned his wife and left town with a woman also said to be a hussy, men apparently being putty in a woman's hands. There were boys' and girls' indoctrination groups—the Royal Ambassadors and the Girls' Auxiliary (sex discrimination formalized). I rose to the heights of the RAs, standing strong against sin and giving demonstrations of such examples as the terrible effects of alcohol on the body. I used rubbing alcohol, not knowing the difference; it has striking and, to me at that age, alarming effects on a raw egg, which was intended as a surrogate for our bodies and minds.

I was also adroit at "sword drills," which were contests where we held a Bible with arm extended downward. On the leader's enunciation of book, chapter, and verse, we whipped it upward—more or less like a sword, I suppose; the Bible was considered our protection against Satan so the drill may have had a symbolic meaning. We flipped through until the swiftest and most biblically literate participant found and read the designated section. We went to overnight Bible camps every summer. At one, a scandal rippled through concerning a song leader spied behind the stage one evening holding a girl closer to his body than concern for her soul actually required. At another, we were asked if anyone needed praying for. I lifted my hand, thinking it couldn't hurt to have a little extra support. (All eyes were supposed to be closed except the fellow's in charge.) On getting home, I was invited to our preacher's office to do that praying and explain why I needed it. I felt betrayed and couldn't tell him what I needed praying about, because I had forgotten. I think it was just a moment of enthusiasm. For a few pre- and early adolescent years I was subject to such moments, sometimes even working to "save" migrant children from perdition, whether due to misguided Catholicism or some other deviation from the one true Protestant path. I am still in touch with one of the subjects of my salvific efforts. The conversion didn't hold, but he did all right, regardless; against all odds, he graduated from college and became a civil engineer and eventually public-works director in several large cities. This church and the religion it represented would today be considered part of the evangelical Christianity cohort. Biblical literalism and infallibility, facile judgmentalism, moral simplicity, arid and astringent spirituality (if it may be construed as such): it knew what it believed. In the absence of competing views, it was good enough for me. I seriously doubt that anything could have led it to plight its troth to Donald Trump as has happened with the modern versions of evangelicalism. Its standards were more severe and implacable, and surely it would have found the means-ends betrayals of the moderns incomprehensible.

During my third-grade year, our little country school closed and the students were bused fifteen miles to a somewhat larger town, which at the time seemed the height of urban sophistication. I was always a good student, so there was never any doubt about my going to college, especially since my mother insisted I was bound to become a doctor or lawyer, the height of aspiration at the time.

Two particularly interesting things happened in high school. During 1962–63, my senior year, when the civil rights movement was gathering a momentum to which most of us there on the Texas plains were oblivious, a family moved to town that was different from most of the locals. The father took over the little newspaper as publisher. The oldest son was my age and we became close friends, which is surprising in retrospect, since I was so conventional and he was not. He smoked, was bilingual and very bright, and knew the world more thoroughly than I. Once when we were having coffee at a local café, some young Black men entered and were directed to the kitchen, the only place they could be served (standard southern practice in 1962). My new friend had us pick up our cups and join them. It was a near revolution for that little town and certainly for me. We were close friends for the next thirty or forty years and then drifted in different directions. But the spark of new thinking had landed on combustible material in my mind. It might otherwise have been a long time igniting, and I remain deeply grateful for the friendship, which I consider an important formative factor in my evolving character. How I managed to be open-minded in that country setting and with my family background remains a mystery.

The other interesting event—what else could it be for an adolescent boy?—was my discovery of sex. I won't say much, but for that last year of high school it was about all I could think of. My girlfriend and I were equally lit up by the discovery, and all was bliss until we went to college and she betrayed me with another boy, delivering my first dose of deep grief. (I mean this; I was pained in my soul, and only the ministrations of the high-school friend spoken of above, who was then my roommate, boosted me from despair with a copy of *The Little Prince,* amphetamines, and a willingness to listen and console.) There could have been an earlier and different kind of grief—she missed a period while we were in high school and feared she might be pregnant. Obviously this would have been a life-changer for both of us, especially her, since abortion was unheard of out there on the frontier. I pictured her disappearing into that void where girls sometimes were taken for publicly unmentionable reasons, often to homes for unwed mothers, but true salvation belatedly flowed from her body when her period returned, bringing jubilation in tow. As evidence pointing to humans being slow learners, I don't recall that our sexual habits changed; we continued tempting fate and were lucky to escape the potential consequences.

If I worked at it I'm sure I could find more to talk about from childhood, but I find that it doesn't much interest me, which seems strange in a project like this one. I know the period helped make me who I am, but it feels remote and uninviting. It was prosaic and conventional, and I did what was expected of an oldest son destined to strive upward. Even so, I think a small seed of my future attraction to Nature and solitude may have been sown, even though I was surrounded by cotton and grain fields and farmsteads. The little village was perched on the side of what was called the Draw, the remnant of an ancient river, now mostly farmed but preserving a sinuous median that was wild and somewhat mysterious, although no river flowed through it during my time there. It had been abandoned by everyone but me since it was considered useless, and I often hiked alone down its winding course before serious adolescent concerns captured me.

When it came time to leave at eighteen, neither family nor community pulled me back emotionally; mostly it was a time and place to get away from. Despite my trepidations about embarking on the next stage, I was sure college and independence would make for a more satisfying milieu. Yet in saying this, I have to wonder how much I unfairly discount about the time before. It hardly seems reasonable or normal that one's childhood would feel so inconsequential, especially for one well instructed in psychology and social work and the knowledge of those experiences that help to make the man or woman. What am I leaving out?

It is impossible not to notice my ambivalence about recounting events of my early life. It really was a generally placid childhood without major traumas such as death, divorce, or disease (or unplanned pregnancy!). But in recollection, it feels like a period not experienced for itself and the intrinsic goods of childhood but for preparation; future life was thought to depend on the record one was assembling—not the kind of pressure so many children today are said to labor under on their way to ensuring success (the infamous and mislabeled "meritocrats"), but not altogether dissimilar. Within a culture dominated by economic values, perhaps that is what childhood becomes, except for the rebelliously insightful, a point I had not yet reached. But strangely, even seen as a time of placid preparation, I have a hard time crediting it, seeming almost to think of myself as having only a tenuous existence before the independence of leaving. Is it the temporal remoteness or repression?

Given my eventual career as a psychotherapist who shared the usual preoccupation with clients' early years, I am compelled to pause a bit longer over this. We are well aware these days, as was Erikson, that the foundation, the strengths and weaknesses and many of the themes of our subsequent years, are set in our beginnings. That was naturally as true for me as for anyone, so why does my childhood interest me so little? I wonder what the feeling that it was so inchoate a time and one with so little sense of agency may have to do with it. Despite my apparent successes along the child and adolescent way, I don't look back with satisfaction or remember much that brings a smile. Was it more an endurance trial than a time of conscious discovery and excitement? Or do I overlook its joys and high points? It is surely ironic that the time of greatest importance to composing an enduring self becomes for the later version of the person the least interesting of all. I may have hit on the explanation above—a child's lack of felt agency in relation to adults and until his own adulthood may lead to unfairly discounting the period as almost an embarrassment to the adult independent self. How do others feel when they look back in their later years? There is much that puzzles me about this.

I cannot speak for my brothers, but one singularity for me lay in my constant fear of the anger of a borderline abusive father. This led to mild separation anxiety in my early years and a slight sense of failure, since I believed I must somehow have invited the rejection. Having worked as a therapist with a multitude of abused or neglected children, I know this feeling to be normal, but of course, this recognition came too late to help. Fortunately, that feeling was not determinative, only a minor presence in my growing consciousness. My mother was a reliable and attentive caretaker but oriented mostly around survival and endurance, not uncommon among her generation, whose youth was dominated by the Depression, poverty, and World War II. My family was emotionally and materially austere; both my aversion to anger and the emotional austerity have, in attenuated forms, stayed with me. My shyness, which surely connected in some fashion with these other dimensions, was also a significant factor in how I managed my childhood, my adolescence, and even parts of my adulthood. But the early embarrassment over its existence eventually turned to recognition that it encouraged a reflectiveness, inwardness, and independence that have served me well.

I remember some early experiences related to dogs that surely connect with my eventual evolution toward animal rights. In my family and probably most others in the hinterlands, "pets" had a precarious existence. They were not allowed inside our home, and no one considered building a fence to contain them or a shelter a worthy expenditure. Veterinarians were unheard of. Dog food consisted not of something bought at the store but whatever scraps were left over from meals, whether abundant or nonexistent; with three sons we undoubtedly fell more toward the scarcity end of the scale, from the dog's perspective. Companion animals, as I call them now, had two main sources: neighbors had puppies to give away, or an abandoned dog found his way to your door. I remember one of each whom I was close to. One was a cocker spaniel I witnessed dying under the wheels of my father's truck one morning as I climbed on to the school bus and rode away, leaving the dog dead on the side of the road. (Why didn't I leap from that bus screaming, to hell with getting to school?) The other was a mixed-breed dog, the source of many litters born under our house, who in time disappeared. As my father came into the house one day I asked if he had seen her. He replied that she'd been run over days before. When I wept, he excoriated my emotionality. My feelings for the spaniel had been equally strong but were suppressed, owing to my refusal to demonstrate emotion on the crowded bus. A little girl sitting beside me cried for us both. Other dogs died of disease or moved on. It was a mostly indifferent and often cruel world for dogs, and I learned to protect my feelings for them.

The positive spin I've put on my early shyness is the way I came to feel about it, but it wasn't always that way and assuredly not when I was young and most in its grip. At the extreme, shyness can be paralyzing, which I thankfully never experienced. But its characteristic social anxiety was sufficient to limit the relationships I formed. In high school and even college, asking a girl for a date was such a heart-racing, sweat-inducing challenge that I sometimes wondered if loneliness might not be preferable. I've read that 40 percent of kids describe themselves as shy, but I don't know how meaningful that is when you consider the range of discomfort the word can imply and what can feel like the shame of admission. Many parents consider it a handicap requiring psychological treatment—sometimes it is. That virtually all children are born with at least a slight degree of social anxiety implanted by nature is bound to be the case. No matter how reliably supportive one's parents are, the world is a big place with an abundance of strangers. Evolution might well favor anxiety's caution over confident heedlessness early in development. In my case I also attribute it to uncertainties derived from my family matrix. It took me more time than it should have (I sometimes think, but then, when is the deadline?) to form a clear and accurate self-image; as that happened the shyness abated, but never completely. It was an abiding presence that I give some credit to for my inquisitive and reflective nature. If asked, I'd have preferred a different source, but I wasn't asked, so there it is.

Since sociopolitical events had a major impact on my ethical development, I must reflect on the 1950s and early '60s. During the Korean War, some now nameless person shared with me the observation that war was a permanent fact of existence, a disturbing thought that stayed with me. I was sobered by it because it seemed a dangerous and dismal way to live, even to a seven-year-old. The memory may have stuck because it turned out to be mostly true of the post–World War II American way of doing foreign policy and remains dangerous. How could it be otherwise?

Then in 1960, there in our little outpost of the Southern Baptist Church, high anxiety of a different sort filled the pews at the fearful prospect that a Catholic might become president and turn the country's leadership over to the pope. Catholics were only a small degree less worrisome than communists in that church.[2]

When Kennedy won, the Vatican dread mounted but slowly drained away when no papist abyss opened up. We were also conscious, even there at the end of the figurative road, watching cotton grow, of *Sputnik* and the anxiety it brought as well as the Cuban missile crisis. Because I was an able student and enjoyed science, I was encouraged by teachers to learn more physics, presumably so I could grow up and help design nuclear weapons to defend us against the implacable communists.

I realize how prominent fear was in politics where I lived—and for that matter, still is around this country. The civil rights movement was distorted by anxious Whites and both closeted and overt racists to fit that same foreboding template. Is it possible, I wonder, that the baby boom generation—born on the heels of the "good war" and imbued with continuing fearfulness throughout the Cold War and then faced with demands for racial equality in clear violation of American caste system presumptions—developed psychological proclivities toward generalized anxiety and acceptance of militarism linked to that? Preparations for war were always mandatory, not by choice, of course, but owing to the perfidy and sinister schemes of our unrelenting foes. The momentum and incentives wrapped in that package seem to have defined the political times of my entire life. Would a less fearful country—and despite our bluster and delusion that is what we seem to

---

2. A few years before the election, I had an aunt in another part of Texas who was deeply imbued with Baptist convictions. She had a son in high school who was threatening to drop out and marry a Latinx girl. My aunt was aghast and fought it and won. It still is not clear to me which was more frightening to her, the prospect of my cousin being a dropout, his marrying a Latinx, or her Catholicism—Collectively they'd have driven a less obstinate woman to despair. Eventually my cousin became the essence of orthodoxy, but he had managed to take his bat to the plate and whiff three quick strikes in that early venture into nonconformity.

be—have been so quick to turn 9/11 into a "war on terror" rather than see it for what it was: a limited strike by a few marginal, cave-dwelling extremists who happened to hit the jackpot beyond their wickedest dreams?

I am no historian, but I see abundant evidence in the American past of intolerance toward anyone labeled *other*—that is, fundamentally different from and assumed to be less than the Euro-American prototype. This kind of attitude generally carries a freight of undefined anxiety and fearfulness under the surface. The Native American expropriation and genocide along with slavery and post–Civil War violence and oppression against the new Americans of African descent are emblematic. And I wonder if the post–World War I anticommunist frenzies, aroused by the emergence of revolutionary Russia—which was by no means a serious threat to U.S. national security—did not betray the presence of those same unconscious fears. Unlike the Natives or the "Negro," the Chinese, Irish, and other immigrants, all of whom were objects of periodic violence and hostility for a variety of motivations, the faraway Bolsheviks were fancied a real threat to national existence, not to mention American ruling class power. This specter dominated U.S. foreign policy until 1991. But in only a decade, before post–Cold War peace could be confidently declared and a few free breaths of exhilaration and relief drawn, terrorism arrived. Those in charge of the national fear generator could now identify new threats, new reasons for the populace to quake and say yes to new weaponry, new battlefronts. Do we use fearmongering as a substitute for national reckoning with who we are and, concomitantly, as a reliable economic engine and career vehicle for a few self-proclaimed "tough-minded realists"? It also is a perfected rationale and subterfuge for imperialist strivings, which took root during WWII and took flight with the demise of the Soviet Union.

Memory is unreliable; it contains shards of past reality combined with new ones added and old ones deleted or altered into a picture that changes with age and experience. However real and complete a memory seems, it is always partly unconscious confabulation, shaped to fit a present self-concept; past features are changed according to whether they now feel pleasing or congruent or simply because experience reshapes recollection according to its own inscrutable machinations. I keep this in mind as I write. There's no point in lamenting it; better to be honest and know it happens, mostly in ways that escape our awareness.

But this doesn't make recollection worthless; rather, it contains its own truths, in part *what really happened* and in part what we now find plausible on the basis of our memory's fit with the person we have become. This has been called *narrative history,* meaning it is history that begins with past events that provide plots and players in stories we tell ourselves and others, and that change with the years. Narrative history seems a strange and improbable way of moving through time and memory, but it's how each of us does it while fashioning our own. Any good psychotherapist understands this and takes it into account when a client's *anamnesis*, her telling of her life story—not her history, her story—spools out in session after session. Let's remember also that our present versions of memories, the fashion in which we construe them and the way we interpret them now—these have their own truths to reveal. For instance, if I have made decisions, consciously or unconsciously, based on the belief that an event was "$x + 1$," it hardly matters that in reality it was only "x." My *operative reality*, my patterns of living based in my recollections, was the former, although this is not the whole story. The direct effects of x would have been unconscious, even if my future views looking back have moved toward $x + 1$.

In short, we can never have a full accounting of how we got to the present. But we have the stories, and usually they will do.

Here's more of my early story. We lived fifteen miles from the small town where the bus delivered me to school. Mother worked there while Dad worked where we lived. Money was always tight. Extracurricular activities suffered from both the distance and the shortage of resources. In a different setting and circumstances, I might have become an athlete or musician. I enjoyed both and wanted to participate fully, but it wasn't possible. I understood then and still do, but with regret. Instead, I was a young scholar, diligent, always reading, excellent grades. The standard family pattern of the oldest child carrying the burden of parental expectations, which typically moderate with each subsequent child, fitted us as well as it did any family. I was alone more than I wanted but not isolated. When I was in the middle grades, I met a boy who became my best friend from then until our first semester of college. I'm sure this friendship was as vital to my emotional well-being during those years as my later one with the iconoclast who moved to town during senior year was to my subsequent social consciousness. I dated reasonably often during high school and had friends. As a senior, I began dating the girl I have described with whom I discovered the joys of unrestrained sex (well, as unrestrained as possible in the back seat of a car). We indulged as often as possible, and I remain grateful to her even in light of her subsequent betrayal. This, I believe, was surely a good thing for my developing psyche, since it hastened me into individuation and maturation as I dealt with my grief and it further separated me from hometown connections.

Other than their providing the usual (for those times) developmental foundation for adulthood, what else can I say about those years that has had evident expression in my adult self? If I had to put one word on this period (1950s through early sixties) it would be "stable," just as society at large during that time is generally described. I wonder if twelve years of rural cultural stasis helps explain my adult propensity to wander. I have liked finding professional positions in new towns, fulfilling their expectations (and often more), and then moving and starting over. Even now, retired, I spend close to a quarter of every year in my camper, staying days or a week in a favorite place and then moving to the next one.

I went into and through the university with a continuation of confidence in my intellectual abilities, but their expression was impeded by my reticence, of which the experiences of insult and intimidation imposed by my father were a part. Buried in my unconscious has always been a fear that expressing anger or outspokenness meant danger. That fear has been a source of self-restraint that I do not like but never was able to fully eradicate. It did not inhibit my arriving at, say, radical political conclusions or becoming a responsive therapist or a productive leader of nonprofit organizations, but it made me more comfortable with an active observer role rather than pushing myself forward. Notwithstanding, I made good and effective places for myself professionally and otherwise, but sometimes I would have enjoyed indulging more outspokenness.

And yet, and yet...this reluctance to bring attention to myself undoubtedly was the beginning of something else I deeply value. Over recent years I have come to the poignant realization of the destructive effects of ego and hyper-individualism on spiritual, ethical, and societal domains. One of my favorite citations is from the late philosopher and novelist Iris Murdoch, who spoke of the "fat, relentless ego" as the chief enemy of the moral life. Clearly true! And it also precludes one's emergence into spiritual awareness. Society and politics, too, degrade when they are associated with self-centered pursuits. Individuals incorporate the most disparate qualities. Who knows if I would have developed my ethical compass in accord with these insights if I'd also been vigorously extraverted?

The most vital emergence during the period I've been describing was an incipient social consciousness. Seeing those young Black men shuttled into the kitchen of that rundown café as part of the everyday racism of late 1950s and early 1960s American life began my inward turning toward understanding and rejecting what I had accepted as simply the way things were. I never shared the racism of my environment, but I don't remember questioning the "whites only" bathrooms and fountains and the clearly second-class status of Blacks and Hispanics either. I lacked something inside that could have delivered me from observation to judgment on my own—some sort of freedom to assess and critique. That miserable little café and my following the unknown Black men into the kitchen began to uncouple me from the assumptions of my environment.

That turn might have come earlier, but it didn't; I was still too young and unready. Our little town took several years to implement school desegregation after the Supreme Court's Brown decision in 1954. My recollection is that it came in 1959, when I began high school. Probably only a few hundred Black people lived in and around the town, with all of the townies in the "flats" across the railroad tracks, well separated from the White and even the brown populations. The Mexican Americans attended school with the White kids, except during harvest season, when the migrants were generously given shortened days and in some cases an alternate school in order not to interfere overly with their work in the cotton fields. Black children had their own exclusive, tumble-down schoolhouse in the flats. If other White students had worries about desegregation, I didn't know about it and had none of my own. All I remember about the integration of our school were occasional fights between White and Black kids. These gave me pleasure, because the main instigator was a White bully who was prone to losing his temper easily and shouting racial slurs, whereupon he was usually thrashed and slank away, bloodied. Since I was occasionally one of his victims for other reasons, I looked forward to his humiliations. He was a memorable example of the problems that come from lack of self-control. No matter how many times he forgot himself, screamed "nigger," and found himself thoroughly beaten, he did not learn either restraint, more effective pugilism, or a more enlightened racial consciousness. My pacifist soul reproves the violence but admits to a smile even today at the memory. He deserved what he got. The school was successfully integrated, but the racial groupings were not.

A side thought: I sometimes describe my sociopolitical philosophy semiseriously as radical egalitarian communitarian anarchism. Each word has a referent arising from a specific set of concerns; in the context of the present discussion, radical egalitarian applies. I have said I never shared the racism that suffused my early environment, but even I have to wonder about the accuracy of that recollection. Since racial assumptions were as ubiquitous as the air we breathed, it is reasonable to ask if I forget, or have suppressed the awareness, or if in transcending those assumptions I simultaneously lost touch with their previous residence in my mind, scant and passive though it may have been. Each is possible; I know of some who declare that no one is immune to the disease. But if I was infected, it was asymptomatically. I never used racial epithets and was uncomfortable when others did. Also, I didn't make invidious differentiations among those I came in contact with, and as mentioned earlier, I befriended a migrant worker in whose home I visited frequently (very unusual back then) and who remains in touch today. The injustice of bigotry was never anything but obviously true to me once I asked the right questions and made the right observations, and at no time have I ever felt fundamentally superior to anyone for any reason, whether racial, educational, intellectual, or whatever. If my sense of having never partaken of racist toxins is true, or even if it only became true unconsciously over a short time, this would surely constitute a lucky virtue within that context but not one I strove for; it just seemed who I was for reasons unknown but appreciated.

Feeling superior to another person forgets, or does not care, that we are each a composite of many qualities and that anyone's excellence at any of them is largely contingent on circumstances—more bluntly, a matter mostly of luck—and is often offset by less admirable qualities. Analogously, the meritocratic notion that ability plus effort equals earned success fails to notice that neither ability nor effort are independent variables. They are dependent on a host of known and unknown influences and the successful "meritocrats" should be grateful for their good fortune rather than prideful at their "merit." Equality, we should hardly have to be reminded, speaks to the dignity and moral worth of the other, which have nothing to do with good or bad fortune or their results. They are intrinsic. Radical egalitarianism finds no reason for anyone to feel superior to any other. Some of us go so far as to include the nonhuman realm, believing that the whole deserves equal moral consideration with the human parts. It seems almost trite even to talk about these matters, an example of belaboring the blindingly obvious. But American history shows that whereas egalitarianism may be obvious rationally and ethically, as a practical matter bigotry in every conceivable form remains a persistent force in the national psyche—one that growing numbers of us despair will ever fade away or even be contained and its effects neutralized.

As for those other two concepts in my philosophy,

communitarian and *anarchist*, the first comes from the conviction that the value of community in American society is too little appreciated; we prefer individualistic conceptions that fail to recognize our dependence on others, which begins in the creation of our embryonic being and never ends. We are what our relationships have made us, or if you prefer, what we make of ourselves within the context of our relationships, but still with their assistance. How could we come to be healthy individuals and personalities without them? Good societies and good people depend mostly on good communities, which is why I claim the communitarian label as both aspiration and conviction.

As for *anarchist*, I have learned that its underlying philosophy, though diverse and ordinarily misunderstood in the details, matches my suspicion of power. This is not to deny the role of legitimate, accountable authority in community, society, and nation, but I came to believe, especially over recent years, that power has a mind-altering and addictive quality that few handle well. My version of anarchism incorporates strong communities because they are good and essential in so many ways. One of which is to keep authority in check, to slap it down when, as usually happens, it overreaches and claims too much for itself.

By my junior year at the university, I was working with campus civil rights organizations and once joined a group traveling to Alabama for voter registration efforts. I also worked with others in support of the Rio Grande Valley (south Texas) farmworkers' strike. At the same time as these were going on, I was active in antiwar efforts. In short, my university experience, along with the inspiration of my unconventional high school friend, made me a very different person from the one who had left the Texas Panhandle after high-school graduation. Childhood had been a time of easy acceptance of the way things were, the commonplaces of rural mid-twentieth-century Texas life, but fortunately the wider world of the university helped to open eyes and mind. Thankfully I also found an abundance of material to exercise them on. Obviously I'm not thankful for racism, war, and economic injustice but for their rising to national consciousness and the opportunity they gave me to do something about them—also, to help me become a better person as I challenged them.

As I look back on it all fifty years later, it is debatable how much has really changed. Jim Crow has more or less been forced to retreat, or alter its strategies, but bigotry persists and has its own political party that has, among other retrograde actions, found creative substitutes for the poll tax and literacy tests to suppress minority voting. Vietnam was a strategic and moral disaster whose continuing effects include a deepening sense that government will lie about anything when it considers it useful to its interests to do so (as do the corporate world and many other modern realms). American militarism is, if anything, a more pernicious influence on world affairs than ever. Its costs to the country in lives and resources, political irresponsibility and mendacity, citizen disengagement, and opportunities foregone, along with the hidden moral and spiritual decay that comes with turning away from the death and destruction done in our names—all of this hardly suggests a nation on the way to building a more honorable and humane culture. Economic inequality and injustice boom and enable the ruling class to implant itself securely, virtually untouchably, in control. Finally, the willful ignorance that supports the denial of anthropogenic climate disruption and the disasters it portends, not to mention the moral loss when dishonesty is accepted as normal—these, too, are part of what seem to me roiling cultural and political failures that appear likely to become worse and possibly develop into outright autocracy. And we had such hopes long ago. . .

I link what came to be my pacifism with my reaction to the American government's decision to prosecute the Vietnam War. That we lost that war is irrelevant to my judgment about it. Rather, that it happened at all and was conducted with such vicious disregard for the casualties and for facing the truth about what was happening and terminating it— this added up for me to rejection of war as an acceptable way to pursue our interests and to deep and enduring suspicion of ruling class motives and integrity. What seems to me definitively wrong is the American readiness—the alacrity even—to turn toward violence and threat, seemingly unconcerned about the destruction we inflict in other lands. Compare our absence of empathy for those killed *over there* to the rabidity of our response *here* to a single assault on 9/11. Since we spend as much on our military as the next eight, nine, or more other nations combined (depending on the year and how the calculations are done), it can hardly be a surprise that we are quick to put it to use.

It is one thing to speak of these matters intellectually, as if they were part of a study of international politics or political philosophy, and even to note how they influenced my individual development. But they also had an even more crucial personal aspect. I graduated from the university and went off to the University of Chicago Divinity School to study ethics and society. That was in 1967, when the Vietnam War was raging. I'd spent my college years protesting, but the war makers failed to notice. The military draft was chewing through the ranks of young men who lacked the physical defects or family resources to avoid it. Graduation brought the end of my deferment. Memory having faded, I assume I took the gamble of hauling off to divinity school on the assumption that my draft board might infer I was studying for the ministry (which I wasn't), and grant a deferment. Ministerial studies were deferrable but did not include studying ethics mostly from philosophical perspectives. This is embarrassing to suggest, as it would have lacked courage and honesty, but I don't know how else to explain my decision to go to Chicago, except perhaps as a classic display of denial, or perhaps, simple bad judgment. The board was not fooled and classified me as 1-A; I had become a prime candidate for the war machine. After considerable soul-searching, I applied for conscientious objector status but was denied because my objection was considered only ethical rather than religious, even though a flock of five clergy wrote letters declaring otherwise. Sooner than anticipated, I received a draft notice. I went for my physical, passed, and was sent down the hall for swearing in; an attorney had told me to cooperate with everything but the final fateful act. I refused to step forward. This ceremony was more than mere ritual; stepping forward was in fact the formal acceptance of departure from one world into a very different one. I had forewarned the draftee processors of my intentions; to prevent contagion, I was treated to the ceremony alone. The swearer-in repeated the ominous formula a second time. I remained mentally steadfast, although in truth I wasn't so confident about my feet; I was nervous and had the fantasy they might move of their own volition.

Afterward, I was not allowed to ride the bus that had carried me sixty miles for this much-dreaded encounter and walked off in search of Greyhound. A few months later, the federal legal authorities, surprisingly, asked my draft board to reconsider. They did but arrived at the same conclusion; again I was called and again I declined. Prospects seemed bleak, but I was recompensed by a new sense of integrity, knowing what I was risking for principle.

I appealed the board's second decision and appeared at a draft board meeting in the Panhandle town of Muleshoe with one of those clergymen in tow. In explaining his vote against my appeal, one of the board members, a local farmer, explained that the world was like a hamburger and the communists were taking methodical bites out of it. This made it imperative that I offer my body to help stanch that dire process before the hamburger was consumed. No one noticed that his geopolitical view, which carried the day against me, had nothing to do with the validity of my claim for classification as a C.O.

I expected eventual trial and imprisonment. Until I turned twenty-six (the end of eligibility), I never heard a car door close outside my home without thinking it might be the authorities come to take me away. Even though I had a romanticized view of what prison would mean, I was a nervous wreck while waiting. But they never came. Despite the anxiety, I was proud to have stuck to my convictions. I don't think I have ever been tested in such a crystal-clear way since then. I have to believe the experience left me with self-knowledge not otherwise available.

Another incident that happened during this time sealed my convictions about violence and its primary vehicle, guns. I attended the University of Texas at Austin; in August 1966, the summer before my senior year, the Whitman massacre occurred. It was launched from the University Tower, the tallest building by far on campus and near its center. I was always aware of it, owing to its grandeur, its pealing bells marking every quarter hour, and its top-to-bottom illumination in orange whenever athletic victories warranted extra celebration. I often retreated to the observation deck for its views of city and horizon and at times for the feeling of separation it allowed from whatever might be bothering me.[3] Charles Whitman was

---

3. And here is another loss comparable to affordable higher education and amity at the airport, which I discuss below: before the killings, I could hop on the elevator, ascend to the top, spend as much time as I wanted, and go back down with never a question asked, a backpack pawed through, or pockets emptied. Today it is closed to public access except by appointment at certain times and days of the week and accompanied by a university employee.

a Vietnam veteran who may have been impelled by a brain tumor or overwhelmingly painful experiences. For whatever reasons, he led off the night before by killing his mother and wife. The next day, he placed an arsenal of rifles, handguns, and a shotgun along with hundreds of rounds of ammunition in a trunk that he wheeled to the elevators and up to the top of the tower and began randomly shooting: sixteen people were killed and thirty-one injured. It was one of this country's earliest and deadliest mass killings and is considered by some to have launched the mass-murder trend that persists and flourishes even now, fifty-two years afterward. As I write on this October day in 2018, blood is still being cleansed from a synagogue in Pittsburg where an anti-Semite killed at least eleven and wounded others only hours ago. In this country, one is never at a loss for examples of gun violence's assaults on peace and personal safety. Who can fail to notice the contrast in the national reactions to three thousand Americans killed by foreign terrorists on 9/11 and the three thousand Americans killed every three months with guns fired by fellow Americans—a terrorizing spectacle of its own? Obviously, weapons wielded to kill fellow Americans are a sign of freedom, whereas those used by outsiders are just another sign that they hate our freedom (see George W. Bush, September 2001). For me, these are good reasons to reject the thinking that fetishizes guns in lieu of honoring life and for choosing nonviolence as the ethical alternative.

I have been trying to identify early influences—the waters of my immersion as I moved and was moved in time's current. The period that has held my attention runs from my birth in 1945 to the late 1960s. Calendar time is curiously linear, even though built on the cycles of

Earth's turning on its axis while circling the sun. Our solar system moves around the galaxy, which moves through the Universe, which mysteriously expands in all directions: everything in unceasing motion. Every year begins where it started in relation to the sun, but we have each moved another year away from birth toward death. When I think about this and realize that some physicists question the nature and even existence of time, I don't know what that could mean. Time registers change, if nothing else, and transience is a principle of life. Time doesn't pass; we pass through time. We picture it as linear or cyclical, but perhaps it is both, or neither; rather, it may just *be*, and it is our existence within it that we are picturing. This perspective seems both linear and cyclical, but that is in the story and its telling, not in time.

Since high school and undergraduate studies filled most of the 1960s, along with my first foray into graduate school, and my university was a central location for much of the countercultural and political ferment of the time, I need to think more about the effect of other influences beyond what I've said about the origins of my commitments to peace and social justice. (These words sound almost anachronistic now that rust covers them owing to their cultural desuetude.) I've always looked back on that period with satisfaction, since it led me in directions I have been glad for, not to mention that it was an invigorating time to be alive and young. I overstate by only a little when I say that the period before university, living out there in that small rural world dominated by agriculture, fundamentalist religion, and convention, felt comparatively inert. The world according to Eisenhower and Billy Graham was well established and thought to be in good hands. We were not encouraged to query these accepted truths. I was a product of that time and place and, except for those revelations about racial segregation when I was a high-school senior, I left for the university nearly as intellectually innocent as the day I was born. This was a general truth about many young people in those times and places, but I tend to believe my naiveté was even more pronounced than others.' That may not be fair, but it feels true, and in light of the oppression at home and in the local culture, it probably is. I was saved by innate curiosity and openness to different views and have always been grateful for whatever configuration of genes and other accidents allowed that to be.

There I was at university in the mid-sixties; the sense of my accelerating intellectual and cultural awareness was palpable. How anyone then could have avoided it, given the ferment of war, racial reckoning, and life-style experimentation, I cannot fathom. Not that I signed on to everything, I'm sorry to say. My excessive self-restraint persisted and cost me the robust participation in sexual adventures for which I longed. It also may be that those early Royal Ambassador demonstrations of the dangers of evil substances precluded my indulgence in drugs. So my times high on magical chemistry and erotic ecstasy were rare. Intellectual and social-change endeavors had to do. I'm sure they served me better as years passed, although I am damned if I don't wish I had cut loose and experimented more.

Symptomatic of my personality imbalance at twenty-one—too much mind and too little body—I met a friend's sister in my final year at the university. We dated and married right after graduation. A more pluperfect expression of shared emotional immaturity, conventionality, and fear of the future can hardly be imagined. The marriage started its downhill trajectory on the honeymoon. It may have been prophetic that I was struck on the foot by a stingray, the most painful physical experience of my life, when we visited the beach on our way home. Fortunately for both of us, the marriage ended after two years.

Reaching my twenty-fifth year, I had one aborted effort at graduate school and one divorce under my belt and waited daily to be arrested for refusing induction into the army. Prospects for this former co-valedictorian of high school and honors graduate of the university weren't looking too good but, oddly, I may have been in better emotional and psychological condition than ever. I felt free and open to the future, a seemingly new feeling that resulted, I believe now, from stepping off the assembly line carrying me thoughtlessly toward career and family—in Zorba the Greek's words, "the whole catastrophe."

The impetus for leaving my marriage and the assembly line, as well as starting and stopping a second attempt at graduate school, was desperation and yearning. Fortuitously, I found an outlet in human potential encounter groups, which were flourishing at the time. My young wife and I attended one of these, where I met and fell for an exotic, to me, married woman, and with the permissions granted by such groups, pursued her. Thus ended my marriage. I began a short-lived but intense and transformative romance with this woman, but her marriage, unlike my own, survived the upheaval. I soon dropped out of grad school once again. Moving into a small, borderline shabby apartment, I began what was easily the most socially involved and sexually enthusiastic period of my life, which lasted eight months. Layers of shyness fell away as I was involved with a tightly bound group of human potentiates, to coin a usage, and discovered how much I had missed by not being more in the company of women.

I don't want to pass over this period too briskly. My relationship with the new but married woman was transformative, as I have said, but it was part of a transformative period. I think of it as the third event up to that time that was essential to my up-and-away development out of the personality and mind-set that had been formed by my family and rural public-school experiences.

The first of these was the visceral, visible recognition of racism and segregation. I had always lived among Black and Latinx people who had almost exclusively low-status positions such as migrant and other farm workers, housekeepers, and "hands" in various small businesses; this was normal, as if part of the natural order of the world. I thought nothing of it, and although the status differential was obvious, it didn't translate in my mind as inferiority. Even so, I was too thoroughly imbued with the customs of that environment to question how things came to be that way and whether it was right. As I think of it, though, my acculturation wasn't complete, or I would have concluded, as others did, that in fact it was a sign of the naturally inferior working for the naturally superior. I've no idea why I did not take that step, but since I hadn't I was open to the revelation introduced by my high-school friend at that café. Our being served in the dining area and the Black men in the kitchen, where we joined them, was no part of any natural order that I could perceive. It bore no parallel to the farm worker in relation to the farm owner; we were all four equal in just wanting a cup of coffee. Three years later I was registering Black voters in rural Alabama and being accosted by White men who were sure I'd be better off if I'd just "go back home where [I] belonged."

The second transformative event was the experience of four years at the university. Having begun high school two years after *Sputnik* struck fear into American hearts, I had been encouraged to focus on science so I could help protect what was then still called the nation rather than the awkward "homeland." Science was crucial for the space race, the arms race, the race against communist subversion and its quest for world domination (a quest under different rationale the United States had taken for its own). This was the conventional, conflict-driven wisdom conveyed to us by the "establishment" of leaders who, had they been more nuanced and competent and less aggressive and duplicitous, might have had room for a more balanced perspective. I tremble at the memory that people who were promoting the production of tens of thousands of nuclear weapons, and assuring us that "mutual assured destruction" was sound foreign policy, had the lives of humanity in their hands, while their minds wandered the nether regions of fear and ambition. And still do. Progress in the homeland is a spotty affair.

When I left for university, I assumed I would accept my share of the responsibility for national defense like any good citizen. This was not onerous in that I enjoyed science and math, which were said to be our conveyance on the road to victory. My father having been in the army air force during World War II, I even decided during the first semester of my freshman year to join the ROTC. It was not a marriage made in heaven. I couldn't tolerate the regimentation, had a hard time keeping my shoes spit-shined, and never got the hang of marching in formation. By the end of that first semester, I had washed out—and not only from the ROTC. When I discovered the liberal arts and humanities, my compass shifted away from science, helped along by the Kennedy assassination, civil rights ferment, and the intensifying war in Vietnam. As it became clear to me that imperfection and moral failure were no strangers to America, I realized that all the world's flaws were no longer exclusive to the Soviet Union and China, our communist bugaboos. It was not necessary to see our adversaries as innocents to recognize that my own country had considerable blood, literal and figurative, on its hands. Science fascinated me, but it did nothing to help me understand how that blood had gotten there. A large part of my intellectual activity since has been aimed at that understanding and using it to assess conditions within and among nations, especially the conditions of my own, which in general I would say are less than edifying.

My third and final transformation came in 1970, with

my involvement with human potential groups and many of the people drawn to them. I can remember saying at the time that it was like having windows opened that I didn't even know were there. As my social anxieties abated, I realized the pleasures of intimacy, emotional and physical, of which I'd known too little. I experienced joy in altogether new forms and degrees. I enjoyed music and dancing and time with new friends. In short, I launched into a social and libidinal flurry and in the process came to a different sense of what and who I was—more capacious and free, with fewer constrictions and fears—and liked it. I also met the woman who became my second wife, "A," with whom I spent the next twenty-nine years. Near the end of that grand year I even found the answer to the question I'd been asking: would I ever find work that appealed to me? My two brief periods in graduate school had been aimed at an academic career, and I'd changed my mind before starting law school, so my lack of direction was evident. I was enjoying myself, but the prospect of a lifetime of odd jobs did not inspire me.

At one of our human potential gatherings I met a woman who was a clinical social worker, a line of work I'd never heard of, but since she was attractive and friendly, I was anxious to listen. By this time, late in 1970, I'd been sensitized to human relationships and emotional tides by the encounter groups I was attending as well as informal gatherings of the like-minded and my serial romantic engagements, so the idea of counseling troubled individuals and families felt like a natural extension. I was admitted to the University of Texas Graduate School of Social Work. In 1973, I left with a master's degree in clinical social work and went to work at a nonprofit counseling center. A page had turned, the stream of my existence bent and widened.

❧

A pause before considering where the current took me. The agonies of the Vietnam War and awareness that American militarism has been a constant component of our foreign policy since the end of World War II have been among the major influences on my ethical and political development. They have made clear that our domestic violence is consistent with our international behavior and that violence in whatever arena is rarely necessary or uplifting to the human spirit. Hence my pacifism. It seems to me that every American must be affected in some measure by unavoidable habituation to our violent ways, by the moral injuries they precipitate, and by the lost opportunities for building a more life-affirming and convivial society. Lives cannot be understood outside the context in which they developed. I've wanted to learn more about both my life and the surrounding history during its first twenty-eight years. This shouldn't be confused with self-therapy, although they may at times intersect; it arose as a stirring of curiosity while I hiked in the desert and remembered my first time there thirty years earlier. That desert setting was deeply familiar, especially as I walked to remembered sites to see how they'd changed and to reflect on my passage through time. When left alone, things in the desert change slowly. It felt obvious that the desert's permanence, especially the great rock piles, hills, and mountains—with Joshua tree and cholla cactus more closely fitted to human time frames—made a striking counterpoint to the growing signs of my impermanence. My changes are similar to the landscape's, only swifter. I am bound sooner than it to expire, disassemble, and fully return to Nature, as I am increasingly aware.

Situations that stand out among those first three decades of my existence must include the Cold War, which always carried the possibility of nuclear catastrophe. I don't know how many others of my generation consider the Cold

War a personally shaping occurrence. It became something like elevator music, a background presence, easy to forget except when something threatening happened: the Berlin blockade of 1948–49, *Sputnik*, the Cuban missile crisis. But backgrounds have a way of engendering foregrounds, the Vietnam War being a prime example. That disaster has led me to occasional dallying in counterfactual fantasy: suppose we had drawn the appropriate lessons from it, had taken seriously our moral guilt as a nation, had recognized the futility and deep wrongness of imperialistic imposition and violence? With those perceptions and a chastened national soul, what if we had dramatically changed our ways? What if we had shrunk our military, closed bases and brought troops home, supported the United Nations and internationalism, focused on peaceful initiatives abroad and a nation-building at home that spread its benefits more equitably for the good of all? Those actions would have made us a very different people and place. The intervening forty-plus years would have seen Americans shaped in very different ways than we have been. I would even venture a guess that 9/11 would not have occurred, since our bullying tendency to provoke others would have been curtailed. Imagine what a difference that would have made in the national psyche, not to mention the athletic events, courthouses, office buildings, and so on that we could enter and leave freely, rather than under the steely gaze of people bearing arms and standing behind metal detectors. But that is counterfactual not merely in the historical perspective. We would have had to be a very different people within a very different society; we are not a nation that did what it did through inadvertence.

Even though the effects are hard to measure, I do not doubt that the Cold War had distinctive effects on my mind—on everyone's mind. How could persistent survival anxieties not damage people's equilibrium and their confidence in existence, no matter how industriously   those anxieties were repressed? How can awareness of the eventually disastrous consequences of anthropogenic climate disruption not be equally damaging, despite avoidance and denial by many and the inattentiveness of others? But the latter is like a slow, progressively fatal disease—the eventual calamity, though certain, is distant enough to make imaginative apprehension difficult for many people, despite the growing and darkening symptoms. And besides, it is easy to assume that when worse comes to worst, today's adults will be dead and thus mostly unaffected—another emblem of the national psyche. Thus, climate change is even easier to disregard than "the bomb." Who cannot be impressed by the human capacity for delusion and suppression? Even I, who think frequently about the existence of these threats, have become blasé, although in an abnormal way: I figure humans will get what we deserve (even though degrees of individual guilt vary hugely). I can't say I grieve at the prospect of *Homo sapiens*' self-inflicted extinction even while wishing we could manage it with less damage to the remainder of Earth's vast life and still-stunning beauty. I don't deny the sadness of our wandering off the edge into oblivion, nor do I welcome it; I only deny that we are innocent and that it would be tragic. What can be said about a species that knows, or could know if it looked and bestirred itself, that it is marching toward self-induced apocalypse even though it could, if it would, stop?

A little explanation is in order here: I sound misanthropic but am not. What I am, though, is someone who does not believe that humans are transcendent beings—above, beyond, separate from other creation—and I see what is glaringly obvious: we are bad for the Earth and other existence. Like the rest of life, we have a distinctive role to play and distinctive ways of playing it with the distinctive capacities we have been given, but that's not good enough for too many of our species members. Humans are free riders, parasitic on Nature; we don't give anything to biological existence, but we take a lot. Even at death, when we could return our bodies for other uses, we choose to go up in crematory smoke or seal ourselves, suffused with chemicals, in caskets and vaults—forever separate in aspiration, I suppose. Compare, for example, how much ecological loss will result as insect numbers and vast portions of myriad members of other classes of life continue their downward plummet with what would be lost if human numbers crash similarly in consequence of climate change. Notice as well that the insect disappearance is caused by human actions and that our own demise will also be human caused. Can we face the fact and its meaning that the loss of insects would be a disaster for life and Earth, whereas the demise of *Homo sapiens* would be a benefit? *Modern* humans, Americans most particularly, have chosen to be unbound by the rules of the community, to always put ourselves first and the rest be damned. Our behavior puts the larger community at risk, and we know how we would respond if some other species created that risk. We have been heedless and show few signs of the self-awareness that could rein it in. That is what leads me toward complacency at the prospect of our extinction.

To summarize the period's major influences as I experienced them in preparation for the next chapters: the Vietnam War and my confrontation with the Selective Service System, the civil rights movement, undergraduate and graduate school during periods of social and intellectual ferment, marriage, divorce, remarriage. For personal rather than cultural effects, I must include the four years between receiving my BA and beginning studies for the master's in social work—a period of confusion about the future, positive emotional development, and direction setting. Except for university studies, I'm struck by how much that affected me was connected with war and other conflicts, although in the eternal yin and yang of existence I notice too that nonconflictual goods, such as the human potential movement and associated relationships, were influential. Also, I responded to the conflicts with efforts to reduce them in my small way and to do my part to alleviate injustice and emotional suffering where I could. Nothing stops any of us from turning negative circumstances into grist for reflection and amelioration. Were the generation before me to make this accounting, they would cite the Depression, World War II, and memories of World War I. Perhaps they would find the implications even more poignant and disturbing than I do as I consider the role of conflict and deprivation in human development. Those who are insulated from these experiences miss more than they know, not that that's a recommendation of conflict and deprivation.

Having mentioned the Cold War, I realize I've never read any research on what the psychological effects of its forty-year duration were on those of us born near its beginning, but I'm sure studies exist. For that matter, I'm not sure we could say it really ended when the Soviet Union dissolved at the end of 1991. Maybe that was just a pause during which we engaged in a variety of other deadly disputes (Iraq, Haiti, Somalia, Yugoslavia, Bosnia, etc.) while waiting for the official rebirth of a new Cold War, which appears to be gestating right now. In lieu of examining research evidence, I can only speculate that so enduring a hostile impasse, carrying with it the apocalyptic potential it had and still has, is bound to have engendered high levels of insecurity, latent and disguised anxiety, cognitive distortions, and inurement to militaristic excesses—all much different, I am sure, from what an emphasis on peacefulness would have led to. The arrival of terrorism and our responses to it fitted well enough within the broad milieu of our perennial conflicts that it easily made a home where the communist menace once lived. I maintain that we did not have to allow ourselves to be so thoroughly determined by these experiences—conditioned to hostility, fear, and militarism as the preferred responses, as if we had no other choices. A better society with better leadership might have tried harder to resolve conflicts less threateningly and to calm rather than agitate the population. The consequences of the route we took instead have been immensely destructive to lives and property at vast financial cost. I even wonder if our response to human-induced climate change might be different if we weren't so hardened by cold and hot wars and the cultural ambience they have created. Perhaps the human psyche can manage only a limited amount of disaster potential over a given period of time.

CHAPTER 2

CONSOLIDATION: MIDDLE YEARS

THERE WAS MORE TO MY middle years than preoccupation with climate disaster and American militarism. There was anticipation of death. Not from heat stroke or bombs, but as a natural condition of life, its outer boundary, which I couldn't see but knew I would someday cross over.

It began in the late 1970s, when I was in my early thirties. I had been working fulltime as a psychotherapist for five or six years and so had been introduced to an array of psychological issues by several hundred clients. The initiating spark is lost in the mists of memory—Was it certain syndromes or certain clients or a mosaic of encounters and concerns that brought it forward? Or none of these, just life itself? I saw it as a philosophical/existential confrontation with an admixture of discomfort at the knowledge I would one day cease to exist forever. How strange to imagine! The feeling was not morbid or anxious, just inquisitive, along the lines of the verse in Psalms (why do I remember this; it isn't from a text I've ever drawn from) about numbering our days in order to get a heart of wisdom.[1] Since my expiration

---

1. I just looked up that verse—Psalms 90:12, a prayer of Moses. It follows a depiction of days falling under the wrath of God, filled with toil and trouble. For these reasons, I guess, those days are thankfully short, ending "like a sigh." I affirm the psalmist's wisdom and accept that suffering is part of our lot, but not with the dismal vigor of David.

date was presumably in the far-off future, death still did not seem altogether real. It was more of an abstract idea than an absolute certainty. Maybe I'd find a way to avoid it, or it would forget about me, might have been the fantasy. But in the light of day I knew quite well that it was real and that avoidant behaviors were nonsensical, self-defeating, and would conflict with conscious, meaningful living. At that still youthful point in my progression, though, actual dying was less urgent than incorporating the knowledge of eventual death into my consciousness in a way that would reap the benefits of its contemplation: I assumed that bringing future death into present awareness would help me keep a sense of proportion during the predictable events and unpredictable vicissitudes I would encounter along life's way as well as help shape whatever spiritual aspirations I might form. Remembering its transience would add gravity to my life's choices. Self-absorption would become ludicrous in light of the self's brevity, whereas attention to lasting realities, to truth, beauty, and goodness, say, would offer a deeper, more fitting, more fulfilling realm of absorption. Knowing that time is finite, I could remind myself to use it consciously and well. Furthermore, the more I held death in mind and bathed in the calm light of attentive reflection, the more natural and acceptable it should become. Anxiety at the prospect would abate even as the reality grew nearer. Envisioning the post-death eternity without me with the same detachment as the pre-birth eternity without me would follow. To say that life is short hardly does justice to how very, very short it is. Not even a blink of the Universe's eye. So pay attention.

One aspect of this psychological/philosophical project stands out for me. Socrates and a host of other ancient, admirable people were quite clear that their central concern was to fashion a good life, a large part of which meant *tending one's soul*. In later years Aristotle spoke of this as seeking *eudaimonia* (a flourishing life) and Cicero as the *summum bonum* (the highest good). Religious and philosophical thinkers have taken up this concept in various forms periodically ever since. These ideas speak of the ends for which we should live and the ways of life most conducive to realizing them. Within the context of contemplating my eventual death, I could think of no better guidance than to consider that my life's time would be well spent keeping these notions of ends and values brightly in the foreground with death in the shadowy background—death as termination, soul tending as the path leading toward it without fear or regrets. I can't say precisely how successful I've been, but my steady consciousness of this path has made a difference—a big one, I believe.

As I say, I do not remember what drew me in this direction, although it could have been encountering Elizabeth Kubler-Ross's books on death and dying, which would have been helpful in working with certain of my therapy clients. After considerable time in reading and reflection, I realized that intellectual and contemplative attention to death could take me only so far. It remained ineluctably abstract. A near-death experience might have helped, but it didn't seem appealing. Even if I could have arranged one with the certainly of survival, that knowledge would of course leave it still unreal, even if less so. I arranged instead for the intake office at the counseling center where I practiced to send me all cases where death in any fashion was part of the presenting problem. I also began volunteering at a hospice and co-led a support group for seriously ill cancer patients. Soon I was surrounded by sick and dying people, immured in mortality. Even the co-leader of my support group died. Abstraction receded.

Lest one wonder, I did not see these people as mere subjects for my learning more acute awareness of death's reality. As I did with virtually all my clients, I came to care about them, grieved at their passing, and came to admire how almost everyone died in an eventually accepting and emotionally dignified manner even when their disease was ugly and messy.

One I recall who did not was a young and very beautiful woman who came to my office seeking what I did not have to offer and unable to accept what I did. She had had great plans and now was forced to watch in anger, fear, and pain as her beauty was ravaged and as the terrible graffiti of lines drawn on her body guided the radiologist's relentless machine as it futilely tracked the lineament of her cancer. Then, as a final insult, her hair fell out. Her dying was miserable; everyone who cared about her experienced a share of it. The only time I remember seeing her at peace was when she was in the casket. I believe that, to her final breath, she could never accept what was happening. Her denial and anger made the inevitable all the worse, all the more unacceptable, all the more painful and agonizing. Death's potential meanings were lost in her anguish and rejection of dying.

I spent over a year working with people whose final chapters were in sight, ending only when I moved to a counseling center in another city, this time as executive director. Had it worked? Had death become real? Could I count on keeping it effectively present in my mind? How much difference would it make to my attitudes and decisions? I can say only a few things about it now with much certainty. (The closer death comes, the more I will know.) Death has in fact been a reliable presence in my awareness (so much so that my wife occasionally looks at me with a look of incomprehension and concern). From time to time it has smiled knowingly at me, bringing thoughts and visions bearing my own *memento mori* (a "reminder that you will die"), reminiscent of those found in Platonic, Stoic, and Christian philosophy and that often appear in religiously themed art. Now that I've reached the age where it is losing abstraction, I have a strong sense of nonanxious acceptance that death will surely come, sooner than later at this point, and is natural and okay. My study of Buddhism and Stoicism also contributed, even though I've not approached them with mortality as a focus. Since there has been an abundance of animals in my life, there has also been an abundance of death, their lives being so comparatively short. I remember a few years ago digging a grave for one of our small dogs. Once the hole was dug and he was tucked in, I stood back and looked and was struck decisively with the sense of how fitting it appeared. He was cozily ensconced in the Earth, which welcomed him back as I covered him with soil.

Thoughts of death cross my mind almost daily, usually only in passing but sometimes in ways that I pause over. The need to assess and make decisions about my heart condition has had the effect of moving my attention from thinking of dying primarily as a more or less slow process to recognizing the possibility of mortality as immediacy: of dropping dead on the spot or, what feels close to the same thing, being deprived of many of my favorite capacities by a stroke, the most likely calamity to befall from atrial fibrillation. These latter prospects have the effect of drawing my attention more intensely to living consciously in the present. I know the activities that most matter to me, and I intend to give them their due. If I die in a place I love, in the company of a loved one, or while engaged with endeavors I consider meaningful, I will have done okay.

I have also come to realize that my early anticipation of a conscious and rational dying experience in which last words could be spoken, my life's time reviewed and parts of it savored, and then passing on with curious attentiveness until the light faded away . . . all of this was probably naive and idealistic. Few deaths are so generous as to allow a stately procession beyond the horizon, so to whatever extent those things are to occur, they must be incorporated into earlier periods of reflection; dying itself may well have other business to do when the time comes, possibly painful and drug addled.[2]

As a coda to these years of dealing with death, I recently made arrangements for my wife's and my postmortem disposition. I felt no presentiment of imminent need, no morbid preoccupation; I am several years older than my wife and a planner by nature, which she is not. I considered it a convenience and a burden removed from her, since she is likely to survive me, and she agreed. We will not be embalmed. We will be buried (on the wildlife sanctuary, near that dog I mentioned) not in caskets but in shrouds and laid on woven carriers. These will be put two and a half feet deep in the ground, the shallowest burial the law allows, in order to be closer to the most biologically active soil and thus more quickly taken up by other lives for their own purposes. (I joke that the good news is people do live forever, but not consciously or intact.) Our body/selves decompose, spread out, and are ingested by microbes, fungi, and countless tiny creatures and eventually scuttle or fly away as parts of still larger lives. I consider this the most pleasing thing of all about Nature's way of carrying on, of incorporating my demise into her further needs, and am grateful that she has allowed me time to participate and, at the end, to yield this small return on her investment.

For twenty-one years (1973–94) I built psychotherapeutic and administrative competence and (mostly) enjoyed working in five mental health agencies scattered from Georgia through Texas to California, with a two-year diversion to Alaska. There, I contracted with the state to serve

2. If psychedelic enhancements are available when the time comes, as they were for example to Aldous Huxley, would I want to go out that way? I'm not sure. I'm only sure of not wanting to linger in a highly impaired, mentally compromised state.

as a court-appointed guardian for abused and neglected children in state custody, meaning that I represented their interests in Children's Court and in dealings with state and private social service agencies. In 1986, I became restless. I had continued my reading in philosophy and ethics, and I considered a return to graduate school. In the serendipitous way that things sometimes happen, I became friends with a historian on the faculty of the Institute for Medical Humanities at the University of Texas Medical Branch, which was nearby. As I spoke to him of my long interest in philosophical ethics (twenty years by that point) and a possible return to school, he suggested I become a student at the Institute, which was just beginning to accept PhD candidates and had more faculty than humanities students (those not studying medicine). I leapt at the chance, applied, was accepted, and began. Since the courses were small seminars and tutorials, and I had flexibility as head of the counseling center, I could do both full time. I felt immense satisfaction in being a student again, especially in the informal and intense milieu of six to eight students working at different times with perhaps ten faculty from all around the humanities, and with no thought about credentials or work-related benefits. The faculty's primary roles were teaching, research, publication, and introducing medical students to interfaces between humanities and medicine; courses included the history of medicine, literature and medicine, and law, ethics, sociology, and religion in relation to medicine. Programs such as this one had begun mostly in the early 1970s, when technological changes in medical interventions, such as *in vitro* fertilization and other reproductive techniques, were arising and promising to expand and confound traditional ways of thinking. It was considered prudent for medical schools to have at least one philosopher hanging about to offer ethical counsel. A few of the programs, like mine, took off and covered the territory about as thoroughly as one could imagine.

Initially, I was most interested in medical ethics but in time moved toward environmental ethics, which became my real home.

I remember the precise moment when this turn was stimulated, as well as the place, and it was far from library or seminar room. I had bought a weekend property on a small piece of lakefront land in the forests of East Texas and spent most of my free time there. I hiked in the forest and, although not an enthusiast, fished occasionally. One day as I lifted a minnow to impale on a hook for bait, a thoughtless act I'd performed many times, I watched his reaction, which was what I have called ever since a silent scream—his mouth flew open and he squirmed in obvious distress before accepting his fate. I was shaken by the realization of how much suffering ignorance could cause. That evening I prepared our usual lakeside dinner of barbecued animal parts: chicken, pig, and cow. It neither looked nor tasted as before. I had been ruined as a carnivore. With no preparation for the role, I had been moved into an animal-rights conception of appropriate relations between human and nonhuman animals and became a vegetarian, which has continued ever since. It didn't take long before I came to the same sense of moral duties in the realm of human relations with the natural world. My environmental ethic fell into the range of what are called ecocentrism, deep ecology, and ecofeminism. For me this became a conviction that the rights, needs, and very being of the nonhuman realms were rightly seen as sharing equally in the beneficence of existence and as deserving moral attentiveness equal to that we routinely offer, or pretend to offer because we know we should, to fellow humans. A tiny fish led the way.

But not only the fish. I had moved into a different frame of mind as I studied and spent time at the lake. One night I lay near the water's edge, looking at stars. I ended up spending the night there, intermittently sleeping and being absorbed in the water, the trees, the rustle of creatures moving around—and those stars. It was close to the unitive experience spoken of by mystics, and I was decisively moved by it. I was fortunate to have a philosopher as my dissertation advisor (a woman with a keen sense of Nature and the physical world, owing perhaps to her early years as a nurse) who understood and nurtured my investigations. The fish had help in my awakening.

In a few years, it was time to write my dissertation, which was to become a study of how rights of Nature and rights of animals—human and nonhuman—were interconnected and how an ethic of respect should shape our relations with all. As dissertations tend to be, it was ponderously titled: *Martin Buber's I–Thou Relation within the Sphere of Nature.* I resigned my position at the counseling center, loaded boxes of books and a World-War-II-vintage Royal typewriter into a pickup camper, and headed west for on-the-ground research and writing. Martin Buber and a variety of other philosophers provided inspiration from the human side; John Muir, Edward Abbey, Joseph Wood Krutch, and others did the same from the side of Nature. I wanted to walk in their footsteps, sometimes literally, as I read their books, interpreted their philosophy and ethics, and allowed myself to engage as deeply as I could with desert and mountain. The Sierra Nevada and the California and Arizona deserts became my teachers.

That was 1988, and it's hard to believe now just how ignorant I was about the nitty-gritty of Nature. My time in East Texas forests and beside the lake was about the extent of my exposure. My deep attraction to wider natural spaces was essentially romantic and intellectual, which does not mean it was insipid or altogether abstract but that it lacked exposure and experience leading to direct, unmediated knowledge. I knew intuitively that the natural world was right for me, that it spoke in a voice I could respond to, but I didn't know where the affinity—really, the love—came from. The national parks and other public lands were the best places to learn, and that is where I went.[3]

The source of my affinity ought not to have been mysterious; that it was indicates how many of us humans have allowed ourselves to separate psychologically and spiritually, even physically, from our inherent ground in Nature. Just as people become deeply divided within themselves when values, emotions, thoughts, and inborn proclivities become incongruent with each other and with surrounding reality—as they face internal conflict and anxiety (existential arrhythmias, I call them, analogous to those of the heart)—they can fall into a parallel situation with the natural world, our place of emergence and our home, even when we're alienated from it and forget. Either or both of these splits in personality mean less wholeness and so less richness of experience, less apprehension of reality. Meaning suffers. As I worked to repair my damaged relation with Nature, or allowed it space to repair itself, I was renewed.

After seven months of hiking and note taking, immersing and reflecting, reading, writing and rewriting, I finished, endured my orals, and was sent off with my new degree. I turned the camper toward Alaska, where I arrived three weeks later. From initial seminar to completion, my final foray into formal education was all I could ask for, a wonderful experience.

And more than that. The seven months as scholar-anchorite affected my attitudes toward just about everything. Although never a workaholic, I was heavily focused on work, but afterward it became just one of the important things I did. Squeezing in time away from work to spend in natural settings became equally important. I was always a heavy reader, but my reading moved from professional publications toward philosophies of Nature, animal rights,

---

3. To those who consider drilling oil, cutting trees, grazing cattle, and mining ore the highest uses of these beatific places: I suggest you take another look, reexamine your souls, and let your taste for beauty and natural goodness run free.

and natural history. My beliefs in humanity's (self-)eleva-
tion to the earthly apex and status as practically the sole
carrier of moral value fled like darkness at sunrise. Finding my species to be a member rather than the rightful
owner and dominator of the life community was liberat-
ing, but also alarming: our breaches of respect and comity,
the self-centered damage we inflicted, the general lack of
awareness... The cultural alienation that had taken root in
my mind owing to America's wars on fellow humans was
reinforced by recognition that our wars on Nature were
indulged with similar motivations, destructiveness, and
lack of conscience. Violent grabbing seemed to be just what
we did and who we were.

It was not just books and my extended presence in
prized landscapes that turned me. Along with the joy of
beauty and Nature's goodness, I encountered the grief of
their losses. Although the reality of climate change and
its certain consequences was beginning to be addressed,
that wasn't what initially caught my attention. At that stage,
the most dramatic evidence for humans' abuse of Nature
came in my trips to East Texas. Driving through clear-cut
forests had the strongest effects on me. It was obvious
that the deliberate destruction of an entire forest or a large
part of it in virtually an instant implied the destruction of
countless animal lives and their homes and habitats—the
loss of an ecosystem, precipitation of suffering, and an
impoverished landscape. I knew there were better, more
peaceful ways to cut trees for lumber, but ways that meant
less immediate profit per acre, making them unacceptable to industrial-scale tree harvesting, which seemingly
marches to the beat of but one drummer. The destruction,
the death, the profit-seeking...and the equally egregious
offense of what was left after the massacre was accomplished. Ugliness—terrible, revolting, stomach-turning
ugliness; land littered with slash that was too much trouble
to put to use, land scarred and compacted by machinery,

land mortally injured, land whose abundance had been taken and replaced with desolation. To this day I cannot encounter a clear-cut without revulsion.

I was touched as well by less dramatic abuses. Living on Galveston Island and jogging on the beach most mornings, I found it littered with wave-brought trash from boats and the oil-drilling platforms visible on the horizon. Drilling also led to oil spills, much of which landed on the beach. I had grown up in agricultural country before the onset of indus-trial farming but over time witnessed its expansion and the imposition of monocultures nurtured by chemical fertil-ization and protected by poisons. As the environmental movement took shape, it was good at pointing out habitat losses and species extinctions, toxified air and water, and so on, while pressing for protection of special landscapes and native wildlife. What the environmentalists were not good at then and even now was confronting the economis-tic assumptions and practices that are societally accepted as definitive of progress toward better living. The belief that Nature is only a bundle of resources awaiting trans-formation into commodities and profit, and the assump-tion underlying this notion that materialistic aspirations are all that matter: until this framework changes, all of the patching, preserving, and frantic ameliorating pressed by environmentalists will come to rather little, as the present rollbacks by a president and party that stand foursquare for exploitation and commodification grandly demon-strate. Recognition of the intrinsic goodness of being has been driven from the land—not that it ever had much of a place once the indigenes were exterminated or oppressed in line with those same assumptions.

The abuses disturbed me enormously, of course, but as I suggested, it was the beauty and spirit, the palpable mystery and entwinements, of natural landscapes that turned my head irrevocably and had the greater impact on me. What more could I want? And for those theistically inclined, what more could they need as sign of God's hand on the Earth? An overflowing gift was there for accepting.

An early sign of the gift, powerful and definitive, came when I reached the Sierra Nevada on my dissertation quest. Over the preceding days of driving a thousand plus miles, I had endured bouts of high anxiety. What on earth had I done by leaving a good job and taking off on a romantic journey that might only expose my incompetence as writer, Nature explorer, and scholar, and having no notion what I would do when (if) I successfully finished? But then I turned west off Highway 395 in eastern California, ascended the mountains, and entered Yosemite National Park through Tioga Pass at a ten-thousand-foot elevation. I spent days in Tuolumne Meadows on domes and trails, moved farther west and hiked a sequoia grove, turned and drove for miles high above Merced Canyon, and then descended into Yosemite Valley. My anxiety had submerged and been forgotten somewhere along the way. Mostly, I now thought about the impossibility of what I was seeing. Earth could not do these things with itself—but it did. I mean this literally: I fell in love.[4]

When my dissertation was finished, I was forty-three years old. My career in mental health was fifteen to sixteen years along its way, but beginning to feel like more of my past than my future. I now had a PhD irrelevant to my career but deeply relevant to who I was becoming. I had remarried in 1970, this time to "A," a woman who had two young children. Thus I gained the experience of stepparenthood, which I did not relish. I'd never had a moment of wanting to father children, but during this phase I probably experienced the same assemblage of satisfactions, frustrations,

---

4. At the end of 2018 I published a book called *Reverence for Existence: A Way of Knowing,* which describes in detail what I refer to here.

and disappointments that most families endure, along with some unique to stepfamilies.

Considering how I felt about my family of origin, especially about my father, my sudden immersion into life with two preschool-aged children deserves attention, since it was a prominent feature in the next fifteen to twenty years of my life. When we start new families, we naturally bring with us residues, mostly unconscious, of the families we grew up in, so the sudden transition was bound to stir things internally. At the beginning, I was so entranced by the children's mother that I failed to realize what I was getting into. The younger of the two was a particularly sensitive boy, more obviously hurt by his parents' divorce and therefore more emotionally changeable, even though his father continued to be a reliable presence and caretaker and both parents were committed to cooperation for the kids' benefit. They never wavered in that resolve and were admirable, mutually supportive parents, but this was occurring in the early 1970s. In those days, it seemed that practically everyone was hell-bent on "self-realization"; all of us adults in the children's lives shared that affliction. Thus, none of us was precisely a beacon of stability, which of course affected the children. Even so, in retrospect I see that those cultural and emotional forces notwithstanding, the natural parents were unwaveringly dedicated to their children's well-being and surrounded them with abundant and unremitting love, a blessing too few children of divorce enjoy (too few children of any sort, perhaps).

It is impossible for divorce not to be wrenching for children (not surprising—look what it does to the adults), even though guilt drives many divorcing people to deny it. However, it is equally true that continuity of caring, reciprocal support between father and mother, and the unvarying message that they divorced one another but not the children and that their loyalty to them will never falter—these go a long way toward mitigation. "A" and the children's natural father were exemplary in these respects.

The stepparents, on the other hand, floundered. We meant well, for sure (I can't speak for the father's new wife, the stepmother, although it appeared to be so), but I swiftly realized that parenting was not a natural role for me, either by preference or by constitution. Still, I felt a responsibility to the children and their mother at least not to be harmful. I succeeded at that, as far as I know. I cared for them and engaged with them as much as I could but never quite worked out the best balance between caring presence and guiding/judging parent. Regardless, for the most part we achieved a *modus vivendi* that worked and sometimes even crossed over into genuine closeness. In the insightful words of the little girl at eight on a day when I apologized for a grumpy period: "Well, you weren't the one who decided to have kids." My minimal aspiration was not to repeat my father's behaviors, which I had so disliked as a child (as an adult as well) until I was able to lay the feelings about them aside, and at that I mostly succeeded. I was more willing to engage with them, although less than what I imagine as ideal, and I was not punitive. Even when feeling most afflicted by child presence, I rarely forgot the problem was primarily internal to me. Neither "A" nor I believed in corporal punishment, so that was never an issue. For the most part, I kept my frustrations contained, which means I didn't inflict them directly on the children, even if I never could completely conceal them. I suppose that made me a more or less normal parent in that respect.

I've never considered it useful, either in therapy or everyday life, for adults looking back on childhood to blame their parents for this or that character flaw or neurosis they've grown into. We are each a product of far too many contingent occurrences, known and unknown, for that to be completely fair or accurate. Even so, any aware person is going to want to understand as best they can their relations with parents, what were significant events and ongoing dynamics, what seemed helpfully formative and what did not, and so on. I cannot know but am inclined to believe that if my father's children, my brothers and I, had appeared to give him parental satisfaction—a few signs that he sometimes enjoyed and wanted to understand us and help in our progress toward adulthood—if these things had happened, then I might have been drawn to have children of my own. That's just a surmise, a hypothesis. But I realize, too, that my preference for tranquility and long periods of aloneness were themselves not predictive of a soul yearning for fatherhood, so my surmise may be erroneous or just one of the factors. I'll never know, but I have no procreative regrets. That may be the best sign that, whatever made rocking the cradle aversive, it fit my nature.

I also know from years of simple observation of families in public places and of working in marital and family therapy that people gravely err in assuming that because they are married they must become parents. Human overpopulation is one argument against it, but closer to home, not everyone is equipped for the job emotionally or by predilection and personality. It is serious work of a sort that requires the frequent submerging of selfish ego in favor of doing what's best for others. I know of no studies that dare to suggest parenting is more pleasure than pain, all things considered, after eighteen or so years at it. Parents surely feel ultimate satisfaction when the job is done well, and a sense of a duty fulfilled and even pleasure in their children's presence as adults and eventually in the grandchildren, but getting there is a hard row to hoe. And I doubt seriously that many of the "I can have it all"–type individuals who become parents these days manage to reach their lofty, possibly delusional, ambitions. (And if they imagine they have, it may be because they asked too little of themselves as parents, with the result that their children become disgruntled spectators of the parents' ascent.) I have as great admiration for good parents, as I have for anyone doing anything well. When I witness good parenting, I am invariably moved—just as I am oppositely moved by the sight of parents with eyes glued to their little hand-held screens while their preschooler stands idly by.

During 1989–1990, a year and a half, "A" and I lived in Alaska. (The older child was on her own by this time and the younger lived with his father.) This move was prompted solely by our attraction to a remote and beautiful land that in imagination (and eventual reality) was imposing as few places are. We rented a house hanging on the side of a deep glacial valley and had the pleasure of watching the progress of termination dust, as early snow is called, slowly whiten the opposite peaks and work its way downward as the days beat their inexorable rhythm toward winter. Single-engine airplanes flew up the valley below us, and occasionally we found grizzly bear scat nearby. Mount Redoubt, a volcano a hundred or so miles southwest, blew fumaroles daily that we could see from the living room. Overall, it was a wonderful time in a wonderful place but not intended for permanence.

Then it was back to the Lower 48, followed by a couple of years as the head of a community mental health center, the realization that that phase of my life had ended, and, in 1994, my move into animal-protection work. I don't think it was just the temporal proximity, but it seems as if the last twenty-four years since that move have been the most meaningful ones, although I'm not sure about that. Therapeutic involvement with people trying to make better inner and outer lives for themselves fascinated me, but as time passed I was increasingly doubtful about humans' capacity for significant change, at least through psychotherapy. People are not exactly fixed in nature and behavior, but by the time they give therapy a try neither are they creatures primed for easy renovation. Changing minds and habits is a formidable enterprise. No one becomes who they are at any point without reason. Humans are surrounded and permeated by forces that resist change.

But crises, impasses, difficult transitions, and clear demon-strations that old ways no longer work have a way of desta-bilizing those forces and creating space for new directions. Important changes sometimes happened, much to my satisfaction as well as the clients'.

Working with and for animals raises far more ethical questions than does working with people. We assume we know what we owe each other, whereas our acknowl-edged obligations to nonhuman animals remain in flux. My long-standing interest in practical ethics and my more recent engagement with Nature almost guaranteed I would find the animal world, and by extension the natural world, deeply engaging of both ethical reflection and affection. For now I can say, looking back at my first twenty-five or so years of adulthood, that they encompassed the satisfac-tions of meaningful work and continued education, a good marriage to a fine woman, and in addition, the chief and most far-reaching development of the period: my growth into a lived philosophy of reverence for Nature and moral respect for the rights and needs of everything that is part of it, from animals and trees to ecosystems.

This last element was a long way from where I'd started as a young enthusiast for Southern Baptist reli-gion; a long way even for old leftist political associates like my friend from high school who couldn't get the inclusion of Nature and animals into a theory he believed could include justice only for humans. I came to see that all injustices have a common core, that in whatever area they appear they share a dismissal of the intrinsic value and fundamental needs of other beings. Speciesism, racism, authoritarianism, militarism, economism, sexism: the template always calls for hierarchies of individuals and classes variously characterized by egoism, fear and resentment, entitlement and intolerance, and sometimes violence against those considered less worthy of free lives and respect.

Reverence for Nature became part of my being, first implanted by experience and later by conceptualization. One of the attractions of ancient philosophy is the prominence it generally gives to justice as a central virtue; some early thinkers even thought that justice alone might encompass all other virtues. I can see why. If we care to be just in our relations with others (whatever or whoever those others might be), we will incorporate reason, generosity, sympathy, objectivity, a commitment to truth and goodness—and perhaps most of all, restraint of ego accompanied by the recognition of oneself as only one among many.

While I'm here, I want to say a few words on behalf of my Southern Baptist origins. It was a religion I happily fled once adulthood beckoned; it didn't offer me anything of a truly spiritual nature. Its belief system portrayed God as transcendentally judgmental. We were expected to mollify his ire at our persistent sinfulness as much as possible—but paradoxically, we could call on him whenever we needed help. I was an obedient Christian soldier for several years; for some of them, I fully expected to receive a *call* to prepare to eventually head to Africa as a missionary to heathens, but the wider my world became as I grew older, the narrower and less fitting this religion appeared. And when I ran smack dab into adolescent sexuality, it didn't stand a chance. Even so, I give credit to that early churchgoing for my developing a strong conscience (too strong sometimes) and a sense there was more to the world than was readily visible, which had much to do with honoring right over wrong, care for others over self-seeking. As a religion, it was too limited to get much past yearning for salvation and everlasting life and so had no response to what I inchoately yearned for, but it knew sin backward and forward. I retain that knowledge, in altered and attenuated form. I will also add that although the salvific purpose did not speak to me, the sense that we should live for purposes that are more than meet the eye did. Conscience plus an ultimate purpose—it was worth the effort and I acknowledge debt where it is due.

Even so, if I may wander briefly into the present political scene, the vast acquiescence, even enthusiasm, that evangelical Christians have offered to Donald Trump, even going so far as to propose that he was anointed by God to fulfill the role he took on [???], is a sign to me of a lethal deficiency in their religiosity, one that unconsciously I may have recognized early. Their spirituality and ethical commitment appear subordinate to their desire for immediate political gains (e.g., antiabortion legislation) and for theologically authoritarian control of the country. Such fundamentalist orthodoxy would make unselfish love secondary to the safety and security they imagine they will feel in a society that justifies any desperate means of attaining it. They are not *too much* religious; rather, *too little*, if imitation of Jesus is the crucial guide. They are noticeably vociferous in claims that their religious freedom is under attack on multiple fronts by implacable secularity while they work tirelessly to suppress the freedom of others (for example, through outlawing abortion). I have no problem with their private decision that abortion is not acceptable according to their religious convictions, but their determination to make illegal the expression of different convictions by others contradicts their supposed commitment to freedom of belief. I have heard them described as believing that life begins at conception and ends with birth, meaning that once a baby is born, sometimes into straitened circumstances, their concern ends, just as it seems to end at the executioner's death chamber and the war machine's latest death-dealing foray. The belief that a fertilized egg is a fully accredited moral person relies on a particular religious ontology that neither science, philosophy, nor most other religious systems will support. The effort to impose it on others strikes me as both arrogant and tyrannical. I admire a wide variety of religions and the people who sincerely represent them, but the people I have just described are not among them.

In full disclosure, I also have to add that that little church where I grew up must share responsibility for making some sins very attractive to me. It used to be, and maybe still is, that country churches had annual, sometimes semiannual, revivals. Preachers from afar would be brought in for a week's worth of sermons and soul saving. I assume this was a sign of recognition that resident preachers' ability to lash consciences with stinging condemnations of sinfulness, baleful warnings about hell, and promises of salvation for those who would "confess" and swear to put sin behind them and change their lives might have lost novelty and effectiveness through familiarity. It might also be that as a visitor the revivalist could remonstrate and vibrate with a passionate intensity that the resident couldn't routinely match or been chary of exposing to people he saw on a regular basis. These revival weeks were fully charged with the Holy Spirit, as we used to say. I very clearly remember one preacher who materialized for his period at the pulpit when I was an early adolescent and for whom fire and brimstone were merely a warmup for the incandescent heart of his sermons. The mistake he made, at least for one young, impressionable listener, was to vigorously, albeit obliquely, confess his own pre-salvation sins so evocatively that I could not help fantasizing about just what he had done and how inviting it sounded. The image and the temptation were with me for a long time before I could either let them go or yield to them, the latter having become preferable.

Benchmarks along the way: I note the effects of my particular family dynamics and of growing up in rural Texas; my choice of conscientious objection in the context of the Vietnam War; the dynamics of marriage and husband-hood; my development of a radical left political orientation despite being surrounded by a radical right family and rural culture; emergence from my shell of self-doubt; and finally, my choice of career direction. It is clear that the experienced continuity of a life incorporates punctuations along the way that infuse and sometimes disrupt its even flow. Thank goodness. The disruptions and how we manage them probably deserve the most examination and appreciation.

This brings me to thinking more about my marriage experiences. I consider myself a passable but in some ways inferior kind of husband, mostly owing to my solitary nature. For instance, I began writing several months ago, camped alone in the desert. Now I'm back, alone and writing in another desert. I've been married or living in sin, as my mother referred to it, virtually my entire adult life and yet never fully fathomed marriage's hold on my imagination and choices. I was always conflicted about it; always returning to its fold. I have been married three times, but it's a toss-up whether the first really counts since I was twenty-one and she nineteen, and we were preternaturally ignorant and immature in the emotional realm. I refer to it sometimes as my "learning" marriage: two and a half years and it was over, with little to dissolve but the legal tie. Neither of us knew why we were there, what was required of us, what to expect, or how to conduct ourselves after wandering into it. It was a marriage in name only. Besides our youth, part of the problem was that neither of us had been exposed to the best of marital models growing up. Her parents had divorced when she was young, and her father was an alcoholic. Her mother never remarried and nurtured a robust disdain for males. My parents didn't divorce but showed little pleasure in each other's company, with scant conversation or laughter and less affection. I am almost surprised they conceived three sons, given the absence of overt intimacy.

During my career as a psychotherapist, much of my practice was in marital and family therapy. With struggling couples who had children, I often expressed the insight—which I had learned along the way—that about the best gift parents could give their children was a happy marriage. Child management is one thing, but a child's daily experience of parents bound in a reciprocity of respect, caretaking, and deep satisfaction at the good fortune of having found each other is a gift beyond measure, a gift that keeps giving over a child's lifetime. I never had any desire to father a child, a feeling I know partly derived from the lack of this kind of experience along with the sense emanating from my father that his sons gave him no pleasure.[5] In fairness, as already mentioned, my avoidance of fatherhood is bound also to have had something to do with my aversion to chaos and my attraction to uncomplicated time alone or with my wife.

My first "marriage" ended and was followed by the quasi-Dionysian period already described. Then I met "A," who was my wife for the next twenty-nine years. After that ended I found myself with Lynn, the woman with whom I've been living and/or married for nineteen years. Adding it up, I have spent forty-nine years married or cohabiting over a period of fifty-one years. Whether passable as a husband or not, I am clearly a marrying sort of man. But why? I enjoy solitude more than most people do. Over the past couple of decades, that solitude has meant spending three to four months every year alone, camping and hiking in the mountains and deserts. Even at home, I spend considerable time in my study reading or writing. I don't enjoy the company of most people, socialize only occasionally, and am never found at parties. Both "A" and

---

5. As with so many men of his sort, the grandchildren my brothers provided gave him delight. I suspect their fecundity drew him at least a little closer to them than would have happened otherwise. My childlessness formed another missing link in our capacity for relating to one another.

Lynn have had enormous patience with me, although it must also be true that the freedom this gave them was to some degree welcomed. They are independent and very involved with animals, work, children ("A's" from her marriage before me), and social or volunteer engagements, so in that sense they were built for a husband like me, or at least well equipped to cope. But I have wondered why I didn't reverse the order of things and live alone while forming nonresidential commitments in lieu of residential marriages. I attribute it to convention, the primordial fear of losing what I didn't hold sufficiently close, and to enjoying reliable companionship. Marriage is a balancing act, but I might have tried balancing outside marriage. And in periods of retrospection, that sometimes seems as if it would have been preferable, although I'm not sure that isn't merely a form of the "grass is greener" syndrome. It is hard to believe I could have been wrong forty-nine out of fifty-one years and not have it revealed to me before now, when I've entered the last stage of life.

There's much more I could say about these marriages and the transition from "A" to Lynn, but I won't, even though I intend this document to be open and honest. Speaking more would carry me into private realms where I would not venture out of respect for them. I will only say that I love them both and have immense admiration for each. I consider it one of my life's blessings to have lived major portions of it in their presence.

The decade on which I place such importance, 1963 through 1973, ended with the start of my mental health and social services career, and I imagine that much of the reason for my taking to it with such enthusiasm were the events of the preceding years. The agencies where I worked had counseling and therapy components along with, variously, programs aimed at child abuse, homelessness, substance abuse, and domestic violence. I believed in what we were doing and that it made a difference in many lives. I gained the insight from family therapy that working with problem children without also working with their troubled families was usually of limited value, since the latter's influence was stronger and more pervasive than the therapist's. It now seems equally apparent that many of the therapeutic and other intervention efforts mentioned could bear little lasting fruit, since racial and class oppression, along with an entire menu of other societal failures, ground on, more or less oblivious to their casualties. American society seems never to have consciously, intentionally, and lastingly organized itself to ensure the common good. We operate in an atomized human environment lacking the solidarity of care that could prevent or mitigate many personal pathologies and much suffering. I eventually concluded that our society is seriously lacking what I call a basic respect for life, and that a major sign of that was its willingness to allow large numbers of vulnerable people to fall through its cracks—and a world-record number of others to be banished to incarceration and forgotten about. Ironically, the endemic failures are mostly generated by society itself, which therefore finds it most comfortable to disregard them. Its individualistic rationale covers a lack of humanity. Vulnerability tends to be treated as personal failure and as misuse of everyone's intrinsic free will, even though it's clear that freedom of will is quite limited, more for some than others.

For three years during the late eighties and early nineties, I did not work in mental health settings. For a third of that time, I worked on my dissertation and completing my doctorate; I spent the remainder in Alaska, drawn there by its natural wonders and the desire to experience them directly. My work there with abused and neglected children in state custody did nothing to contradict the view I'd developed about the vulnerability of the relatively weak to powerful cultural forces. When I returned to the Lower 48, I spent two years as executive director of a community mental health center, day by day feeling the deepening of my concern that too much effort was going into bandaging victims, people whose wounds generally required more intense and comprehensive intervention, never mind the benefits of a societal context more structured around humane values and caring practices than our own is. My energy for the work was fast being depleted; my experiences in natural world settings, launched originally at my East Texas retreat and then working on my dissertation, had enlivened a desire to work on behalf of Nature and animals.

As mentioned earlier, I did not embark on this writing with the thought it would become as critical and emotional as it occasionally has. But I see now it was inevitable. How could a life story told with particular attention to the concurrent, turbulent events that shaped that life not have moments of heat, much of which derives from sadness at what seem to me lost opportunities to cultivate communal goods? Even so, as I think about these emotions and attitudes now, I can't help wondering how they evolved as they did and why these particular concerns took hold of me as they have. My present convictions began coming together at university and evolved and matured over the succeeding years; I tend to think they were close to their present shape when I reached my forties (the late 1980s and early nineties), although naturally modified since then by age, experience, and study. They feel coherent and consistent and have become a large part of who I am. The attitude I have come to refer to and write about as *reverence for existence* expresses my conviction that respect and compassion are the right way to live toward others, any and all others and toward *being* itself. Pacifism; promotion of justice and egalitarianism; recognition of the rights of animals to their own versions of life, liberty, and happiness; veneration for and protection of Nature, including its biodiversity, beauty, and natural climatic and other processes: these cover the attitude I'm talking about, which I regard as the positive counterpart to the criticisms I have offered. Without a compensatory vision, criticism is unbalanced.

I cannot be simplistic about this. These words speak to whole realms of current reality and my view of ethical responses to suffering and injustice. But I also know that others could affirm many of these words as written and still support attitudes and endeavors that I object to. I remember once talking about animal rights with a man who steadfastly claimed a powerful respect for animal welfare but who also thought uses of animals for food and research were acceptable if conducted with care to mitigate suffering. Words are only words and can open quite different individual meanings. I don't write these pages with evangelistic motives, although I occasionally write essays with an explicitly advocative or expository purpose but not with confidence they will change many minds (some of these compose the second part of this book).

Most history and autobiography begin at the beginning and work their way forward. Mine has meandered, but I hope not confusingly. I didn't want to describe sequential segments of time and life so much as I wanted to understand better how I arrived at the finale of a life now approaching its last years, which meant that atemporal associative processes sometimes intervened. I have been critical of directions the culture has taken, and yet I somehow managed to build a good life within it. If so much was so bad, how has that been possible? Since I don't find nourishment in bitter fruits, some explanation is needed: I really have achieved most of what I wanted and am content with my life more often than not, even though I would prefer to live in at least a dozen other countries than the United States.[6]

I have been lucky. Being White and of normal abilities have given me a leg up to begin with. (On the other hand, it is morally unlucky to live in a caste culture where those features matter so deeply.) The contingencies that formed me were mostly positive and supportive of building an adequate life; I surmounted those not so positive and most of the terrible things that might have happened did not. I thank a solicitous fate rather than meritocratic virtue for what has gone well. I attribute my ability to be satisfied and dissatisfied at the same time mostly to the belief that, regarding the controllable aspects of life, I could in fact choose my own direction, and the uncontrollable could be managed. I recognize how much we cannot control. Will my airplane make it safely to an airport? Will a virulent disease or aggressive brain cancer strike me? Will thermonuclear war end it all? Of course, despite these possibilities, I believe with the Stoics that I am free to take an attitude toward them that allows for their acceptance, the idea being that one is free to choose his interpretations and reactions and that this freedom trumps circumstance. I believe this while recognizing the challenge of it and my limitations in carrying it off, especially if that airplane were plunging earthward, out of control. More to the point, since most of the contingencies we face are not so cataclysmic, I have felt free to choose among the controllables—there might be fewer of those than we realize—and to do so according to my central aims and values. Even when the military draft threatened to carry me off to prison, I made my decision feeling that it was my choice rather than theirs that I would act on. It also helped that my aspirations, which were not low, were

---

6. "Love it or leave it," as those in favor of the Vietnam War put it on their bumper stickers, would seem an appropriate response to my words, until you learn that retirees are not welcome immigrants in most countries.

for achievements that were up to me, such as assuming a more responsible job or graduating with a certain degree. I could be diligent, even knowing I might not be brilliant, which was out of my control. It also helped that fame and fortune were irrelevant to my life planning. My experience, then, has been that recognizing and acting on what I could control, while relinquishing concern for what I could not control and assuming a genuinely unperturbed attitude, have allowed me to be mostly satisfied. This is in accord with Stoic doctrine and it has fit me like a glove.

I have mentioned the other factor that helped make this plan work. The capacity to detach ego from surrounding events, while still caring that the good is done, allows us to remain tranquil even when the good is not done. One is engaged with the community or an endeavor; he feels a duty to work hard toward building the good and is accountable for seeing and acting on that duty, but without egoistic involvement his concern is only for the good and not for himself. Insofar as I have kept these thoughts in mind, I have managed to be satisfied even though lamenting the harms done by an inhumane society. Detachment is not indifference.

I return to 1995, when I left mental health behind (professionally) and took up the new work of animal protection. This was the result of what that little fish had started back in Texas ten years earlier. My entry into work for animals could not have happened within a more propitious organization, the reasons for which I will describe below. But before that, I remember another notable experience that seemed to predict my eventual move into work for animals.

The minnow I had encountered was supported in his influence by an avian friend who appeared very near the same location in East Texas. I discovered a pair of grackles who appeared to have fallen from their nest. (I now know I should have made greater effort to see if parents were still around and to fashion a substitute nest if they were. But I didn't know that then and they were hungry and bound to be in danger.) So I put them in a box, took them home, installed them in seemingly comfortable, contained quarters in the garage, and tried to figure out what to feed them, which turned out to be mealworms. Days passed, they grew, and time came for release. We took them out of the garage, opened the box, and stepped back, where-upon one of them flew directly up into an oak tree and sat waiting for his sibling. But sibling, who had never seemed as healthy as the other, could not fly and merely sat wait-ing for I knew not what. The other watched from his limb, called, flew about, watched some more, waited, and even-tually decided he would have to make a go of it alone and flew away. A sad affair for all of us.

I took the young bird to a vet who did tests and pronounced the problem as giardia that had weakened him and stalled his growth. Medication, more mealworms, time for recovery, health appeared, release was imminent... and he flew from the box to my shoulder. I had not tried to make a pet of him but time had brought habituation; he seemed to decide his life would be with me, and I knew that was not an acceptable way for a bird to live. So I built him a nest and perch near the house along with a supplemental feeding station in case it was needed. I left him alone and he ventured around the property and beyond but always returned to his nest at night and to my shoulder whenever he saw me. I assumed wildness would set in and soon he would leave, and it did but he didn't. He was self-sufficient and had mostly graduated from the nest I had built, but not infrequently when I would go outside for any reason I would find he had landed on my shoulder. I did not want this but confess I had become devoted to him and, appar-ently, he to me.

A weekend came when I had to be away and when I returned he was still around but kept his distance. The break in time had had an effect. The next morning I was working at my desk and looked out a window and there he sat in a tree, watching me. We looked at each other for several seconds knowing that something serious was about to happen; I started for the door, he flew away, and I never saw him again. I was glad he had finally realized his true nature and glad for his emancipation. But I wept. A few years later I recounted this story to someone and, to my surprise, I wept again. It was a relationship most unique; I've never forgotten that bird, the grief of loss, and the thrill of his launch into freedom.

People often want to make friends with a wild animal, to somehow penetrate the interspecies boundary—which explains much of the horrible wildlife "pet" trade. Other explanations are not so benign; many cherish the feeling of specialness they derive from the animal's presence or the psychic boost from identifying with it (a certain variety of male is drawn to owning big cats or wolves and wolf hybrids, for easily discerned reasons). Although sometimes a sort of friendship emerges, it is never a good thing for the animal (who should not be captive), for it leads him to betray his nature. He becomes a shadow of who he should be. I fully understand the urge to reach across the boundary. Having it happen adventitiously with that grackle, I know precisely what it feels like, but it is an urge that must be resisted. Admire them in their natural habitats going about their natural behaviors. Show them that respect, and you'll both be better off.

Back to where I started: my departure from the mental health profession and entry into animal protection. I begin with early observations about my new work world, which took a relatively short time to coalesce into a perspective that has changed little over the years since. It is not a world for the faint of heart. Animals suffer vastly and people devoted to them suffer as well owing to their identification, and sometimes over-identification, with animals and what they are made to endure at human hands. Since "animal people" are often far more connected to animals than to people, they feel this suffering and find it easy to locate the source in human behavior. Animal disregard is pervasive, far exceeding people's devotion to dogs and cats and, ironically, not mitigated by that devotion. Sometimes animal people only consider other animal people worth consorting with. They can be loudly self-righteous and indifferent to the effects of their actions and words on non-animal people, or even animal people who differ from them in some respect. They can, in short, be obnoxious. When people identify with so much suffering while knowing it is their own damned species that thoughtlessly or greedily perpetrates it, these feelings are understandable, but not always easy to be around. As a psychotherapist I learned that a caring distance was necessary for me to be useful and not overcome by others' pain. Unfortunately, it is a skill too few animal people could access. They were drawn into the work by their emotions and I think were usually sustained in it by them. This was all a surprise to me when I moved into my new profession and leaves me ambivalent even now: I admire the commitment and moral certainty of animal activists and share their aspirations and values, but I don't generally seek them out for companionship.[7]

I spoke of human death's transit in my mind from abstract to concrete and particular. Now I had a similar experience in a different realm. I had responded to the minnow's pain quite particularly (no more fishing or eating animals) and held that position more or less unchanged for the next few years, thinking it sufficient. I

---

7. I once heard from a friend that one of my employees reported that I had done good things while at the organization but was not a real animal person, owing, I think, to my having a separate life from animal work, which she did not.

had written about animal rights in my dissertation, but it was still rather abstract. Now I realized viscerally that the organization I had been hired to lead was killing animals (euphemistically called euthanizing). That this was the accepted practice among animal-control agencies and "humane" societies, the only way they could see for managing millions of homeless dogs and cats, did not alleviate my discomfort. I'd known about it from the beginning, but the job so interested me that it was easy to accept the rationalizations, especially since I had no experience dealing with companion animal overpopulation and assumed the board and staff knew what they were doing.

PAWS (Progressive Animal Welfare Society) was, in its programs and services, a superior animal-protection organization with a forceful and articulate animal advocacy department, high-quality wildlife rehabilitation, and a companion-animal hospital and shelter that did good work but also was controversial, owing to the killing. Shelter staff were noted for the stringency of their adoption standards and not uncommonly drove potential adopters away in exasperation and sometimes fury over the interrogation they were subjected to. This drove me crazy, as well, knowing as I did about the death that awaited animals not adopted. The board of directors hired me because PAWS' administration was self-destructing, and I had both the experience to deal with that and a compatible animal-rights philosophy. There were conflicts among staff and staff allied with board members, carrying the conflict to that level; board members and management were divided by philosophy and management goals. Standard nonprofit organizational processes were unknown or ignored. The PAWS founder had been kicked upstairs from management to the board, having been outgrown by the dynamism of her organization, but she still exercised psychological control. No one could see how to resolve the serial dysfunctions.

For me, this was the easy part. The hard part was knowing that at the end of each day dogs and cats who had not been retrieved by the people with whom they lived but from where they had strayed, and others who were relinquished by their people for a variety of reasons (many of which boiled down to simple irresponsibility and self-centeredness)—animals no one seemed to want since they had been in the shelter for several days awaiting adoptions that never came, these dogs and cats were caringly (really) marched down the corridor at the end of every day to what was called the "euthanasia" room. And that was the end of them. I couldn't bear it. Even though I'd made a point of observing every other aspect of PAWS' work, as I always did on becoming executive director of an organization and felt particularly impelled to do in this new field, I never entered that room when animals were present.

It took several months of conversations with staff and learning about all the issues before I made the decision to write a short essay about why this killing had to stop.[8] The essay has been lost along the way but I remember the title: "When Will We Stop Killing the Victims?" I distributed it to the managers of all the departments. Two of them agreed that we had to find a way to stop killing, but the third, the shelter manager, was violently opposed. Along with her staff and most everyone working in traditional humane societies and shelters across the country, she was adamant that killing was the only way to relieve the prospective suffering of animals for whom there were no homes; in their view, going "no-kill" was the height of folly. At the time, no-kill shelters were uncommon and always condemned by the traditionalists for their alleged irresponsibility in eschewing killing.

---

8. I never used the generally accepted word for dispatching these animals except when it met the definition of true euthanasia, which is the humane and compassionate ending, or allowing to end, of a life for its own sake when the creature is suffering and no better alternative is available.

I then took the essay to the board of directors, where there was more controversy, but they soon voted in favor. We gave ourselves a bit less than one year to put in place alternatives to overcrowded kennels and thus eliminate any reason for carrying on as before—which we did. There's much more to the story. A year later I published *Disposable Animals*, a book about shelter killing and why it should stop; it described in detail my critique of the rationales for killing and ways to get off the deadly treadmill. (A second edition was recently released.)

The reaction of the animal-loving staff in the shelter to our decision to move toward conditions where they would no longer kill homeless animals was shocking to me and is an example of one variety of human paradoxical behavior. There is no doubt that those in the shelter who had responsibility for the near-daily killing of dogs and cats did so with immense pain (theirs, not the animals'; they did not know their fate). Yet they were totally convinced that not killing was guaranteed to result in animal suffering for which death was the only prevention. So to abandon the killing "cure" was interpreted as abandonment of their responsibility and abandonment of animals to fates worse than death. Such was the dogma. Cognitive dissonance naturally intensified their allegiance. Wavering would allow for the possibility that much of the killing was unnecessary and thus contrary to their devotion to animal well-being. I sympathized, then and now; I know it was painful to them, but the dogma and the consensual validation and their formation of a unique "tribe" of those willing to do the necessary dirty work meant they were trapped in an endless loop.

Almost the entire staff of animal caretakers quit rather than remain to see if the new approach might work (and to help it do so). The morals of this story are many: the power of dogma unexamined (and sometimes unexaminable), insularity, rationalization, long-time habit/tradition—these and more were so strong as to capture people into efforts contrary to their core values and certainly contrary to the welfare of the creatures to whom they were committed. And it is this that I find sobering and eye-opening—that even people with deep moral commitments, and lives largely built around them, can be drawn into beliefs and actions quite at odds with those commitments, even to the point of seeing what they were doing as their true expression. It was almost an Orwellian "war is peace" scenario, except their intentions were benevolent.

After leaving PAWS, I worked as head of two other animal-related organizations for five years and then semi-retired and now work only a few hours per week for Wildlife Rescue & Rehabilitation, the organization my wife founded and still leads. For fifty years I have also maintained a preoccupation with ethics that has varied in intensity depending on circumstances of work and other experience. Broadly speaking, within the field of philosophical ethics, you can differentiate those who focus on theoretical ethics from those more engaged with practical ethics—not that the two should ever be fully separated, despite the inclination of some to do so. Among these are a few who go so far as to declare that theoretical ethics have nothing, and should have nothing, to do with how lives are led. This carries intellectualism and specialization far past where I would ever go.

It seems to me that my personal development in ethics as an adult (after familial and Baptist Church infusions as a child) usually resulted from an experience, or series of experiences, that provoked a practice-oriented response; only post experience and response did I seek concepts to explicate what had engaged me and why and how and where it led my beliefs about practice. I don't imply that

I entered experience in naked innocence, which never happens, but only to emphasize that life more than intellectuality is the prime mover of ethical development. That tiny minnow whom I've made so much of revealed my casual cruelty and led me to quit fishing and give up meat eating. Without his silent scream, I have no idea how long it would have taken me to awaken or even if I would have. That's hard to imagine now but I have to consider it, just as I don't know how enlightened I would have sought to become about violence and war without Vietnam and the efforts of Selective Service to force my participation. Ethical development seems to depend on both inner receptivity to situational claims and to experiences that invite those claims into awareness and action. One can fail on either or both counts, and I am grateful to have found myself embodying the first while facing the implications of the second. Despite my rejection of that early Baptist Church dogma, I say again that I give it credit for sensitizing me to matters of "sin." My secular awakening to matters of moral success and failure enjoyed the benefits without the simplistic judgmentalism or its promise of postmortem hell for those who came up short, a worry I faced for many years as a child.

Both pacifism and vegetarianism/animal rights were my answers to questions thrown at me by life. As I think about it, questions are thrown at everyone, perhaps more often than we realize. I learned from experience and many mentors, mostly people I never met except through their writing, that the shape and meaning of a person's life is a function of lifelong circumstances beyond their control as well as their answers to questions life asks along the way over which they almost always retain some measure of control. Our moral responsibility is to hear and respond, which is exactly what I felt back when I started at PAWS and saw the faces of animals being led to their deaths. My moral consciousness was called to expand once again.

Religious people are supposed to believe that religious commitments supersede or infuse all others, although it seems to me that the contemporary performance of evangelicals I mentioned earlier puts the lie to this for them. I recently read an interview with an evangelical leader who dryly commented that too many of his fellows appeared to have put their politics above their religion, and who could deny it, even if many rationalize? Ethics, I believe, should occupy the same central place even for those like myself who lack conventional religious commitments. Ethics as the pursuit of truth and goodness and as the practice of what is learned in their pursuit ought to precede and shape other values. Ethics should also provide the measuring stick for evaluating the acceptability of different choices and actions. Among the many benefits of this approach, it will help control what Iris Murdoch, as I mentioned earlier, called the "fat relentless ego," which is the greatest impediment to ethical ways of being. If you go in search of the key to ethical success and failure, I believe you will find it here.[9] Since I've raised the matter of what a person can control in becoming who he is, it may be worth inserting here that I consider the idea of free will mostly incoherent and helpful only as a hypothetical for purposes of discussion. That does not mean I consider humans completely determined creatures, composed and shaped like a projectile aimed and fired across space and time, subject only to environmental forces and psychologically conditioned reflexes. But I see no way to avoid recognizing that we truly are formed by fateful contingencies beginning in the womb and continuing until death and that in general we operate guided by subconscious factors shaped by those contingencies—forms and degrees of luck that convert with little or no intentional awareness into choice and action. This

---

9. The same insight occurs in *The Way of the Bodhisattva*, a central teaching in the Buddhist canon: "All the harm with which this world is rife,/All fear and suffering that there is,/Clinging to the 'I' has caused it!/What am I to do with this great demon?" [8.134]

does not, in my view, suggest a reduction of humans to mere automaton-like organisms responding to stimuli with no effective mind, consciousness, or intentions; it is an efficient and usually necessary way to live. But we also know from observation and experience that we are capable of reflecting on self and situation and of drawing on reason, judgment, and ethics, and that in the seriousness of certain moments, we can assume responsibility for our choices. We are not free, but we are responsible; unconscious, automatic momentum can be slowed long enough to pay conscious attention and make an ethically directed choice that redirects momentum. I call this *freedom of the will* and consider that possessing it makes us accountable even as we acknowledge our limitations.

From a silently screaming minnow and a soulfully engaging grackle to the sense of a forest or desert or mountain range as enchanted, rich with wonder and mysteries, the convictions and experiences that led me to what I call *reverence for existence* seem to have had varied provocations. This is not surprising, since what I refer to in this expression is the unity of being—natural and human worlds preeminently. Memory not being altogether reliable, I'm not really sure, but recollection has it that my earliest related encounters in Nature were often painful breaks from the identification and gratitude I experienced. Once I was hiking on the Olympic Peninsula of Washington through old-growth forest; it may have been my first time in a forest like that. Those places, even shrunken as they are by some 95 percent since Euro-Americans invaded and cut-cut-cut, cannot be easily described. The giant standing trees and their naturally fallen siblings, amid vines and green shadow, a jumble of the living and seemingly but not really dead (life permeates every particle of forest space, it seems), a whole imbued with palpable spirit... If I were walking there now I could fill the page with its biography, which would write itself and invite my reverence. I have returned to such forests and many others less dramatic, and always something of this awe-driven experience reawakens in me.

On that first day many years ago, I walked in silence for several miles before noticing that in the distance, the subdued forest light was brightening. I began to feel as if I were readying to leave a theater and seeing the sunlit sidewalk through the glass doors ahead, except in the forest's case the change was out of place. I walked on, still immersed in beauty but with dread coming on. I reached the light and saw that the old forest beyond was dead and gone. It had been clear-cut. The rich jumble of life behind me had been replaced by the jumble of death and dying ahead, everything left tangled, bereft. The border between was almost ruler straight, which was a wonder in itself. I've never been in a war zone, but the pictures I've seen of Iraqi and Syrian cities turned into rubble by explosives, no doubt with blood and body parts moldering with the rest, affect me now in much the way this fallen forest did. Since humans, too, are children of Nature, it feels irreconcilable that our kind would be so destructive of these family members. The voice, the spirit, of the forest embraced me, and the human desecrations made me want to protect it. But in this case, I was too late.

Other times I have driven unfamiliar roads and found myself looking out on open-pit mines, where instead of palpable spirit as in the uncut old forest, the landscape demonstrably suffered. I gaze around their perimeter to see what has been destroyed. The clear-cut forest and the open-pit mine are bookends of a sort between which the less dramatic or smaller-scale desecrations are fitted, and of course they are legion. Some millenarian Christians claim none of this matters because the Second Coming is imminent. Even if that were true, they seem to think their god wouldn't notice or care that his sacred creation could be mindlessly degraded, since this short-term loan was about to expire anyway. From another perspective but stemming from a similar eschatological orientation, it may be that anthropogenic climate disruptions will finish us off. In that case, human destruction still matters to those who love creation, even if our own ugly marks will be expunged in a few million years amid Nature's renewal, which is about the only consolation I can find. We will have reaped what we sowed.

But until one event or another extinguishes *Homo sapiens*—and it seems clear to me that we are a species bound for self-destruction—we are left in the meantime to define our relation to the natural world, even as it frays, shrinks, and loses vibrancy under assault. All of this screams that our relationship has already been defined by the commodity orientation, that nothing out there deserves care except as a resource. So far, under the sway of radical materialism, it is evident that humans disavow accountability for our behavior toward the Earth. It's there for our use. What more is there to say? That's it in summary. But, for me, experiences I have had of Nature's immanent goodness and beauty, immanence that signaled there's much more to matter than materialism has been able to know, led to my reverence for existence, an awareness and attitude readily available to the attentive. In his 1980 book *Gateway to Wisdom,* an introduction to Taoist and Buddhist practices, John Blofeld speaks of this as "reverential awe for the majesty and mystery of the cosmos itself. ... Beauty, goodness and meaning are to be found right here before our eyes" (pp. 11, 15). More recently, in *Landmarks*, Robert MacFarlane notes that a man whom he admired described this as "taking part in the existence of things," a participation that arises "through the particular, the personal, the microscopic observation of all that surrounds us" (p. 106). The bare fact of existence evinces holiness, if I can borrow a religious word and remove its theological implication, leaving still a sacred reality. It's a short distance from there to recognizing ethical obligations to the participants in that reality: human, nonhuman, everything Earthly. I don't need theology for this, but it always surprises me that those who have theology and its creation stories are so often uncomfortable with the notion of a piety-evoking natural existence. They seem to love God but not his creation; I love creation and have yet to encounter their God. It takes all kinds, I suppose, but when it comes to protecting creation, I'd wish for their help.

I have been semiretired for about ten years now and have worked for animal causes for the last twenty-four, including my present work for my wife's organization. People have sometimes wondered what, if anything, it means to have gone from twenty-one years in human-focused work (social services and mental health) to twenty-four oriented around nonhuman animals (of all kinds: companion, wild, and farmed). In one sense, it was only a change of clients, since the goals remained the same—to alleviate pain and improve their life chances. In light of my beliefs about the moral concern owed to all creatures, the underlying motivation was also unchanged. I have sometimes heard the protest that so much human affliction needs attention that it doesn't make sense to worry about animals. In answer to that, I say that all suffering matters and that we have sufficient resources for responding to both human and nonhuman animals, if only we choose to do so. If our adversary is suffering itself, rather than its occurrence only in certain beings, I tend to believe that efforts to alleviate it anywhere help to alleviate it everywhere.

It has been noted as well that humans are of a "tribe" that does not include animals (except maybe Fluffy on the end of the bed), and it is natural that people's first allegiance goes to tribe members. There is truth in this, just as in the observation that in a situation demanding choice and immediate prioritization, our first obligation is to family rather than neighbor. But in accepting that family and tribe come first, we can still see that moral obligation does not end there; we must reach further morally insofar as we can. But it does raise the question how my attitudes toward humans may have changed, even while remaining a tribe member, when my clients have changed.

I approach the question indirectly. It was 1995 when I switched from mental health to animal protection. The remainder of that decade and the beginning of the next were eventful. Two years at PAWS, followed by publication of *Disposable Animals*, whose writing was sparked by my experiences there; my return to Texas and taking a position with an organization that thought itself devoted to wildlife conservation but may have been more a wildlife viewing venue (not a place where I fit well at all, which is why I left); divorce from "A," my wife of twenty-nine years, and meeting my present wife, Lynn; and taking a position as head of an accrediting organization for animal sanctuaries. Work at the two organizations following PAWS was disappointing, the first because its purposes and ethics did not align with mine (which I would have known beforehand if my experience in the field hadn't still been limited or if I'd been more insightful), and the second because it involved work with animal people whom I found almost impossible to work well with. They tended to be small groups operating in relatively isolated locales, too frequently considering devotion to their resident animals all that was required and often lacking basic standards of professionalism and comity. My ardor for animal rights did not diminish, but my desire to work with animal people dissipated in the extreme. I accepted with relief my wife's encouragement to work with her at Wildlife Rescue & Rehabilitation.

Even so, I need to make clear that my distancing from animal people did not mean a parallel loss of respect for the work they did or of my understanding of the psychological and cultural factors that impelled them. I was more affected during this time by political conditions seemingly remote from my immediate experience. The Clinton presidency was a disappointment. It was disheartening to see how power-seeking political nihilists among Republicans following the Gingrich lead could successfully sabotage democratic political processes. It was the beginning of something that has only become more extreme today and that is a clear threat to whatever degree of democracy remains. It should never really surprise us when individuals behave aberrantly and destructively, but it does surprise when they can find enough institutional and even popular support for it to threaten the system.[10] Witnessing this behavior and its persistence and nihilistic effectiveness have been dismaying, even alienating. Honorable conservatives have been too few and too late in confronting it, as have liberals in seeing it for what it is. It is this quarter-century-long incremental coup, not yet fully accomplished but not for lack of continued effort, that encouraged shifts in my views that revealed themselves partially in my switch into work for animals. I did not lose concern for the plight of suffering humans but became more fully aware of suffering perpetrated by humans on animals and the natural world, of the bland acceptance of the casualties, including human ones, by the culture we have made—one that prioritizes commodities over communities and wealth and power over flourishing life in any of its forms. This perception did not point me toward policy or politics for resolution, but instead toward understanding it as something in the nature of our species that did not seem resolvable under current conditions, and probably only partially so under much better conditions. Not a misanthropic conclusion but surely a chastened new

---

10. Thinking analogically, as I have aged, I hope I have grown stronger in the mind (wiser) even while declining in the body. One would hope the political and societal systems would change like a strengthening mind rather than weakening body, but we are seeing that they do not, not just in the United States but in many other countries as well.

appreciation for just how crooked the "timber of humanity" really is and a lost confidence that any amount of milling can remove our flaws.

One perspective on the changes I've undergone is just to say that I have gravitated toward those who are innocent, the kingdoms of life, not including *Homo sapiens*, who are under lethal assault in multitudinous forms by the outlaw species. I am not indifferent to the members of my tribe (all humans, not merely their American version), and even continue to offer assistance to those who are vulnerable and oppressed, but have transferred most of my psychic energy to the wider sphere. I am not drawn toward misanthropy but, even if I were, I would face the irony that only humans can save the wider world from their rapacious or indifferent conspecifics. This seems unlikely; I have become pessimistic about that. But people must try.

My final thought about how my attitude and relations toward humans and other animals have shifted is this: One of the great insights of mysticism, and one that underlies virtually every serious spirituality, is variously expressed, but I put it as experiencing *the unity of being*. As one masters himself and subdues ego and engages with reality in an open-spirited/-hearted/-minded way, he identifies with the well-being of other life very much as he identifies with his own. When I speak of reverence for existence, this is what I have in mind; sometimes I think of it as cultivating an attitude of Thou-relatedness, in the terms of Martin Buber, my mentor. When we do this, tribe does not disappear from awareness but does lose its precedence as the only essential variable for which one expresses compassion. *In extremis*, tribe will still come first, but fortunately we are rarely there and are free to express care wherever we are drawn to expressing it, wherever it is most needed.

Although my story has hardly been arrow straight, looping as it does backward and forward and between personal time and historical flow, I have more or less reached the twenty-first century; I got here at the age of fifty-five. The year 1999 began with predictions of doom. Y2K, aka the Millennium Bug, had much of the world in a dither over fears of computer collapses that would wreak havoc at the crack of midnight on December 31, 1999. But it didn't show up. The new millennium launched with unpredicted mayhem of a different sort on September 11 of its second year (2001). The attacks were not really unpredicted, since intelligence sources relayed copious indications that something seriously threatening was in the offing, but they were blown off by those in charge of a giddy new administration with other things on its mind.

I sometimes wonder if the widely shared expectation of Y2K disaster spoke of something deeper than fear of worldwide computer program malfunctions, deeper even than the ambition of some to make a lot of money helping avoid them (whose efforts, I have read, earned them several hundred billion dollars). Was the anxiety a premonitory projection, the expression of an unconscious realization that modernity and its supposed progress were missing something vital and that the absence might be punished by varieties of unpleasantness? A new millenarianism for the new millennium? Pigeons coming home to roost? Anxiety always searches for a cause, a hook or hooks to hang itself on. Besides the computer conundrum, out in the world there was much to worry about, but too little cultural support for speaking its names. What better than the essence of technological progress, the computer, to become the surrogate for unnamed anxieties? (They were not really nameless, though, just too infrequently named and grappled with.) I'm not sure how seriously to take this speculation, but for real-world sources of legitimate anxiety, I offer the daily possibility of thermonuclear holocaust, anthropogenic climate disruption, and the veritable absence of cultural centers of value and meaning apart from working and spending. Compared with all this, Y2K might have seemed like a walk in the spring rain.

Then, less than two years later, another tragedy erupted—the still ongoing war in Iraq. It does not minimize the tragedy of all those lives expunged by nihilistic criminals on 9/11 to maintain that the American response could have been far more intelligent and measured than it was and to suspect that the complete lack of that kind of response was intentional. Some of the country's leaders were no doubt cynical and sinister in their motivations; many others merely misguided and/or panicky. Most of the population, sensing panic at the top and never wanting to miss openings for the indulgence of vengeance, was more malleable than usual. I do not accept that the attacks on that day had the inherent power to "change everything," as was commonly proclaimed. Yes, they were a shock, especially to a national culture that embraced the mythical notion of American exceptionalism and was unable or unwilling to put the attacks on us within the context of our history of violent interventions into the affairs of other nations. Nor should we forget our war-making in various countries, which resulted in millions of casualties (Korea, Vietnam, Cambodia, Laos)— levels of civilian death and suffering almost unimaginable and exceeding our own on 9/11 by a factor of one or two thousand. On a smaller scale, it's an interesting footnote that the first President Bush's unjustified invasion of Panama in 1989 is estimated by some to have led to about the same number of civilian casualties there as the 9/11 attacks caused here, around three thousand. That loss was proportionally greater for Panama, a much smaller country, but I've not read that it "changed everything" there. It probably didn't, since it was not the first time we involved ourselves in their politics or in those of other Central American countries and Mexico. American imperialism was old hat as far as they were concerned.

As a result of our taking the route of extended vengeance and opportunism, young people today are preparing to graduate from high school who have never lived at a time when the United States was not making war on somebody, somewhere—or more accurately, many-bodies many-wheres. The majority of our people seem to have bracketed off their awareness of what's being done in their name and at their expense, but at what cost to self and society? Rather than what has culminated in the blather of "America First," what if we had had a self-reckoning, a realistic look at the place we'd taken in the world? What if we had started a transfusion of resources out of places where they were too abundant, such as the war machine, into places presently shortchanged but that better serve the common good? Could that happen here?

No, I don't suppose it could. Even then, the circumstances weren't propitious for such reckoning. When a country has been severely harmed, even if not in a way that came close to threatening its basic physical security as a nation (the emotional analog being a different story), the impulse is to hit back, especially for the United States and especially when leadership is drawn to it for its own reasons. It even seemed that every church with a signboard out front forgot that vengeance was supposedly the Lord's as they admonished us all never to forget what had been done to us—as if that would be allowed, as if anyone really believed in "turning the other cheek" or forgiving one's enemies. To this day athletic events are plagued with never-forgetting pregame rituals. Major elements of foreign policy remain held in a death grip by not forgetting and not deciding that enough may have been enough already. Actually, enough has been way too much, but it's not clear when we will recognize that.

A national reckoning in which terroristic violence received its appropriate condemnation and proportionate response, but within a larger framework that noticed the ways in which we have invited violent anger; one that considered alternatives to knee-jerk violence of our own, and what the effects of those responses might have been in lieu of seventeen years and counting of war: could a different country, one with different values, have turned tragedy in a direction that discouraged rather than fomented repetition of tragedy after tragedy, that worked to break cycles of violence through peaceful collaborative ones?

But there's more to talk about in this new millennium than international mayhem. I gravitated into this subject for several reasons and intend more than just geopolitical critique. I want to speak on behalf of the victims, those on the receiving end of our bombs and for those in the "homeland" who suffer from the perverse hardening of citizen souls that is bound to come out of witnessing and accepting but mostly denying (although the unconscious knows) such violence and the gathering of self-delusions that justify it. Our separating of refugee babies from their refugee parents on the southern border, our incarceration rate and methods, our worshipful attitude toward guns, our national indifference to the afflictions of poverty and bigotry, and so on are just some of the symptoms.

The first twenty years of the twenty-first century seem to me mostly dark ones for large parts of the world. Even so, these years have been a time of considerable personal satisfactions as I have done work that seemed useful; spent increasing amounts of time in my anchorite way camped in enchanting natural settings and been inspired by the new understandings they offer; discovered that aging, as I suspected, is not dreadful and has much to recommend it (even in light of its losses), and enjoyed the solidity of a good home and companion to share it. The goodness offered by these aspects of my life has coexisted with dismay about the darkness I described, which I guess makes me consistent with those people that surveys are always turning up who report optimism about their individual lives combined with pessimism about the direction of the nation or the world. On the one hand, it seems odd for people to find their lives so separable from the surrounding currents of existence, but on the other, it may just be an effective survival mechanism, although one increasingly challenged by worries about how the world will be for their children. On that count, few are optimistic. What happens if personal optimism subsumes into the currents of pessimism about the larger world? We may be seeing that now.

Strange to me, this is also a time when things are said to be getting better and better. Even *Time* magazine jumped aboard with an issue in early 2018, edited by Bill Gates accompanied by the likes of Warren Buffett, Stephen Pinker, and others who were ready to proclaim the gospel of optimism. I don't take this seriously, not because there aren't pockets of light in the darkness—people whose lives are genuinely better or less onerous owing to infectious disease control, nutritional improvements, access to better education, and so on—but because these measures, though important, are mostly material and instrumental. If there is an emptiness at the center of many or most people's *souls*; if the peripheries of their souls are dominated by violent conflicts over belief systems, power, and wealth; if political realities are crashing down into permutations of authoritarianism; if climate and nuclear weapons threats continue unabated...if this, then the darkness may prevail despite optimism and its current sources. If the boat is slowly sinking, events in the salons can be pleasing distractions, but how much can they do to keep the vessel afloat?

Yet I'm not grim, only dismayed. Since there's no tyrant's boot on my throat and I have sufficient material resources to meet my needs, I have the privilege of taking all this as material for delving into: as present reality sitting atop history and always calling out for interpretation. I want to be a student of being, in a manner of speaking— of being as *being*, the fundamental stuff of real existence, and being as the passing show "full of sound and fury" and signifying much about the ways of *Homo sapiens.*

CHAPTER 3

CONSUMMATION: LATE YEARS

I FEAR I HAVE ALLOWED disappointment to dominate the last few pages—now to resume a more balanced perspective. I prize equanimity above all other enduring conscious states and know it usually opens a way for responding to suffering with empathy but not agitation—focused energy but not superfluous and overwrought emotion. I have mostly allowed this story to roll out without much formal organization (no outlines or timelines have guided it), and it has turned into something more than a superficial review, which is what I intended. I see a few things differently than I did before, one of these being that my critical analysis has been evoked as much by a wish to defend those who have been made to suffer (human and nonhuman animals, forests, landscapes...) as it has been an intellectual and observational exercise. The dismay, the criticism, all of that are products of engagement, not anomie, but it is time to move on.

The end of this story is coming near. Another recognition that has come from telling it is seeing how many parts of my character and personality had fallen into place by middle age, which did not so much surprise as clarify. Even a change of career from human mental health to animal protection felt more like logical progression than novelty. Divorce from "A" and building a new relation with Lynn was, I think, born in belief I could step aside from the intimacy blockage I had experienced and be reborn, but I found it did not happen. I was essentially settled as who I was and only minor change followed; seemingly I was either less blocked than I thought or more immutably so. The changes that come with age—the desired ones—are matters of refinements, deepened understandings, expansions and contractions. What comes forth is not a new person, but if things go well a newly aware one, adaptively altered toward increased wholeness. A dozen years ago, for example, I discovered that after a lifetime avoiding it, I thoroughly enjoyed opera. How surprising! And sometime back there not too long after the turn of the new millennium I began reading ancient philosophy and found it responded more to my intellectual and spiritual needs than more recent work. And I've mentioned the increased time I spend in natural surroundings and found the ways they, too, infuse my mind and spirit emphatically. This is no surprise but it recognizes an intensification of the distinctive goods I have long found in Nature. Change is unrelenting, but it moves into new and quieter and sometimes deeper forms. We've all known people for whom *aging* is another word for *calcifying*; this may be a greater danger than we realize, at least for some. I intend to avoid that and am hopeful of success. I see that much of that will depend on keeping my disappointments in proportion and unnourished and turning the energy this frees into always renewed curiosity and gratitude for what does not disappoint.

A few weeks ago, my ninety-five-year-old mother died. (She was alive when I began writing.) Her passing was more a relief to herself and her sons than anything else; her body and mind were collapsing and moving on without her. The real sadness to me was that she appeared to stop living years before she died. She wasn't depressed; she just seemed depleted of meaning and reasons to care about much beyond her inventory of things disapproved and disgruntling and her simple certainties. She had no interest in the world except when occasional events evoked her prejudices and, more rarely, when occasional events brought gladness, as when her granddaughter remembered to send a new picture of a great-granddaughter. When I visited her a few weeks before she left her apartment for hospice, she asked if I was a Christian. As the black sheep in the family, I had always perplexed her, and I guess this was a last effort to find a consoling pigeonhole where I would fit. Too quickly I replied "no" and realized I should have sugarcoated it with reassurances about morality and respect for certain doctrines. So I tried to salvage something by saying that I was most philosophically at home within Buddhism and so not totally adrift from religion. That was wholly ineffective against her perplexity, since Buddhism meant absolutely nothing to her except that it was foreign and not Christian and therefore almost certainly objectionable. According to my brother, she remained concerned about this and occasionally spoke about her disappointment—how much out of fear for my eternal soul or dismay at my perpetual unorthodoxy, I'll never know. For her, no religion but Christianity had validity, which ironically is an attitude I've always held against it.

I take one of the lessons from this incident to confirm age-old wisdom—we die very much as we have lived. In part, living is always preparation for dying. Mother was formed for endurance by early poverty and emotional austerity and in this she followed very much in the steps of her own mother. She would endure life to fulfill her duties as wife and mother; with Dad dead, sons who were themselves aging, and grandchildren and great-grandchildren far removed, she didn't have much left to endure for. I mentioned it earlier, but I only once ever heard her reflect on the life she had led. This was a couple months before she died, when I called to ask how she was doing. After recounting her array of debilities, she paused and then said she sometimes wondered if she'd worried too much about saving for a secure old age and whether she should have spent more time having fun. I was stunned and told her I could understand her thinking those things, since for all of us getting old meant reflecting on the path we'd taken getting there. And the conversation ended, as did, I suppose, her passing reflectiveness.

I now remember one other occasion of personal revelation by Mother. After divorce ended my brief, early marriage—the first of an eventual six among her three sons and therefore alarming for its novelty—she decided to fly from her home to mine, something that she had never done before and hasn't since. She thought I must be in need of consolation, and she wanted to offer it. I was far from bereft but it didn't matter; the gesture was so peculiar for our family that I was happy to accept it. During her visit she told me of her distress on my behalf and because she had liked my ex-wife so much. And wonder of wonders, she confessed that as a young woman she had had her own divorce prior to marrying Dad. My silent first reaction was hope that I had a missing father, but it was not to be. So the visit was revelatory in many ways, but this brief time of intimacy was never repeated. Secrets and suppression: not the best way to organize a family.

It sorrows me to acknowledge a reality that makes me wonder about myself: having had both parents die within the past seven or eight years, I feel no loss. Neither did I weep or grieve. Am I missing something vital emotionally? When I have witnessed others lose parents, they seemingly occupied all points on the spectrum of grief, but still I lack a sense of the "normal" and authentic when parents die. My nonreaction feels abnormal, but is it? I am easily touched by all manner of sentiments, sometimes deeply, so why not this? I don't think it's possible to fully understand, but a few thoughts come to mind. We were never a close family, even though in their later years, Mother and Dad wanted to act as if, or wished that, it was. One of my brothers reacted to this by trying hard to be close them all the way to their deaths. The other, with whom I have no active relationship and have never discussed it, appeared as remote from them as I, for unknown reasons, even though he had produced a daughter who in turn produced children who were a tie with our parents that I lacked. I felt that I received the basic minimal necessary nurturance of childhood from Mother and nothing from Dad. The ties between us were therefore weak to begin with and weakened further over time and as I diverged ever farther from their views of reality. For several years when I was young, we had no contact beyond cards and occasional calls. I consider it healthy that I detached myself from any expectation that it could be different; that alone might explain my equanimity at their deaths. There was also this, and it may be the most telling—as my values took shape after I left home for good at eighteen, those values could hardly have been more opposed to theirs, which I consider mostly bigoted and hidebound. To them I was a cipher that they never dared interrogate or make sense of; I reeked of blasphemy and sedition. Mother enjoyed speaking of me as her "doctor son," but it was clearly only a consolation prize. So the wonder I began this paragraph with may not really be appropriate. Genes alone are insufficient to form bonds of filial love where mutual respect is absent, and I have a difficult time pretending.

As I was saying before parents came to mind, we are eighteen years into the twenty-first century as I write today. I notice that world events continue their wayward course, not going in any definite direction that I can detect: perhaps slowly oscillating pendulum-like or, more ominously, retreating a couple of steps for each one forward. I don't think I hear progress spoken of much, as it once was, as momentum toward the improvement of all things, especially material and technological ones. (I don't know that progress ever meant making better people and communities, just better lives based, supposedly, on better *things*.) Tentacles of the internet ("internet of things," it is called) and AI spread ever outward, weaving a net that's meant to contain us like fish behind a trawler, taking us toward I'm not sure what, but it won't include privacy or material simplicity. The conflict and competition of politics carries on as always, only more intensely, it seems.

I wonder why we pay so much attention to that sadly predictable realm when there's so much else to care about and over which we ordinarily have more control. Instead of elections and wars, both of which have become rather remote from the majority of us, I could focus on how some communities are taking hold of themselves and acting to make real improvements in their solidarity, in their schools and streets, in their efforts to ensure that none of their members suffer from avoidable socioeconomic handicaps and other misfortune. And on other realms of creativity, the arts and sciences and humanities, and how they enrich our perceptions and experiences and understanding of how the world works. And how about those still too few workplaces and enterprises that aim to generate profits, share the benefits fairly, and function in socially and environmentally wholesome ways? In large measure, we are what we engage with and think about; we are what we choose to care for, the ways we find to make meaning. I can stop looking in the wrong places culturally even if these more salubrious places are yet small in the big picture. I prize neither positive thinking nor querulous lamentation. I just want to see things for what they are.

Something else I notice, something more personal, is that events in culture and politics that once would have shaped my beliefs and behaviors in the way Vietnam and civil rights once did no longer do. This isn't surprising but it isn't a change I had thought of. In fact, how could they?

With greater self-knowledge came the ability to sort and place them into the matrix of my experiences; other than the 2016 presidential election, nothing much was left that could truly surprise me. As time went on, I was formed. As this century began, during the year I turned fifty-five, I had been who I was for some time. At twenty I strove to make sense of Vietnam and came out a pacifist; I wonder, at the same age, what I would have done with 9/11, or what it would have done with me. I suspect little difference. Even though with the latter event Americans appeared the victim rather than the victimizer as in Vietnam, the truth is that 9/11 did not just happen on September 11; its seeds were planted by American actions in other countries over many years. That makes it explicable but still awful.

As we age, we should be less susceptible to the vagaries of time and circumstance, more solidly built, but at the same time beware hardening of the cognitive arteries. Whether from calcification or in response to emotional needs and anxieties, we are today immersed in a phenomenon I would never have anticipated. Large numbers of people deny or distort reality and in many cases accept flagrant untruths, a large problem because apparently infectious to a great range of people. I have witnessed these changes occur in my family and in politics and commerce and seen how they waste minds and trivialize existence.

I would expect no change so radical as pacifism or vegetarianism in my later years, but things happen. They are always happening—and the mind should notice, I hope with clarity and objectivity even if predisposed in certain directions by experience. So 9/11 and the unceasing war-making that it set off by the United States, combined with the deterioration of our politics, and perhaps most of all, with our unwillingness as a nation to confront the realities of anthropogenic climate disruption: these terrible events and patterns have not set me going in new directions as they once would have, but they have helped to consolidate my thinking and, I believe, deepen my understanding about how humans are built, our flaws and needs, how society works, and of the ways that a small minority can pull the wool over a nation's eyes and manipulate the country for its own interests only. These are important matters to understand, and I see people working to address and change them and am glad for that. For me these recognitions have been mostly cognitive and emotional rather than existentially fundamental, although after November 2016 I amplified considerably my financial support for groups aiming to protect Nature and human rights.

The old expression that "no man is a hero to his valet" is probably true, although I don't think it implies that affection and respect necessarily decline with familiarity. They may actually increase as illusion or idealization decline. Time has the effect of allowing one more and more familiarity with one's fellow humans. There too, any imputed collective heroism, or in the American case, "exceptionalism," that one might have presupposed will take a beating. To know is sometimes to forgive but never to forget all of the ways we fall short of moral ideals and too often even of simple kindness. This is one of the reasons the usual human pride demonstrated when we speak of our preeminence within creation, our superiority to all the rest of life, appears so absurd. Animals and trees are admirable and honorable in ways that humans mostly forgot when they settled down and built cities and armies. As for affection and respect, well, my early views of the species *as a species* have lost all their luster, but thankfully without precluding those feelings toward certain known individuals and a readiness to give them a chance with strangers.

Anyone who writes very much knows it as an activity that intensifies thinking and may even be its own way of thinking. These pages have served that purpose for me. It is useful to consciously place oneself within time and in the doing find that a few new understandings pop up unexpectedly. I mentioned at the beginning the playful debate my wife and I have over when one truly becomes old. I now have an explanatory schema, although I have not yet exposed it to her comment. I declare one's sixties to be early old age, the seventies middle old age, the eighties old old age, and the nineties and beyond borrowed time. Standing as I do in the middle of this progression, I expect to spend my remaining time mostly as I have during recent years: helping maintain and enjoy home, its resident companion, and her organization, Wildlife Rescue; camping and hiking, reading and writing, traveling abroad. These please me and fill my time so much that I wonder how I ever fitted in a normal career. But I do not count on anything; we are subject to all manner of contingency, not to mention simply changing. I jogged faithfully for forty years, even running a few marathons and many shorter races, and assumed it had become a fundamental part of my being. And then two to three years ago, my motivation changed along with less and less subtle physical deterioration. The miles felt more onerous and less satisfying, and I am now a walker with moderated ambitions. When I camp I hike fewer miles, spend more time settling into pleasing spots within lovely landscapes, and work to still the mind to match the body.

As is clear from what's come before, I am pessimistic about human prospects in the short term as well as for long-term survival as I see democracies fail (and many of their citizens voting for that failure) and the thermonuclear sword continue to hang over our heads. I have every expectation that we will fail to act on climate change before the tipping points have been passed and things run beyond our control toward collapse of the climate systems and ecosystems on which humans vitally depend. The recognition that even seemingly well-established democracies such as ours can fail has been a recent reve-

lation to me and a definite surprise, although the suscep-
tibility of citizens in countries without much in the way of
democratic tradition to cooperate in surrendering their
own freedom and preparing for oppression is predictable.
I assumed naively that, whatever our defects, Americans
were better than that, but clearly we are not; the Republican party was quicker to see this than I and has committed itself to midwifing the failure and industriously taking
advantage of it for two to three decades now. And it is
impossible to witness our preparations for a new nuclear
arms race without wondering about the human capacity
to learn from experience: haven't we been through this
once already? Not only that—who can realistically imagine
that those mighty, death-dealing objects can exist indef-
initely without being used, whether deliberately or not?
And why on Earth do we allow those weapons' continued
existence when their destructive capacities so far exceed
any conceivable benefit?

Paradoxically, though, I retain a powerful belief in
the beauty and inherent goodness of existence and of its
savory presence for anyone who chooses to dip the cup
of an inquisitive consciousness into its stream. It is only a
matter of paying attention, identifying with what attention opens to experience, and setting sail accordingly. A
wise book once declared that humans are gifted with an
inherent *will to meaning*, and I agree. But it is fragile and
easily lost or distorted.

We humans live within, are nourished by, and orient
ourselves within fields of relationship(s). The idea of the
"self-made" person is a myth intended to mask this sense
of community, as if the myth maker were embarrassed
by the reality. Whether fields of relationships are energy
fields, force fields, psychic or spiritual fields, we can think

of a field as a sort of ambience, a context, within which we find and define our being and discover what, in turn, the relationships ask of us. I posit an ethic that acknowledges and affirms our immersion within dependent relationships; they are sometimes chosen and sometimes given but always bring with them an obligation and usually a desire to respond according to what care and respect demand for the particularity of each. This may sound odd, as if I'm saying that we must go about the world constantly calculating ethical metrics and rules and duties. Hard cases require us to pause for calculation, but in general once we affirm the equal moral value of other beings and our existential, even spiritual, entanglement with them, the attitude of care follows. Once we experience the deep value of existence, relationships of respect follow naturally.

This is on my mind as I think more about the twenty-first-century portion of my life. One may be mostly who one is, and will mostly remain, by my age, but my feelings and hopes still note how cultural affairs appear to be going. The events of 9/11 and afterward, for example, did not change me substantially, but my judgments about them altered my perspectives on this country's future and dimmed my hopes for a different kind of world. I cannot avoid noticing the parallels between the most recent couple of decades (my sixth and seventh) and my third one. In both periods, political leadership identified a villain and unwisely and often duplicitously went to war against it, found itself ensnared in a violent maze, and spent years refusing to admit the obvious failure and continuing its deadly futility. No wonder the concept of human progress has gone mostly underground. Thankfully, age brings with it a stronger capacity for detachment, or as it used to be put, for being *philosophic* about things. The more I know or surmise about human nature, the more philosophic I need to be. We seem to be unique among the species of life—no other animal has the capacity and inclination to consume the Earth (to their detriment), to dominate it far beyond what practical need and good judgment would advise, and recognize that it puts at risk not only its domination but its civilizational existence. We are an evolutionary mutant; I don't know what can save us.

And yet the irony is that we also have the capacity to know this about ourselves and the capacity to fashion ways of life that not only are self-protective but that also allow us to flourish. The people I know about who manage this operate in ways that are less vulnerable to seductions and distractions and focus on the meaning of what they do and how they live. They sometimes form small, informal communities of mutual support, they choose materially fairly simple ways, and they do not highly value accumulation. They strive to do what they love, tend to be kind, and usually have some sense of participation in the spirituality of worldly existence. It is not a complicated lifestyle, but it is difficult to carry off, since it goes against the accepted cultural ways that come to most of us with mother's milk. I have a vague recollection of a story I once heard from, I believe, Judaism according to which as long as there was one righteous person in the world, God's spark would not go out. That's how I feel about the sort of people I'm describing; they provide the sparks of goodness that may not save the world but will give it value and demonstrate meaning while it lasts. They are reminders.

I have been fortunate that my ways of making a living have introduced me to a goodly number of such people. Some worked to get a homeless drunk off the streets; others help a girl heal from sexual abuse or a woman from domestic violence. Others provide therapy for dealing with emotional traumas or focus on community conditions that permit or foster trauma. Most recently I have met people who feel the pains of abused and exploited animals and fight to heal them and others who recognize a dismal future with climate change unabated and ring the alarm.

None of them feel we've made sufficient difference, and many increasingly despair at the apparent prospects, but all recognize the necessity of caring for being, the implicit call of reciprocity for gifts received.

I have just finished reading for the third time Peter Matthiessen's book *The Snow Leopard.* The first two times, fifteen years ago, I read it back to back, something I hadn't done with a book before. It has an allure for me that I find hard to define in its combination of spiritual journey, hard physical reality, the power of Nature, and scientific inquiry. Matthiessen spent close to two months of climbing through snow and icy waters and up and down thousands of feet of elevation changes reaching as high as 17,000 feet, of being almost constantly uncomfortable, ill fed, and in danger. Yet much of the time he felt more spiritually elevated and attuned than ever. He returned to the lower lands, where it was still autumn, and prepared to go home. In a day, he went from the ethereal to mundane reality, a transition that came hard.

> Now I am spent. The path I followed breathlessly has faded among stones; in spiritual ambition, I have neglected my children and done myself harm, and there is no way back. Nor has anything changed; I am still beset by the same old lusts and ego and emotions, the endless nagging details and irritations—that aching gap between what I know and what I am. I have lost the flow of things and gone awry, sticking out from the unwinding spiral of my life like a bent spring. For all the exhilaration, splendor, and 'success' of the journey to the Crystal Mountain, a great chance has been missed and I have failed. I will perform the motions of parenthood, my work, my friendships, my Zen practice, but all hopes, acts, and travels have been blighted. I look forward to nothing.

But then came the following day:

> We climb onward, towards the sky, and with every step my spirits rise. As I walk along, my stave striking the ground, I leave the tragic sense of things behind; I begin to smile, infused with a sense of my own foolishness, with an acceptance of the failures of this journey as well as of its wonders, acceptance of all that I might meet upon my path. I know that this transcendence will be fleeting, but while it lasts, I spring along the path as if set free; so light do I feel that I might be back in the celestial snows.[1]

I cite Matthiessen at such length because the extremity of his experience and the clarity of his conflicts over integrating its dimensions with normalcy—"the aching gap between what I know and what I am"—express so well what I have experienced, albeit with lesser acuity, and what I think most of those who seek greater reality and deeper awareness experience. I see more clearly than when I began writing how much disappointment I feel about directions my society is taking and how little my participation seems to have meant and the hundred ways that I have come up short. Yet I also know the exhilaration of being here, of seeking such truths as I could find, of being engaged, of accepting my failures, and of finding meaning despite the imperfections. I emphasize this because the disappointment and the exhilaration are two aspects of the same reality; the better I can hold the disparate parts together the closer I come to full understanding.

Having drawn on Matthiessen's wisdom, I will now call on Robinson Jeffers to help me move toward the end with a tone I've wanted this story to convey. It's from his poem "The Answer":

---

1. Peter Matthiessen, *The Snow Leopard* (London: Folio Society, 2018), 257–58, 260.

Integrity is wholeness,
the greatest beauty is
Organic wholeness, the wholeness of life and
things, the divine beauty
of the universe. Love that, not man
Apart from that, or else you will share man's
pitiful confusions,
or drown in despair when his days darken.[2]

Months ago as I hiked in a California desert and realized the love I felt for the place and all it represented—this Earth, the beauty and goodness of it, how it had helped make me—I felt drawn to a better understanding of my relations with places like that, and with the people and events I have known. Somewhere in that hike I started thinking about the years I have lived and how time, Nature, and history conspired to bring me to that particular place with the particular feelings and thoughts I was having. So with no real plan for what was to follow, I began to write. I knew that people do not make themselves. When people turn attention to it, they find that their *self* is an elusive creature, one I have come to consider not just ephemeral and fleeting but a transient compound of experience, relations, and body/mind. Not quite the "emptiness" of Buddhism but close. All this is interwoven with consciousness—netlike in fabric—and mostly following trajectories guided by its weave. I wanted to better understand how I had been woven and what had led to the trajectories I took. All of the words that preceded these right here are the result, and as I happened to read the Jeffers poem I thought that in far fewer words, albeit words less specific, he had summarized my project: "the wholeness of life and things,/the divine beauty of the universe./Love that...." We all fail miserably to live up to the goodness of the place we live—this Earth—but the

2. Robinson Jeffers, "The Answer," in *The Selected Poetry of Robinson Jeffers*, ed. Tim Hunt (Stanford: Stanford University Press, 2001), 522.

gift of existence, and the time to have made right ways to live within it, and gratitude for both, will be the last thoughts I have.

CHAPTER 4

LAST THOUGHTS ABOUT DEATH AND DYING

BUT WHAT OF DEATH, THE specter that I know has begun to cast curious glances my way? To the extent that genes are an indicator, I can look forward to perhaps twenty more years of life, since my parents died in their mid-nineties. I'm not optimistic about that, but who knows. Whether twenty or more or fewer, the years amount to very little in Earth time, even if not insignificant in personal time. I am at the stage of neither welcoming nor fearing death. As losses mount and debility accelerates, which to some extent they must, I can imagine moving toward death in a welcoming state of mind.

I know some who regard human life as absurd in light of its transience and limitations, its smallness from the Universe's perspective, and the lack of evident inherent meaning. With or without a belief in God, it is easy to see our lives as paltry and too often frittered away on distractions, meager purposes, and destructive and unethical activities. From what perspective can humanity possibly be seen as an image of the godly, as Genesis suggests?

Except for a few months as a callow undergraduate student, I have never been drawn to the absurdity hypothesis, even though I cannot dispute its rationale. Who could argue that most, or even many, of us make good use of our lives? I think, metaphorically, it must sorrow *Being* deeply to observe how reliably we come up short of even moderate aspirations to good and meaningful lives. What I have appreciated about existence, though, is the chance it offers to see and marvel at reality and to discover ways to find and create meanings during my few years of consciousness. Not a promise but an opening.

As for not fearing death, I have described how an early preoccupation with dying was a beneficent endeavor and contributed to my comfort with knowing that nonexistence always yawned underfoot and that it would one day seize me. More important, I now believe, has been my immersion in the natural world over the last half of my life. I used to spend large chunks of time hiking in forests. From a few feet above the ground, except for occasional snags, which themselves are virtually hotels for insects and birds, the forest is trunk, limb, and leaf standing, reaching out, and quietly absorbing sunbeams in verdant splendor. It offers silent testimony to life abundant in soil and atmosphere, majestic in its gnarly being. But look to the ground lest you stumble over fallen dead trees and the duff from years of fallen leaves along with the insects, fungi, and more that have joined them in the fecund tapestry of death. Existence for the standing forest is rooted amid former life. The distinction between life and death becomes almost insubstantial, mere formality.

Nature illustrates the cycles of life and death, the rightness of each stage, the transitions from one to the other. Individuals die for the sustenance of wholes. One stage cannot happen without the other. The notion that we could or should live forever is an alien intruder, a desire of individuals who forget their place. We exist at the sufferance of wholes and ultimately for their good, not ours. I think it impossible to feel the being of Nature, its generosity, perdurance, and creativity, and not gladly accept its conditions.

ESSAYS

PREFACE

THE THOUGHTS AND OBSERVATIONS THAT follow were written during the late teens (of the twenty-first century, not my own) and unpublished except on my blog, a site that exists in almost complete obscurity. I feel compelled to write about things that capture my attention but am completely inept at finding ways to enter the "marketplace of ideas" to present them. I usually feel satisfied if I can state with clarity an observation or two about current happenings and then move along to begin another. But these essays seem to me organic with the preceding autobiographical and historical material, so I hereby append them with these few words of explanation.

One of my favorite words happens to be Greek: *ataraxia*. It refers to a calm state of mind, serenity, equanimity without passivity. It is energetic while unperturbed. The ancient Greeks, as well as Taoists, Buddhists, and adherents of other spiritual practices, believe it is the best possible condition of one's mind, a medium for mental clarity, and the condition most conducive to progress toward wisdom and enlightenment. I not only like the way the word rolls over the tongue but also seek, and often find, *ataraxia* as my own state of mind. *Ataraxia* does not deny that events matter or that danger and suffering are real, only that mental perturbation is neither appropriate nor helpful as a response. Some occurrences have serious consequences, but the truth is that few matter as much as we believe they do (in the big picture and over time), and fewer still are such that we can control them. In all events *ataraxia* facilitates correct decision and right action.

In contrast with this ideal state, I sometimes feel myself losing equanimity in the face of events that I allow to distress me. Violence, egocentric disregard for the needs and rights of others, greed, dishonesty, injustice— these things upset me and I sometimes find myself writing commentary as a response. So I vacillate, while not relinquishing my belief in the superiority of *ataraxia* no matter what is going on and what I am saying about it, and I always return.

I feel a degree of responsibility for hurtful actions around me insofar as I can imagine impeding them even a little. The ataraxic aspiration does not deny responsibility but rather complicates it. Whereas earlier in life, as I have described, I had active, physical ways of confronting, say, injustice, at this stage I am left with words and support for those taking an activist approach. If we are all responsible in some measure for conditions around us, then we are all obliged to act in individually appropriate ways to improve them. These essays are my later-in-life effort to contribute to thinking about reasons to strive for change.

NATURE'S WAYS

CHAPTER 5

BECOMING ELDER

I AM CAMPED IN THE northernmost reaches of the Sierra Nevada in California, a place I've come to faithfully for many years. I used to hike a lot of miles in these mountains. Now it's fewer and more selective miles but with no net loss in my portions of inspiration and satisfaction. The years have piled up and delivered me to territory not reached on even the longest hike. Some call it "elderly," an adjective I eschew because it resounds of consignment to irrelevance. Call me an elder instead. In many traditions, that word has an affirmative ring to it—rather than pointing out those who have been discarded, it recognizes that those traveling this new-for-us landscape might be privy to special knowledge. I will add, however, that at seventy-five I feel only a newcomer to the territory and may have only the glimmerings of such knowledge, although hopeful of more.

How does the elder I have become feel when he watches those he was among only a decade or so ago launch extended hikes while he is only writing about them? On one hand is nostalgia; there was great joy in the exertion, the sights and smells, the beauty, and the conscious deepening of his union with Nature, a deepening that felt somehow connected with time and distance, with immersion. On another, serene acceptance: he had

to cross those regions to get to this one, and present satisfactions are infused with former ones while enriched by
new vistas. It is remarkable what can be discerned on
slowed and shortened walks.

Where was the boundary between the territories of
then and now? It was more a permeable borderland than
a gated "exit then/enter now." There were several years
during the period of moving into my early seventies when,
I see now, mind/body were preparing the way. I had been
a jogger, a road racer, and an occasional marathoner for
forty years, beginning at the age of thirty; then the miles
became less inviting. The same with my hiking; I'd discovered my affinity for long mountain and desert treks over
thirty years ago, but more recently, the miles came to feel
less necessary. I sensed no change in my desire or my need
to be in natural settings but a new willingness to be less
physically active there.

Motivation had changed and it seemed the legs put
up no argument; it was probably a joint (both meanings
of the word) decision. As above, I had twinges of sadness
but mostly acceptance; it felt right. My other interests were
relatively unchanged but the proportions shifted. I will
note that in the midst of these changes I developed atrial
fibrillation, which has the unfortunate effect of reducing
stamina; climbs are harder now, especially at higher elevations, but this seems consistent with the new trajectory I
had already begun even if more abrupt and definitive. I
confess, though, that it's the only change I actively dislike; it
feels imposed rather than appropriately emergent with the
years. This attitude, however, makes assumptions without
foundation, since I know that organisms like me are built
to wear out, often announced through a wide variety of
unpredicted signs that nature is taking its course.

I have few needs additional to those associated with
survival: being frequently in natural settings, reading
widely, writing, enjoying the virtues of solitude. My time in

camps has not changed—still three months or so a year—but I read more, write more, and indulge in more contemplative time while physically covering less of the landscape. I also have a wife, who doesn't come along, and we enjoy a home together and other interests. I consider the simplicity of this existence a genuine good, with the parts rather easily kept in balance most of the time. Even so, elderhood is not the easiest stage of life. It is a time of loss and change, the same as all stages but with different losses, and changes pointing toward endings rather than continuations. Many of the crucial questions have been adequately answered, but new ones, and new versions of old ones, still appear. They often congeal, I tend to think, around this one: How do I do this aging thing right? By "right," I mean appropriate to my nature as well as to aging's trends and imperatives; meaningfully; ethically; sufficiently attentive to deepening of spirit. Also, how much attention should I pay to health issues? Am I as prepared to die as I believe I am?

While walking this morning I smelled the woods—an olfactory response that has always been part of my engagement with the Sierra—and the familiar scent aroused memories as well as thoughts about present and future along the lines just mentioned. This is my first trip since I spent two weeks in Death Valley in January (it's mid-June 2020 as I write). The time between trips has naturally been dominated by COVID-19. For my wife and me, the virus has been no more than an inconvenience—wearing masks and distancing at the grocery store, handwashing on return—and sheltering in place is hardly noticeable since our lifeway is already consistent with that. But we make fewer spontaneous outings, and those are restricted by closures. The big loss was a five-week trip I'd planned to begin in early May, camping, ferrying, and touring around southwest Canada, particularly the coast. Maybe next year instead, although I realize as an elder that "last chances" have a place in my mind now that earlier life was far less familiar with. The trip I am on now will last a few weeks, visiting whatever I can find open around the Sierra. Considering the solemnity I'm feeling and the thoughts I'm having, I wonder what will come to mind.

What is reality? That is way too big and mysterious a question, so I'll try this one: *What is real within the bounds of life as I know or imagine it?* In a sense, this is the unspoken question behind most of the choices we make over the course of our lives and is especially prominent, though hidden, within the big ones. It seems to me that the assemblage of our responses is how we build character and find value, for the realities sought are those that make a purposeful life. The work I've chosen, the places and people I've loved, the ways I've focused my personal or solitary time—all reveal what I have considered most real, meaning what is most essential (as opposed to inessential or trivial), most meaningful, most consistent with how I envision my *self* within the greater Self of existence as I experience and imagine it. The most distinctive exemplars of those who seek the true fullness of reality are found among sages and mystics, but they are not as common as they once were, and I can only aspire.

It has seemed to me as an elder that the reality questions come with different aspects and different gravities than they did during earlier periods. Setting off on a career or marriage at twenty-five is clearly a major step but not necessarily final. Mistakes can be corrected. Starting over is always possible. (I've had two or three careers, depending on how you define them, and two marriages, not counting one that was early, immature, and brief.) But now the plenitude of time that I once assumed has transmuted into a state where the terminal boundary hovers on the horizon, no longer a mirage but definitude, with the date perhaps set and certainly anticipated but not showing on my calendar. I have moved into the period for which the philosophical study and reflection on death as existential condition that began in my thirties has prepared me. This is vital to recollect but not what I'm thinking about right now. Practical matters still make demands. "Last chances" require consideration. Decisions feel closer to final.

For instance, if it continues to become ever more evident that the United States is neither a united nor a viable nation but rather a house that was built on sand—rich and powerful but internally decadent, bigoted, violent, hyper-materialistic, undemocratic, and sunk into egoistic individualism at the cost of solidarity—ought I not to expatriate rather than feel myself complicit by my presence in all this? Could I live with the losses? Would it be worth the wrenching changes? In this as in so much more, margins of error have shrunk, choices become more final. And this one, decisively, was not one I would ever have imagined considering.

Then this one: Where do I draw the line on allowing myself, with whatever health-related maladies arise, to move into a medicalized state of being? I watched my parents, who died in their nineties, spend their last fifteen or so years engulfed in medical appointments, hospitalizations, rehab, home health care, copious pharmaceutical inputs, and worst of all the sense of themselves as dependent creatures of the medical industry. There were many times I was sure they should have been told there was nothing more to offer for this or that problem or pain but were instead sent to another specialist (passing the bucks, so to speak) or tried on another pill or another procedure. It was not a good way to live and certainly less so as a way to prepare for dying.

My philosophical/spiritual preparation for death is well on its way, but before the ultimate need for it arises I ask to what extent I should submit to the regimens of medicalization? How much medical misery might a few more months or even year or two be worth if spent largely perambulating between treatment centers and in persistent pain or discomfort and inexorable decline? After my first appointment with a cardiologist for evaluation of atrial fibrillation, diagnosed by my general practitioner, I left with prescriptions for four medications, none of which I was willing to take. But as the risk factors mount up—blood pressure, cardiac deficiencies, all those mysterious readings from blood samples...then what? Aging is a risk factor all by itself, regardless of who is doing it and in what condition, something hard to encompass until I remember that we are all built for obsolescence. When does wisdom intervene on behalf of evaluations and treatment despite my aversion versus wanting a clear picture of my condition even if I most likely refuse treatment?

Then there are the more mundane questings. As a younger man still interested in friendly smiles and other affirmations from women whom I considered attractive, I was never sure how I appeared to them. Sometimes I thought I was desirable, and others not in the least, so I stumbled along in ignorance but doing okay. Now the interest has declined, but I doubt it will ever disappear, and my perplexity is all the greater. Just how old, how decrepitly ancient and wizened, do I look? Were I playing the field, I'd be a mass of uncertainties. A brief look in the mirror and I see my face as of thirty or forty years ago. Closer scrutiny, and especially the testimony of pictures taken back then placed alongside those closer to now, remove all doubt. I have changed, and not for the better. But how bad is it? I can never decide, but I might lean toward despair if I were not sufficiently detached and if the yearning had not diminished as it has.[1]

---

1. In one of his final songs, Leonard Cohen said he didn't need a lover because "the wretched beast is tamed." Older men, I think, usually experience this, but the tameness comes in degrees.

I think the chief reality issue for elders is one that is always with us, even if not much attended to in younger days: contingency and its unpredictable incursions. Humans are spindly creatures with vulnerable foundations and always subject to falls, metaphoric and actual. Once it was only a matter of jumping back up and hoping no one saw me; falls are invariably humiliating. Is there something metaphysically symbolic about them? For me now, a fall carries more risks than merely to pride, and the return to verticality is more of a challenge. This is all obvious. The important issue, here and about the state of our elder body in toto, is how we distribute our attention. I want to be alert without excess and most of all not to become so over-attentive that every twinge sets off concern. As we obsolesce, it seems that twinges multiply and could easily become preoccupying. One cardiologist told me that he had patients with A-fib who were so anxious about the symptomatic arrhythmia and instances of heart-rate fluctuations that they would barely leave their beds.[2]

As I said at the beginning, I am camped in the mountains, at an elevation of about six thousand feet. I've learned a formula for dealing with the breathlessness of climbing brought on by my altered circumstances: aging + A-fib + elevation = I'd better have sufficient time on this trip for physically adjusting to the variables as I climb. When I forget, as I did a few days ago, I'm reminded, while feeling almost bad enough to want to join that fellow who never left his bed. I offer this anecdote to suggest one of the forms of consciousness that elders can adopt and still do things that are important to them.

A philosopher whom I admire[3] and who advised me on my doctoral dissertation once wrote a paper that I still

2. It's time for such people, I would say, to do serious work on their attitude toward dying and learn acceptance, and then get up and on with life.
3. Sally Gadow, "Body and Self: A Dialectic." *Journal of Medicine and Philosophy* 5, no. 3 (1980): 172-185.

have thirty-plus years later. Even as a relative youngster I knew it contained wisdom I would return to someday. She described what happens with the body in aging; she called it a "subject body," meaning that it can take on a life of its own seemingly separate from you the inhabitant, you the consciousness, and will demand attention and accommodations. This is inevitable, but how we attend and accommodate are crucial. One does not want to move toward hypochondriasis or psychosomatism or even preoccupation; tranquil alertness might be the ideal, with an emphasis on tranquility. We should be satisfied to die at any moment while remembering that death is not on every moment's program. Most of the subject body's grumblings are explicable and survivable, so we might as well relax—which is far easier to do if the above steps have been attended to.

One of the difficult challenges for me as I entered into this territory was how to interpret the changes. If I see I have slowed on my hike, is that because I am now older, or have neglected my conditioning, or having a bad day, or just being more anxious? If I can't think of the word I want to express myself, what does it say about the state of my aging mind? The same goes for declining memory. I know that the state of my attentiveness and concentration are essential to psychological and spiritual functioning, but they can become distorted (think again of that person captive to his bed) and lose their greatest value if they turn into neurosis. As much as possible, I avoid interpretive scrutiny of changes, just make note, and go on.

But it is not the physical aspect of elderhood that most interests me, even if it can be, with the right attitude, the source of great humor from time to time. A serious clown, a gloomy trickster, neurotic and ready to completely take over the show if allowed to—give the body a foot and it will try to take a mile. Nonetheless, it can be understood and remain the friend it always has been despite its recent tendencies to whine.

It's the consciousness, the mind, that makes or breaks the elder. Eudaemonic aging, as I will call it, incorporates many virtues. Spiritual awareness one, as is acceptance of the transience of all things (except perhaps the Cosmos, always changing but enduring). Unending curiosity is another: What is this world really about? Why do humans squander the great gift of their birth? Why did they create the present morass of unhappiness and delusion? At what point in our evolution did we make the fateful turn? Look at all that's happening and try as objectively as you can to picture where it will go and how it will end. Better than that: be present in Nature, experience it directly, spend time with the many good books that confirm how sentient and intentional are our fellow creatures, plants and animals and fungi. Cultivate equanimity—the attitude of an interested spectator—and gratitude.

A few years ago I had an endoscopy. Going in, as an experiment on what the dying light of my life might eventually be like, I vowed to pay close attention to my mind as the anesthesia did its work. I thought the transition from conscious to not might be a foretaste, a model, but it didn't work—at least if the reports from those who've had near-death experiences are credible. They are to me—not in the sense that what they say happened literally did happen but that the emotional/spiritual tone and course of the process that led toward but did not arrive at death sounds intuitively right. Serene and accepting, we know the sun is setting for our last time—followed, in my estimation, by dissolution, my personal completion as my nonself particles merge into new life forms. But on the table, with the anesthesia flowing in, I drew a blank. I could never recollect any aspect of the transition; a switch flipped, and I was gone. I was glad to have made the effort. It satisfied a piece of my curiosity.

Spirit, acceptance, curiosity, and beyond acceptance an affirmative belief in the rightness of death, mine included—these and more build the attitude I seek. One of the reasons humans have created the morass I mentioned above lies in our species' movement toward feeling ourselves separate from Nature, as if we were beings different and superior to all other forms of life. We self-alienated from our source and in lieu of reverential engagement and gratitude, we chose to extract everything extractable, to commodify creation—and not with a gentle touch. We orphaned ourselves at the price of our wholeness and the spirituality known in the communion of existence. Alienation makes death fearsome. "Ashes to ashes, dust to dust" sounds one way at someone else's funeral, but for the fearful it's not terribly reassuring when anticipating his own. It should be. I'm in no rush to join the soil but I find the picture of it, when my time comes, exhilarating in a way. It will be my recompense for the gifts I received, my fulfillment of the contract implicit in coming to be.

Degree of alienation is probably the central determinant of how well a life goes. If, as has been said and I believe, we die in the manner we have lived—that living is in part preparation for dying—then our end time will vary with our alienation: from ourselves in our potential integrity; from other people and Nature; from our possible experience of the ultimate, the absolute, the pervading spirit of existence. What about the question I asked about reality? As we reach union, experience solidarity, know the taste of what the wisest seekers of all philosophies and religions have sought—tending to the soul, as Socrates put it—we move past alienation, which I think might be an elder's greatest insight.

Chapter 6

What Is It Like to Be a Human Wondering What It's Like to Be a Nonhuman?

OVER RECENT YEARS PUBLICATIONS HAVE appeared bearing titles such as "What is it like to be a [tree or bird or...]?" Others ask "What does a [tree or bird] know?" People have noticed that the evidence of their senses and of research points to forms of experience and intentionality among the supposedly lesser beings that exceeds what they were taught in science class. The same applies to what we generally assume about plants and animals compared with humans. People ask, "What the heck is going on out there in the other-than-human world? What should I make of it?" This seems to me a positive sign of increased human alertness, especially if followed to its logical conclusion, which is recognition of unity amid continuity and diversity.

What is going on out there is amply described in the books I alluded to, which summarize it as thought, emotion, relationships, behavior, awareness, problem solving—on levels that boggle our innocent minds.

Here's what is going on out there. Neither plants nor animals are mere automaton-like resources placed on Earth solely for the benefit of humans and without an independent reality of their own. What we do matters to them (obviously), since our acts have a decisive impact on whether they flourish or crater. They do not merely swoon before the machines, or anthropogenic climate disruption, depletion of numbers, destruction of habitats, extinctions. They try to adapt and make the best of it. It is a valiant effort, but the statistics on degraded landscapes and depleted species and falling absolute numbers of plants and animals show they are losing.

Those losses are not the point here, however, for they are a story often told and systemically unheard, or too little heard and not effectively attended to. The point here is *what* is lost along with the numbers: the myriad individual beings and the intelligence that has guided their kind through history and evolution; qualitative, even spiritual, losses that would be easier to comprehend if happening to human neighbors (albeit those losses are often poorly attended to as well) and that have more in common with the human realm than we realize. I will focus on two aspects of this loss.

Even with increased attention to animal and plant sentience, many observers are vigilant to avoid a bugaboo that deeply disturbs them: the curse of anthropomorphism. Despite the evidence of other intelligences out there, pleasure, intention, affection, and so on are considered human characteristics, and these observers believe that attributing such experiences to those others is therefore a case of the curse. It has seemed to me that those who define themselves primarily as scientifically-minded types and who write about the living world, especially animals, are among those most haunted by the insidious dangers of anthropomorphic toxins and are assiduous in guarding against them, at least publicly and professionally. So creatures of the natural world are called resources, and their social activity is mere instinct, territorial display, mating ritual—anything but what it looks like. Sometimes these activities are purposeful and other times maybe just social or joyful, like birdsong in the morning.

The central problem underlying the anxiety over anthropomorphism is that it rests on a silent assumption: all the traits that humans display from time to time are perforce human-owned traits. They are ours alone and make us special within the scheme of creation. The examined history of human–animal relationships covers a lot of territory, but above all one element stands out—humanity's determination to differentiate and elevate itself in relation to all the rest of existence, almost as if we were formed separately by a different god or creative force. Related to the others only instrumentally. As one early commentator put it, the only reason animals were created alive was to keep the meat from spoiling.

That the assumption and the fear of anthropomorphism run deep is revealed when even people who observe animals closely and are regularly astonished and delighted by them feel compelled to issue caveats. In an article in *The Atlantic*, Jenny Odell says that, "[David Sibley] writes that instinct is more than merely programmatic: Birds must be motivated by something like feelings. 'I realize this is enormously anthropomorphic,' he notes, but nevertheless, 'maybe the feeling an oriole has when looking at its finished nest is similar to the feeling human parents get when we look at a newly painted and decorated nursery.'"[1] If the attributed feelings are anthropomorphized projections of the observer, then they must not really exist, Or if they do, they are something else that looks like without truly being feelings of satisfaction at, in this instance, a job well done. Sibley strengthens his defense against anthropomorphism, unconsciously I imagine, when he refers to the possibly satisfied bird as "it" rather than "he" or "she." Since an "it" is an object, it would be incapable of feelings.

---

1. Jenny Odell, "Why Birds Do What They Do," *The Atlantic*, June 2020.

Later in her review, Ms. Odell discusses the greater ani, a species of cuckoos native to South America, who form co-parenting groups that engage in formidable communication circles where vigorous chatting and body movement occur several times daily. She comments: "They inch closer together, cocking their heads slightly, seeming (from my anthropomorphic view) to be listening attentively to one another." What else would they be doing, for goodness sake? What is humanizing about recognizing animals doing what they actually appear to be doing? What's to be afraid of? They are obviously communicating. Isn't the danger of failing to credit behavior that one recognizes as being what it is, *and* similar to what humans do, as great as that of denying or minimizing it out of fear of the curse?

The books I referred to at the beginning of this essay imply one alternative to human ownership of those supposedly human traits, but not one they seem aware of or, if they are, want to accept. Here it is: Existence itself comes complete with an entire repertoire of traits and capacities and actions that are there for the taking according to species need or desire. Together they compose one of the streams of being that creatures may dip their cups into and extract what they will. Animal satisfaction at a job well done may not be the same satisfaction I experience, but it is probably quite similar, the job really was well done, and I have no reason this side of vanity to deny the possibility. John Muir commonly encountered "joyous" streams cascading out of the Sierra Nevada. Having seen them myself, I don't quibble—they are joyous as I would be joyous if I were a stream.

Of course, Thomas Nagel raised the decisive red flag against my imagining what it would be like to be a stream back in 1974. His eminent and much cited article "What Is It Like To Be a Bat?" made clear in a scholarly, philosophical way the impossibility of my successfully knowing that. I can imagine what it would be like for me to be a stream or a bat but not what the actual experience of the stream or bat *qua* stream or bat is for them. If I could genuinely imagine it, I wouldn't still be me. Still, although I acknowledge my limitations in this respect, I have other capacities to draw on. I know what it is like to be a being, to exist on this Earth, and through the gifts of sentience to experience it, to taste and smell and respond, to make relationship with it, to live and eventually die. And I can imagine some degree of similitude among the others and myself as we abide and act and add to the rich goodness of it all, this world we love.

Going farther—and this is the second point I wanted to make—I don't even need the ethologists, mycologists, and botanists to continue to display, research project after research project, that those beings they put under the figurative microscope really are pretty damned amazing. I already know that because we share a world, one from which humans, apparently alone within creation, have psychically expatriated themselves, forgetting that this emigration will never work in practice because reality has even us in its grasp. Sharing the world and appreciating the gifts that have made my life work in the ways it does, I cannot but realize that among those gifts are the other creatures who make it complete, whether their demonstrated capacities are astonishing or mundane. I honor them as fellow travelers through this realm.

We know about the four cardinal virtues—justice, courage, temperance, and prudence. Plato included a fifth: piety. I can, if I wish, move into the sense, the spiritual sense, of communion, the unity of beings within Being. And the conclusions about my place here and what I owe those others arise naturally from that experience. Honor and respect; do no avoidable harm. These will work; one need not anthropomorphize here. Humans must choose these attitudes, but for the other lives, their versions appear to come naturally.

CHAPTER 7

FIRE EARLY & LATE

IT IS SUMMER MOVING INTO the fall of 2020. California has been burning for almost four months, with over three million acres incinerated by mid-September and more on the horizon. Thousands of fires, many beginning small and some merging to form bigger ones. It is a record year in a period of climate disruption when records are made only to be broken, frequently before people have recovered from earlier calamities. For some, recurrent evacuations are becoming the norm.

I had been wanting to camp at Lava Beds National Monument for the past six months, but the coronavirus kept it closed until a few months ago. Before I could arrange to travel north, wildfire set in and closed it again. Fire burned 70 percent of the monument, meaning over 32,000 acres; I don't know how much burned around its boundaries. A few weeks ago, like a battered boxer up against the ropes, it gathered itself to try once more and reopened. I am pleased it did and am camped here as I write.

The fire burned completely around the perimeter of the campground. In some places it leapt in and took out trees, brush, signs, and picnic tables, but left it about three fourths intact, due apparently to a fortuitous combination of light wind, the encircling roadway, and valiant firefighting. I bow in gratitude to both humans and Nature on the assumption it was a collaboration to preserve this green island in the dark sea surrounding it. I've found a fine little campsite and recognize the flip side of fiery tragedy is that it keeps the crowds down. I have the place practically to myself.

I have been here a week and plan to stay at least one week more. The trails are closed, but with the roadways bårely traveled I can walk them to observe, take pictures, and experience the aftermath of what fire does to a landscape.[1] What you saw here before the fire was rolling country to the north, with remnant volcanoes and hills and buttes separated by flatland covered mostly in bunchgrass, sagebrush, rabbitbrush, and swathes of lava flow inserted with easily imagined violence. The middle third of the Monument, where I am, retained most of the grass and shrubs and added juniper, which flourished during the decades of fire suppression—probably the most extensive, ultimately destructive, and wrong-headed failure to have ever been visited upon the forests; throw in its opposite, clear-cutting, and you wonder any forests remain on the continent.

I've never lived anyplace where juniper was appreciated—it is the pigeon of the plant world—but the wildlife and I like it: for birds, reptiles, and a few others it is excellent cover and shade, and for me the species here grows upward rather than mostly outward (as the Ashe juniper tends to do in Central Texas where I once lived) and so makes finely shaped trees, though not nearly as tall as the few ponderosa pines found well-spaced among them. They are migrants, or remnants, from the southern side of the monument, which is more elevated and thus favorable to the pines.

---

1. "Protecting the resource" is what trail closing is called—an unholy phrase that is too often used about natural things. I'd like to scour it from the tongues of "resource professionals" as thoroughly as the fire did the ground; "resource" degrades whatever piece of Nature it refers to.

Many areas are still almost exclusively lava field with only occasional plant growth, although it always surprises me to see large trees and bushes that found a way to root and flourish amid the gnarly lava, seemingly against the odds in this arid country. Lava flowed out of the volcanoes here sporadically for over 100,000 years in molten luminosity and now the land has once again been burned and newly blackened. Born in fire below, lava hardly notices fire here on the surface. I wonder how long it will take for it to break down and become part of the soil.

Since junipers were the predominant tree, their dark deaths are most apparent. I say "deaths," but I can't help wondering if there's a chance some could come back. I see on the trunks of those that were chain-sawed that the fire damage was only superficial, barely penetrating and sometimes only scorching the bark. The leaves on most of those still standing are all burned away and on others roasted in place. Grab a handful, and it turns to organic dust. Could new growth return next year for any of these? I've seen flowering trees bud early in the spring, only to be crushed by a late freeze, and still come back. Can these junipers perform similar magic? Doubtful, I'm sure; their foliage and high oil content make them too thoroughly burnable even when heartwood appears sound.

I see many burned shrubs where new growth is already emerging from the roots. As a source of inspiration, the sprigs of green foliage arising from blackened, burned roots and standing beside the dead limbs of their forebears can hardly be matched. I was surprised by the first ones, and then suddenly I saw them everywhere. Over the coming years, I will be interested in seeing how it all comes back, the stages and sequences and species. If it does come back. Reality impels us to realize that many ecosystems around California will not return to their pre-fire condition. For example, forests will become grasslands, owing to climate changes that for the foreseeable future have altered rain and temperature patterns that were the historical environment in which forests prospered. This Lava Beds land was already arid, so what happens when it becomes more so? The answer for many of the natives is probably that the collection of plants and animals that flourished here were able to do so only conditionally and the terms were narrow and may now have been exceeded. Hot and dry was fine; hotter and dryer may ask too much.

A burned landscape is invariably grim, black and death-filled, with abundant visible evidence of real loss and mental stimulus for imagined losses. How did the snakes and lizards manage while hiding underground? How many mule deer were brought down by smoke and then incinerated? What about coyotes and rabbits and ground squirrels? It seems quiet—have the birds mostly left for food and safety? No, some are still around. The only specific news I've heard was from a ranger who said the rattlesnakes had become quite active, which I surmise is out of desperation. Presumably rodents also managed to hide underground, but what happens to the predatorial dance when there's no cover? What are the rodents eating while waiting to be eaten themselves? Who, if any, benefit from the fire while all await new growth? I picture a lot of death and adjustment over the interim. Even so, I saw a hefty bobcat scurry into a rocky depression as I walked this morning and am reasonably sure that during the night coyotes yipped. Animals are resourceful creatures and know more than we about what it will take to resume their normal lives.

Knowing that most ecosystems have incorporated periodic fires into their repertoire since their time began consoles and reassures me. No matter how ravaged it appears now, it will return surprisingly quickly, even if altered. But future promise does not negate present loss. I love the characteristic look and smell of this landscape, especially when the rains have come, and now I look out from my roadside walks and it is gone. Yet I also notice that each day I am less affronted by its grim visage and become more comfortable with the new format. Bare, skeletal branches weave shapes that weren't visible before, graceful, sometimes eerie lines, reaching black wands toward blue sky. These first impressions of end-time desolation begin to give me the sense of transition rather than mere ending, of landscape pausing to draw new breath with hints of things to come in the hopeful green sprouts.

It is one thing, of course, to understand that fire is normal, that new green growth will return, and that life and time will march forward. But we may never be able to think that way again. Now and for centuries to come, we will live under a weather regime that will dance to the tune of an increasingly disrupted climate—more heat, drought, flood; more extremity and unpredictability; more species losses and forever altered ecosystems; more calamities of water and food shortage. After each catastrophic event we will wonder what it would have been like if we had had the sense to do what was necessary to preserve the climate that was. The loss, and the guilt that should accompany it, is an analogue writ large for the grief I feel amid the relatively emptied landscape before me.

Perhaps it's just my fading memory, but I don't recall being struck before by the land being so thoroughly scoured of life and organic detritus by fire. Because so much that grows in aridity isn't even head-high and visibility thus extends to the horizon, it is easy to forget how much grows here. But because most of the growth is low, it burns readily. Once gone, it leaves a peculiarly mottled, gravelly patina, desolate to the eye. Apocalyptic may be the word. It reminds me of battlefields after trench warfare or of Hiroshima after the bomb.

There are more fires to the west, I hear. For most days over the last week, smoke has dominated the sky. I can look almost directly at the morning sun, a beautiful, deep orange circle painted by smoke. I can barely smell it but don't have the most acute olfactories so it may be stronger than I realize. My eyes tell me that if it gets much thicker, it will be time to leave. The horizon is obscured and the buttes little more than outlines themselves. Paternalistic as the rangers often are, this is one time they say we're on our own to decide. They don't measure air quality and it's up to us to determine when it is no longer acceptable.

After twelve days I am forced to leave; the smoke has grown heavier and I don't want to subject my lungs to further assault. The experience of being here after fire has been different than when I've been here before, but I am sorry to leave. I have adjusted to the changes and can even sense that the fire was cleansing and has opened space for renewal in new combinations of arid lands flora. Park Service employees had periodically, here and there, thinned the juniper during recent years, which means their jobs become easier. Instead of that, they can monitor new growth and eradicate saplings where they return too eagerly, too prolifically. I don't know enough about the natural history of this place, or how much of a genuine problem the juniper is, to judge but I hope they will use a light touch. Decisions about what should and shouldn't be allowed to make their place within a landscape ought never be done without careful thought, for considerations of both ethics and ecosystem dynamics.

As I leave, I think about how I am drawn to volcanic regions. Here in Lava Beds there are none of the more energetic signs of subterranean unrest as there are south of here in Lassen Volcanic National Park: the boiling, vaporous mudpots and springs, steaming fumaroles, and sulfurous ponds. Here there are only the signs of what once was: lava tube caves, remnants of cinder cone volcanoes, and ground sprinkled and often immersed in the rough dark lava of congealed basaltic flows. At Lassen there is a spot on the east side of Boiling Springs Lake where I always spend time to stir my imagination with the odorous, turquoise colored two- to three-acre pond where steam rises from fissures along its banks. What is happening below, I wonder? Does the pond wash away in snowmelt floods and refill, slowly to resume its sultry, quirky pres- ence surrounded by pine and fir forest? The toxic brew will not permit trees or other plants to grow along its shore, but I've never noticed floral damage along its summer-dry downstream bed.

Here in the less dramatic, superficially quiescent region of Lava Beds, it is primarily the sage-juniper landscape with its lava intrusions that holds my attention. As my predilec- tions have changed with age, I am drawn more to places like this, where I can see the horizon. The lava speaks deci- sively of a violent history of change and the near certainty of eventual renewal after volcanic disturbances. Volcanic regions remind me of transience, which is always good to remember. Today's smoky atmosphere strikes a fitting note to that as I drive away.

[From my Journal nine months later]

I have moved several hundred miles north of the lower Owens Valley where I was camped and am now at Lava Beds N. Monument. I was last here late last summer after the fire that burned 70% of the Monument; ironically, fires to the west brought so much smoke eastward that I was forced to leave earlier than I had wanted to; it was like being awash in fire's dominance. I've returned to see how things look nine months later. It's virtually a cliché to speak of how land- scapes regenerate after fires, how most ecosystems have always depended on and adapted to periodic fires, and so forth, which is true and has the added benefit of assuaging the pain of looking at a desolate post-fire landscape. This one was dark and gloomy with bare ground and ashy dirt punctuated by blackened juniper and pine snags standing as if sentinels of what had happened and marching to the horizon. My austere nature faced a stiff trial as I observed and walked around; even useful fires doing their natural work leave the workplace looking terrible. But I remember noticing that after only weeks there were already signs of slight green regrowth, which was reassuring. The problem in these times, however, is that as climate disruption moves inexorably along and worsens, all bets are off that depend on historical norms. To begin with, fires now are more common, typically more intense, and cover a wider extent owing to the desiccation and hotter temperatures of the new climate era. And these very conditions mean that some forests will not come back and more landscapes will turn to arid and semiarid grassland. Each year more of what's left will burn. A few days ago I studied a U.S. drought map and the entire West was in some degree of drought and much of that not merely a recent phenomenon; at my home on the North Coast we are ending our second rain season at approximately half of normal and some say we're actually in a multi-decades drought that is only interrupted from time to time with rainy years.

As for here and now, though, nine months have made a significant difference; grasses and a few forbs are returning and in a first brief walk I've counted three species of wildflowers. I had speculated that maybe some of the juniper would regenerate since their burning seemed superficial, but that was wrong-headed optimism, at least at first glance; I've seen nothing to justify it and in retrospect it sounds naïve. Still, what was consistent darkness, but for a few areas and trees that due to the vagaries of wind had survived the surrounding conflagration, today has a soft green glow decorated with occasional glitter of purple and yellow flowers. The distant view across the relatively flat land north of here is still mostly of those dark sentinels, but looking closer signs of better days coming are clear. If we weren't still in drought, I'm sure it would be even better. But no complaints; the sight before me is like a smile returned to the face of a depressed friend whose grief has yielded to time. Tomorrow I will walk farther and see more.

*5-29: It was cool days and cold nights when we arrived two days ago, but that has been replaced with hot days and cool nights. So Twig and I used the morning to take an ambling walk around what is called Cave Loop, probably three miles or so. Most of the trails will be closed for another couple of weeks so we walk along roadways that aren't heavily driven. I was perplexed at the continued closures but a ranger made sense of it—vegetative cover is slowly returning and since no one sticks slavishly to a trail they keep them closed to protect young grasses, forbs, and shrubs slowly making their return (against the odds, I imagine, since it's so dry); wandering hikers do more damage than we realize in normal conditions and this is a delicate time for the plants whose home this is. So we stuck to the road except in unburned areas.

Fires, like tornados back in the Texas Panhandle where I grew up fearing them, are famous for doing great damage in one spot while ignoring one beside it. Tornados have been known to destroy a house but leave a meal on the table. Fire will burn an area but leave a tree here and an island there or a hillside unscathed. It dances to the winds and whither they goest, it will follow. There is much of mystery to see. In some areas, those with heavy groundcover, it's easy to picture how the fire moved across the land burning everything as it went. In others where the grass and sage and such were thinner, it's not so easy. Strong winds, presumably, flinging embers forward. How does one half of a thirty foot tree burn and the other appear unbothered? The more closely I look the more I see that the desolation of nine months ago has been healed at ground level but skeletons of incinerated juniper, sage, pine, and bushes stand around as reminders and can easily dominate one's perspective; they are not pretty sights. Surfaces also appear grimmer owing to removal of vegetation leaving dark lava more exposed. I wonder if sage and its cohorts will have a hard time recovering; while grasses, forbs, and wildflowers are doing well, I don't see signs of the others' return. I was inspired when I was here shortly after the fire to see green sprigs arising from blackened roots but they don't seem to have come to anything. Maybe it was too early or too dry or just a last gasp, or maybe hungry creatures ate them. Whenever I pay attention I see new signs of my ignorance everywhere. Fire science, botany, geology, wildlife biology...so much more is unknown than known to me. Reading to remedy that is one good way to spend the better part of a life, and there was a time when it was more important than now. I honor that way and at times like this miss it, but not with sufficient motivation to change. Thoreau was still identifying and classifying, writing and organizing his copious notes until practically the moment he died, but he was only in his mid-forties. Muir lived much longer but over the last decades of his life his approach to Nature was less strenuous that when younger. My involvement feels deeper than ever but different in that it too has become less demanding while turning more to the beauty and spirit of the places I go. The balance has shifted.

Hardy little wildflowers have appeared and one could imagine them oblivious to what happened while they lay dormant, but I'd bet not. Indian Paintbrush, ubiquitous at all elevations and diverse habitats throughout the West it has seemed to me as I hiked them, have shown up here but not in abundance. Except for the red Paintbrush, yellow and purple are the exclusive colors, except for the lovely white interior of one plant's dime-sized purple blossoms and a pink flower I saw later. I counted three species of purple and about the same of yellow. It must be late in the season for all these guys. The burn has motivated me toward a more observant trek than usual, which I'm pleased about. Would that I could always be so attentive. I notice how diverse the forms taken by lava as it spread itself around all those millennia ago. There are largish heaps occasionally and then narrow strands winding across the land and then small piles and, most of all, solitary chunks scattered about, not to mention collapsed caves of remnant sluices where the viscous currents wound beneath the surface back during the volcanic periods, rising from well below, and then in time the ground above falling into the emptied space. The Monument is characterized by dozens of these things that did not collapse and where bats find homes and visitors wander and wonder. Although I've entered several of these caves I'm not really drawn to them, much preferring illumination to darkness. (If I continue this metaphor I'll have to deal with the evident analogue: do I prefer surfaces to depth? Better remain literal.)

All things considered, a comeback from the fire is well underway, and I'm sure it would greatly appreciate a few heavy rains to boost it along. No one can resist the pull of spring under any circumstances, but when it comes as rebirth after affliction everything counts, everything is a benediction. Speaking of which, I didn't mention that whatever shape the lava piles take, all are being colonized by growth: grasses, shrubs, sometimes trees. Brave seeds that decided to accept a challenge.

*5-30: We walked again this morning but less ambitiously than yesterday: a mile or so out, a long sit on a well-placed lava chunk, and then back. Twig seems as much drawn to tranquil being-there as I; she shows no signs of impatience however long we sit. The longer we stayed the more immersed I felt in the surroundings. Quiet, still, a solitary bird singing to himself. It's easy to think of plants as Nature's mystics, so complacent, present-centered (here, now), nowhere to go, untroubled. Seemingly placid with what they have even when not every need is met; no complaints. If the elements declare it's time for them to die, I don't picture them happy about it but accepting. The mind of a plant has to be very different from that of an animal; while its roots are busily scratching around out of sight meeting fungi and other plants' doing the same, its aboveground self is immobile except to the breezes and the inevitable changes that all life are subject to: growth, decline, illness, predation, the seasons and the weather. While most animals have territories, that of a plant is comparatively minute extending farther underground than above. Immobility means that many animal concerns mean nothing to them; no going in search of food or shelter or hiding from predators. Except for Saguaros, I don't know of any plant that people with guns find irresistible to shoot.

I speak of a plant's mind intentionally for why wouldn't they have one as we animals do only different? People I call anthropocentrists are loathe to allow any creature but humans a mind; maybe a few primates and cetaceans, perhaps elephants and parrots; the list is short. So even though they tend to identify mind with brain there are clearly many creatures with neurological equipment and brains that won't make their cut. But if mind is a locus for perceptions, responses, relations, feelings and thoughts or their analogues, memory, learning, forms of conscious-ness and selfhood...then surely many kinds of life, even without brains, have minds since they have bodies. My approach to this question is like my approach to other matters having to do with the living world and humans' place within it. I seek commonality, areas of identity and sharing, linkages and community. How are we like other life? Do we not share with it membership in the unity of *being* and therefore compose a commune, a mutuality of existence? I don't expect a plant to use their mind cogi-tating thoughts like these; in my imagination they do two primary activities. They tend to their needs and the needs of many of the surrounding plants, including propagation, self-preservation, various mutualities. And then they stand patiently absorbing the beauty of being. Not mere decoration, resource, or placeholder, they are pleased for their time to be... As was I, sitting among them. And then it was time to arise from my lava perch, watch where I stepped as I returned to the road, and walk back to camp.

*5-31: I don't fear falling into anthropomorphism when I think as I did yesterday. The label is used erroneously far more often than not, it seems to me. I will cheerfully call it anthropomorphism when I read on my almond milk container these words: "Shake me up. After opening, I belong in the fridge. And don't keep me waiting." But if you go far beyond that, I raise questions. Animal affection and joy, grief and sadness, thought and care—I see nothing in existence that suggests these qualities are owned and expressed only by humans. The more compelling question to me is why so many people are so concerned to avoid any appearance of granting animals more than rudimentary feelings, if that, and instrumental behaviors and relationships, concerned only to survive and reproduce, especially their genes. Why the apparent anxiety at acknowledging commonality? Why not rejoice at sharing the goodness of being with other creatures whom both evolution and a receptive and sensitive awareness suggest are fellow travelers through a grand mystery? Love and inclusion fit better than exclusion.

I have a theory about why so many people strain to find differences between humans and the rest of life; it was sparked by something I read in Reinhold Niebuhr while an undergraduate. He observed that humans couldn't decide what they were—were they just matter like all the rest of life appeared to be or spirit, children of Nature or of God? Despite all appearances, our species has wanted to believe the latter and diminish the material aspect. If spirit is too strong a word we might just speak of ourselves as ever-so-different, occupying a higher level of existence, special. I would call it a deeply rooted ontological anxiety; for irrational reasons many humans feel they would lose something in the acknowledgement of shared being in shared reality. Of course, the evidence from both worlds, those of science (evolution, ecology, and so on) and spirituality attests to commonality and the latter in particular recognizes that reality is most deeply apprehended in the experience of deep unity, ultimate Oneness. But unconscious anxieties never give up easily.

*6-1: Since my meditation on plant mind a couple of days ago I have been rereading *The Hidden Life of Trees*[2], a book I'd first read a half dozen years ago when it was published but wanted to refresh my mind about as I have become more intrigued with the notion of plant sentience over recent years. I didn't remember the following thought though it undoubtedly had unconscious influence on my ideas: "So, let's get back to why the roots are the most important parts of a tree. Conceivably, this is where the tree equivalent of a brain is located." He then referenced research suggesting that the key site might be the root tips where chemical and electrical impulses occur as well as molecules and processes similar to those of animals. "Can plants think? Are they intelligent?" He doesn't say and acknowledges that most of his fellow plant researchers are skeptical, to put it mildly, but he is clearly open to the prospect. As am I. This research process and the reactions of the scientific establishment remind me of an almost exact parallel in animal research, which for decades now has been unreeling evidence about animal behavior—their ways of going about the world, solving problems, obtaining what they need, and experiencing existence in their particularized ways and places—that steadily pushes back the margins of what was thought of as their narrow, programmed, machine-like, dully predictable

2. Peter Wohlleben, *The Hidden Life of Trees: What They Feel, How They Communicate* (Greystone Books, 2015), pp. 82-3.

lives. Suddenly they are found to be far more interesting and alive than was imagined and, although it should not have required this, it has sharpened the ethical compass in our relations with them. Animals have lives and ways of life. Don't we owe them moral consideration, too?

Late yesterday afternoon I sat under a tree in camp reading. I had noticed that things were going on within the tree, which is similar to but not a shrub oak, about the same height and density. There were conversations in the form of clicks and occasional particles of moisture would land on my arms that I could only imagine coming from the clicking creatures, bug pee, perhaps, if bugs peed. I had looked and noticed a few cicada-like insects on the limbs, not moribund but definitely lethargic; they moved in response to my approaching finger but not much and not far. They were about an inch and a quarter long with veined, transparent wings that extended beyond their posterior and with orange delineations around their dark bodies. Occasionally it seemed these were joined by others but I wasn't aware of any leaving. I figured they had business to do and left them alone. After a while a small gray bird landed directly above my head and began preening and cleaning his bill on the limb. He didn't seem on a search for a meal but the cicadas (as I will call them unless I learn better) weren't sure and were far more alert than I'd given them credit for. A space 2-3' in radius erupted around the bird and dozens of them sped away, the bird seemingly oblivious. He moved to another nearby limb; another eruption. He had a game going. But then he left, perhaps closer to me than he liked. I had not seen more than a fraction of these insects; their stillness and color tended to blend them into the tree and shadows, besides which I am never as observant as I would wish. Such abundance that I had not fully noticed is part of what interests me in this encounter, but more than that, the creatures had not seen me as a predator despite my size, but they did the see the tiny bird as one despite his size. Maybe this isn't so surprising since humans rarely fly into trees snatching insects for meals and birds do. But I had misread their seeming lethargy and unawareness; before the bird arrived they didn't need to display energy and attentiveness beyond noting and classifying my presence ("tall, two-legged, nonflying, white-haired creature, not an insectivore"), but they were not dozing. In spite of appearances, they knew what was going on around them. Surprises never end.

*6-2: There's an expression I've always liked: "Don't speak unless you can improve on the silence." Wise words but rarely honored. Even I, quiet by nature, have a hard time abiding by them in situations where talking seems called for and where I could not often claim to be improving on the silence by talking. I have been to silent retreats where silence is expected and people go for days with hardly a word spoken and I found it an immense relief; wordless, I felt more peaceful and at home with myself; in the smiles exchanged I was accepted and accepting and felt closer to the others than I would have in a wordier world. A big part of the problem, I think, is that speech is very often less a communicative act than a performative one. Speaking announces a person's presence, declares their mood and personality and something of what they know, establishes status; it creates a simulacrum of relation, which with real, improving speech can become genuine relation but does not often get that far. The simulacrum replaces or fills in and gives the impression of connecting with the listener; it kills time. Often it has a purpose, selling something for instance, and may succeed at that but insofar as it remains instrumental it does not achieve true relation. I wonder what the result would be if every social gathering required attendees to spend their first half hour in silence, even late arrivals who find others whose half hour has expired talking? More silence would offer far more reality to the human world than more words.

I bring this up because Twig and I have just returned, sweat covered and panting, after a hike around what's become our preferred route, the three mile or so Cave Loop, which tends to be less trafficked than other roadways. How grateful I will be that the trails will be open for our next visit. We leave tomorrow and head south to Butte Lake in the far northeast corner of Lassen Volcanic N.P., a relatively undeveloped area at the end of a six mile dirt washboard road. Walking Cave Loop we stop periodically and sit and look at what's around us. The first thing I notice is the silence; there are few human sounds, only an occasional car or airplane. The sounds I hear, gentle, soft, fitting, are from those who live out here: always it seems there's a solitary bird (was he already there or did he fly in and land for the company?), singing for the pleasure of it is my guess or as greeting; flies buzz, insects click, that's it. The speaking of these creatures actually does improve upon, or at least does not detract from, the silence. I can't picture them forced by anything to speak; they don't do it because of discomfort or convention; they have nothing to sell. They speak out of their nature and the authenticity of their being. I enjoy the silence out there and these little punctuations; it fosters connection and appreciation for the goodness of it all. It facilitates a unitive feeling to the extent I am receptive.

I also enjoy the perspective given by elevation change; to the north it slopes downward toward hills on the horizon and it seems I see many miles before they close the view, and to the south it rises and I see a shorter distance. Not to strain for imagery but there's a sort of ethereal quality to the vast northern scene—it encompasses so much that's so varied and suggestive of early volcanic times—while the southern scene is more straightforward and practical. Both, however, reveal how astonishingly prolific the grasses have been in recarpeting the landscape; with eyes only to the ground it's verdant but raise them and skeletal snags remind of what happened. I can't well identify why this particular land affects me as it does, but I'm inspired by it and will return as often as possible.

CHAPTER 8

ON DEATH:
ED & MARCUS AURELIUS

[Note: During the middle of the aughts I spent several summers volunteering for the National Park Service in Yosemite Valley. I wrote this essay during one of those times and include it here because it is still timely and brings from memory two beings I cared much about albeit differently.]

DEATH IS ON MY MIND these days, as it frequently was on Marcus Aurelius's (see Chapter 12). Mostly he thought about his own mortality, as I sometimes do mine. But my present meditation is on the ending of a dog's life, which raises feelings not so different even if less poignant than the prospect of my own demise.

Ed isn't quite ready to die, although he seems close. I don't want him to die but am willing to let him go when I must. Several times I've thought the time had arrived. Each time, he rebounded. I no longer trust my perceptions, so if euthanasia becomes right to do, I will probably wait too long. It is much like with my father who is 88 and about as crippled and infirm as Ed. I often think he is preparing to let go, that the pain, disabilities, and insults of old age have grown so intense and comprehensive that death was finally preferable. But, no, he hangs on, sees another doctor (with generally unsatisfactory results), muddles on. He is evidently determined to hang around until forcibly ejected by the great bouncer at closing time, unhappy but tenacious.

I calculate that Ed is about eighteen. Twelve years ago as I left work he ambled up, sat down in my pathway, looked at me in silent inquiry. It was a face and a look like none before. Where had he come from? The look communicated confidence—the person at whom he looked would make things right—and readiness for relationship. Calm, serene, engaging. But I resisted; I had a beloved dog, Annie, and felt myself a one-dog man. I asked a colleague to take him for a few days while I tried to find him a home. I secretly hoped he would decide to keep him, having lost and deeply grieved his own dog a few months earlier. But he had been hurt and would not incur that vulnerability again. Ed came home with me.

Ed became Ed as a double namesake. I greatly admired Ed Abbey's Nature writing—his take-no-prisoners intensity especially—and while I wrote my dissertation in 1988-89, in which he occupied the better part of a chapter, he died. He was not much older than I am now, but fell prey to some blood disease that I'd never heard of. At his wish, and to their credit, his wife (the last in a series) and friends packed his body in his sleeping bag, took him into the desert, and laid him to rest under a rock pile. I recalled that he had said while healthy that when he died he hoped to be laid out somewhere in the desert and left for the vultures, but I gather that friends and family decided this wasn't prudent, or esthetic perhaps.

The other honoree was Ed Duvin, a good friend, philosopher, and animal rights/social justice activist. Ed Duvin and Ed dog share a kind and gentle spirit, and the former shares as well Abbey's intense sense of the injustices commercial culture inflicts on Nature. Ed dog has honorably represented his namesakes' intelligence, even if not their passions.

Black, shaggy, mixed breed with predominance of spaniel. And that calm and that face. Self-sufficient emotionally, neither fearful nor aggressive, no interest at all in normal male dog posturing and combat. Once when Annie was attacked by a larger dog, who was getting the better of her, I looked at Ed who looked in dismay and aversion at the battle. It did not interest him but he seemed to feel an obligation to the girl who was sharing her person and home, so he stepped over, bit the aggressor in the rear, stepped away. This distraction caught the other dog's attention and I could intervene; fight over. That's the extent of Ed's career in the arena. He preferred serenity and reflection.

He has always been healthy. But for several years arthritis has steadily encroached so now he can barely stand upright and usually needs a helping hand to get there. Sometimes he is incontinent, always to his great embarrassment. He is nearly deaf. The state of his mind is hard to evaluate but he is not senile, at least not fully. The exception to his healthiness occurred three years ago when he suddenly developed laryngeal paralysis and nearly asphyxiated. The country vet recommended euthanasia and in tears I almost consented. My grief may have affected her as much as Ed's condition did—she said I might try a specialist. So I carefully placed his anesthetized and tubed body in the truck and raced to the city. Miraculously, they were able to surgically repair the problem but at the cost of his bark and minor difficulties drinking without choking. He adapted, as animals are adept at doing.

Now he sleeps most of the time and requires considerable care and patience. For a short time, I found myself getting testy and impatient with him. His legs wouldn't straighten and hold, his paws folded under; he might walk a few steps and then collapse. This self-sufficient creature had become terribly dependent. But I recalled that compassion is the companion of wisdom on the path. Some of the most admirable people I have known were caretakers of terribly impaired children and old folks. They demonstrated love in its highest expressions. The world needs that more than it needs more industriousness, progress, or wealth. The people giving and receiving need it. Now Ed needs it.

So I prop him up, carry him, clean his messes. I hope he can deliver himself into death when it feels to him time, or that if he can't he will find a way to ask my assistance with a clarity I can't miss. I'm not a natural caretaker, but he's teaching me. We both gain by this.

Death is death, whether a person's or a dog's. Naturally the prospect of one's own death tends to capture your attention more briskly than anyone else's, but feelings and attitudes about death cross species and ego boundaries as you contemplate the nonexistence of a present existent. Marcus Aurelius contemplated it a lot.[1] Invariably, he described death's approach as something to accept calmly, sometimes even to welcome, and in certain circumstances to precipitate by one's own action. Even so, his preoccupation with death—the need to repeatedly assure himself that it was a natural event with no real sting to it—makes me wonder if there wasn't more than meets the eye. Was there more feeling attached, even anxiety, than he acknowledged? I have too much trust in him to jump to this conclusion; as a Stoic he knew he ought to face death with equanimity, but perhaps he wavered from this occasionally and thus, reiteration on behalf of reinforcement. After all, death radically culminates. We *are,* and then, we *aren't.* No more plans or pleasures, no more experience of any kind. One just disappears...forever.

---

1. There are innumerable translations of Marcus Aurelius' *Meditations.* The one I usually refer to was translated and introduced by Maxwell Staniforth and is a Penguin Book, 1964.

I won't assume that he wavered, but if he occasionally did, is that surprising, even for one with his philosophical commitments? Death confronts us on so many levels. How much physical pain and suffering will I endure? (If a lot, is this Nature's way of making death less aversive?) What will it feel like to see everything that I have cared for fall away as I make the departure? Even though I unproblematically experienced, in a manner of speaking, an eternity of nonbeing before my birth, what makes a future eternity of the same nonbeing problematic? Because I've known life and will lose it, of course, but still, it will be the same state, neither pleasant nor unpleasant because nothingness has no discernible qualities, at least for those who have entered it.

Nothingness: Now there's a notion to wrap the mind around. Emotional reactions are one thing, but intellectually I have a hard time picturing the world without me, although it seems to get easier with time. Is it a logical impossibility? If I try to picture myself not being here, I have to be here, so how can I not be here, even in imagination? And were I not here, no picture at all. Leaving myself out of the picture (or the absence of picture), I try to imagine nothingness *per se*, with no personal referent; no Universe, no-thing. Nothingness, total absence of anything at all—I can't do it—even blankness is a thing. Impossible to imagine no features whatsoever—easier to conceive my nonbeing than complete nonbeing. As with imagining infinite time or space, the mind hits a wall. If the Universe has always existed, that might explain it: speculative nothingness sits comfortably alongside other unknowns, but apprehension of real, total nothingness in a world that has never known it may run into some cognitive limit. I will become nothing, cessation, yet the world goes on as before.

Life is sweet...but the bargain was: accept birth, accept death. It is irrational ever to expect only one side of a duality—hot without cold, up without down, birth without death. No. As confirmed nondualists, Marcus and I must reconcile death with life, must really know in our souls how they are linked, how this unity is essential and proper, how individuality is just a momentary formation within Wholeness. But the mind rebels, thinks it absurd, and always will so long as it remains trapped in separation, which the ego implacably is until it begins yielding to the knowing of higher experience.

Such knowledge is hard to come by. It's why deep meditation, mysticism, nirvana, and all the other terms associated with unitive consciousness refer to an almost unreachable and always elusive state of being. We seek unity but approach it as a fragment of the Whole. Ephemeral and elusive, as testified by every seeker. You can get there but not stay, at least not before death.

What do I hope to achieve in my preparation for death? Equanimity, naturally, but more than that; I want knowledge founded on ineffable experience that dying is reunion, return to source, flowing on. And that while I won't be conscious of the flow once dead, which is poignant but not tragic, I can affirm the mysterious reality of it, applaud my moments of living.

Will it be like my recent endoscopy, where I determined, as the IV anesthetic drip did its work, to focus on consciousness itself, to observe its presence and then its approaching absence? The transitional moment came but I've no memory of it. It seemed abrupt, a quantum change. Where did I go?

I recently read the account of a woman who experienced a massive left hemisphere stroke. *My Stroke of Insight* she calls it.[2] She lost virtually all normal functioning: movement, perception, sensation, memory, words, numbers, the incessant internal monologue. She could easily have died. A horrible experience, except that she was a neuro-

---

2. Jill Bolte Taylor, *My Stroke of Insight: A Brain Scientist's Personal Journey* (Plume Books, 2009).

anatomist (brain scientist) and had a better understanding than most could of what went on. For some time afterwards she was immersed in right brain operations and from this perspective knew vast peace, even euphoria, a sense of being a fluid stream of energy at one with the Universe. She acknowledged times of ambivalence—did she really want to return to normal existence? She came back, but as a different person.

Her story reveals that our very brain embodies duality between separation and oneness, that they can work together, but that in each of us one or the other tends to dominate, to some extent per our choosing. I suspect that that right hemisphere may be the seat of ultimate experience, and that through it, along the way to varying degrees but at the end decisively, one can experience his true unitive being, and death as merely transitional: embodiment... dissolution...dispersion...reembodiments... As clinging to ME and my individuality dissipates so goes the anxiety. A perfect picture of life's flow, filled with billions of daily deaths, from beetle to baron, but never itself ending, always regenerating.

Marcus spoke of death in two contexts: as the conclusion of his life and as one more sign of eternal and ubiquitous change, of the impermanence of everything. He was downright Buddhist in his emphasis. "Time is a river, the resistless flow of all created things. One thing no sooner comes in sight than it is hurried past and another is borne along, only to be swept away in its turn." (IV, 43) "Observe how all things are continually being born of change; teach yourself to see that Nature's highest happiness lies in changing the things that are, and forming new things after their kind. Whatever is, is in some sense the seed of what is to emerge from it." (IV, 36) Recognizing this, "...surely a man were foolish to gasp and fume and fret, as though the time of his troubling could ever be of long continuance." (V, 23)

The river's flow did not trouble Marcus. Stoics are nothing if not realists: Nature's determinations were to be accommodated rather than bemoaned. Impermanence described the way things are, understanding and adjusting were central to his intended way of living. This contextualized experience, including in particular that of one's own self and its duration.

Buddhists sometimes speak of impermanence as if it were in itself a source of our suffering. But it is attitude that matters. Attachment, aversion, and ignorance turn impermanence into an affliction. Nonattachment, acceptance, and wisdom turn it into a condition on the path to liberation. Marcus speaks of ceaseless change and transformation as "Nature's delight." If that appreciation can become ours as well, it leads to a vision that, when deeply internalized, truly makes for delight and solace. "Out of the universal substance, as out of wax, Nature fashions a colt, then breaks him up and uses the material to form a tree, and after that a man, and next some other thing; and not one of these endures for more than a brief span." (VII, 23) In answer to the perennial question, then, the good news is that there is life after death; the bad news is that you won't be aware of it since—body/mind/spirit—you die, dissolve, disperse, sooner and later becoming part of other life. Endless recycling and transmutation. The whole carries on infinitely while uncountable individuals, flora and fauna of millions of species, have their wee moments to dance, sing, look around in amazement, merge back into undifferentiation, and reemerge, rise up in innumerable new forms and do it all over again. Not a picture that flatters the individual ego, its vanities and preoccupations look pretty silly and irrelevant, but exhilarating in its own way.

Yes, it leaves a host of questions, preeminently how best to live one's wee moment, but with proper perspective it is surely a grand performance. "Observe, in short, how transient and trivial is all mortal life...Spend, therefore, these fleeting moments on earth as Nature would have you spend them, and then go to your rest with a good grace, as an olive falls in its season, with a blessing for the earth that bore it and a thanksgiving to the tree that gave it life." (IV.48)

It is one thing to salute the process and another coming to terms with discrete events along its way. I awoke at 3 a.m. this morning and noticed silence. Ed, whose sleep is generally fitful, was motionless and soundless. I was sure he had died. I felt relief for both of us—it is unquestionably time for that olive to fall—but grief and a brief bout of rebellious perplexity inserted themselves. What *sense* is there in all this living, loving, and losing? Then he snorted and woofed: question deferred.

The reflections of Marcus Aurelius on death are legion. You might think it would become depressing, but it does not. His theme is consistent: meet death with calm acceptance (which is something other than resignation) and gratitude for the life one has had, whether long or short. Contemplation of one's death brings beneficial insights, he tells us:

- Realization that life's ending is a mere process of Nature and that it contributes to Nature's well-being;

- Death exemplifies change and as you think about that and all the other changes life has presented you that were manageable, anxiety diminishes;

- Contemplation of death instructs us on relation with God;

- Death is consistent with the plan of your creation and reminds you of life's brevity thus encouraging you to use it for good while you can;

- Contemplation of death fosters acceptance, whether it comes tomorrow or next year and teaches appreciation for what you have had;
- Death is the great leveler; it removes all distinction between kings and stable boys;
- It releases one from having to feel, think, sense, do ...;
- Death finally relieves one of the obligation to deal with "company so discordant."

I suppose we could summarize as "look on the bright side," except Marcus is too serious for that. Death is the great inevitability, the last important thing one does. A thoughtful person wants to do it well. One can rage against extinction, as some advise, but that seems pointless, inappropriate, self-indulgent. Absolute inescapability presents a challenge—I can't not relinquish what has been my greatest prize, so let me understand what it means to live and to die and finally to exit with grace. Even if we lived forever, the question of what to do with your time must be answered, but brevity should add urgency and awareness to the quest. In a sense, "how to die" will have been answered by our earlier responses to "how to live."

If the *Meditations* are assembled in the order that Marcus wrote them (unlikely, but we'll never know), it is interesting that of all the many times he speaks of death, the only two where he hints at something other than its complacent acceptance are in the final pages, when he may have been sick with plague and dying. In the first instance, he asks himself why he would hunger for long life, suggests some possibilities, asks if they are really worthwhile, and concludes: "Then if you think them [the possibilities] beneath your notice, press on towards the final goal of all—which is the following of reason and of God. But to prize this, you must remember, is incompatible with any feelings of resentment that death will rob you of the others." (XII, 31) It seems possible that he had entertained thoughts that more time of life might be good, that there was much he could still accomplish for the Empire and his people, but decided this was unseemly. It didn't fit his world view. Even so, if wanting more of the conventional desires was unworthy, and I don't doubt that he sincerely believed it so, what about lost opportunities to practice reason and follow God? As an intelligent, reverent, morally and socially responsible man, there may have been sadness at the final curtain's falling on his chances to do good for his people and to become a better man. While life surely had its pleasures, for an honorable man it had as well a "mission," and his individual piece of Universal Nature's Mission must die with him.

The final Meditation (XII, 36) once again raises—only to abjure—a suggestion of nonacceptance. "Wherein, then, is your grievance?" he asks about the eventuality of dying. The answer is pure Marcus Aurelius.

> O man, citizenship of this great world-city has been yours. Whether for five years or fivescore, what is that to you? Whatever the law of that city decrees is fair to one and all alike. Wherein, then, is your grievance. You are not ejected from the city by any unjust judge or tyrant, but by the selfsame Nature which brought you into it; just as when an actor is dismissed by the manager who engaged him. 'But I have played no more than three of the five acts.' Just so; in your drama of life, three acts are all the play. Its point of completeness is determined by him who formerly sanctioned your creation, and today sanctions your dissolution. Neither of those decisions lay within yourself. Pass on your way, then, with a smiling face, under the smile of him who bids you go.

Perfectly rational, perfectly accepting of life and death as they come, utter equanimity; exit with a smile of gratitude to the Source, Guide, Master: Universal Nature. (His eventual dying words were said to be: "Weep not for me; think rather of the pestilence and the deaths of so many others.") But was this Meditation born of grievance? He died at 58, encamped near a battlefield. We don't know what he may have been experiencing. I venture to guess he felt ambivalent. Two thirds of his tenure as Emperor had been spent away at war; natural calamities had besieged the empire along with barbarians. He had a powerful social conscience and would have been deeply affected by Roman suffering. How could he not have felt incomplete? There was so much that needed doing: so much good, justice, amelioration of living conditions. (He had sold the royal jewelry to buy food for his people.) At the heart of his philosophic soul he was ready to die ("Such a man's life [one with mind disciplined and purified] fate can never snatch away unfulfilled..." [III.8]), but for the sake of all those citizens who depended on him, he would have been pained not to be able to give what they needed. So it seems to me.

It interests me that with all his contemplation and all those years at war, Marcus said nothing about war itself as a human or political matter. Was it too common to merit notice? Perhaps, but more to the point, his meditations were about self-mastery and self-improvement, about understanding Reality and according himself with its demands and standards. The meditations were spiritual exercises. His meditative interests were self-focused in this positive sense. Forms of social and political organization, his thoughts about them do not appear. This saddens me, for I would like to know what he thought about war, political dynamics, Roman society, marriage, and more. Instead, he tells how the good person, striving to be responsive to Universal Nature, should handle himself whatever the circumstances. Situational variables were always secondary to what one brought to them, his attitudes, beliefs, and self-management.

Having lasted into my mid-sixties the prospect of dying gathers my attention from time-to-time. Previously remote and abstract, it has now moved into the neighborhood and is less of a stranger. And my daily observation and tending of Ed, the recognition that death hovers on his doorstep, prevents any avoidance I might be tempted to indulge. Will he be alive when I return to camp? I never fail to wonder as I approach.

How helpful is Marcus in my preparation for the psychological and philosophical demands of the "last act"? He was described by Maxwell Staniforth, one of his translators, as a late transitional representative of Stoic philosophy. He expressed a wider affective range, more humility, more self-questioning, and even with his thoroughgoing efforts to improve himself and do justice to his role in creation, he was more doubtful about human prospects. He combined deep commitment to duty with pessimism and is all the more admirable in my eyes for his devotion to the good and the right despite the limited impact it was likely to produce, people being people.

In this light, his repeated exhortation to himself about death, its normalcy and beneficence in Nature's grand scheme, the incumbent duty to calmly embrace it as his life's final contribution to the order of existence, fits neatly into his life "project." I identify with Marcus and feel affection and brotherhood and reinforcement from him as I prepare to share the universal end-of-life anxieties and contingencies. If intrinsic meaning and the potential to realize it are given with existence, they are not complete until life itself ends.

This way of thinking has special pertinence as one encounters the usual infirmities of age and confronts the modern, mechanized, profit oriented, and emotionally too often impoverished medical establishment. Its values and practices have become technical and instrumental; they aspire to master death, death the enemy. If one yields, if he offers his body to this machine, something vital to the wholeness of his life course may die before his afflicted, medicalized body, his wonderful mortal foundation, inevitably caves in. By then it has become an alienated other, and the grace of a conclusion grateful and affirming has been deferred, perhaps lost.

Of course, one ought not wait till the denouement to prepare for it. For a change of pace, I have been reading Montaigne's essays and find this: "If I can, I shall keep my death from saying anything that my life has not already said." One readies for a "death with dignity," a notion more spoken of thirty years ago than today, by having lived a life with dignity. Having lived with eyes focused on responsibility to the Real, one might see their death as not only their last important act but as their final reciprocatory offering to the Nature that invited them in and provided for them.

Ed continues to decline and in my exasperation I sometimes feel it is neither far enough nor fast enough. His care has become burdensome. He doesn't sleep well and wakes me several times a night as he flails about unable to turn over. So I arise and rotate him by the legs; not much dignity in that but it makes him more comfortable for a couple hours or so. He becomes as well increasingly incontinent, drinking and peeing copiously, his kidneys evidently giving out.

We drove across the mountains early in the week to see a vet. She and I agreed that we are in the palliative care stage and she gave me steroids and pain meds. Also, enough of a tranquilizer for me to euthanize him if the time comes. He was having a bad day and could not walk or even stand, so I toted him into the clinic, laid him on the waiting room floor, then to an examining table, then back to the truck. Since we were strangers to the clinic staff, we must have seemed queer, like a bad joke of some sort. He seemed virtually comatose the entire time.

But then he has a good day, his mind relatively intact and his suffering minor or at least manageable, dogs being the great Stoics that they are. I dream some nights about old suffering parents and old suffering dogs.

Besides the sadness, and sometimes resentment, I feel for Ed, this situation raises thoughts about ethics, quality of life, and interspecies relationships. It will be grief and relief when he dies, but I don't think euthanasia appropriate just yet. I judge that by what seems to be his state of consciousness, as best I can fathom it. If there were persistent signs of irremediable pain (though animals are loathe to show them), it would be time for him to go. The incontinence is an immense inconvenience to me, but euthanasia is not for my benefit. If he becomes unable to stand on his own at all, combined with the other maladies, then that might make euthanasia proper, as this morbid calculus goes. He cannot raise himself now; I lift him to his feet and he totters around and sometimes tumbles. Still, in his unstable way, he manages and occasionally wants to go for a ramble of fifty yards or so.

Twelve years ago when I wrote *Disposable Animals*, a polemic against animal shelter killing of surplus dogs and cats, I was often accused of failing to understand that "there are fates worse than death." (And deaths worse than fate, I replied.) It seemed a bare-faced rationalization for traditional shelter practice. But the value of life, and what we owe others in protecting and taking care of theirs, are matters that move into murky waters in cases like Ed's, and as I've begun to discover, like that of my parents. For Marcus Aurelius the duty of justice is one most stringent, and I agree with him. But what is justice for a dog in Ed's condition? If he were found abandoned with no apparent attachments, hardly anyone would hesitate to recommend euthanasia. But he has me, and love takes justice and raises its obligations several notches. How could it not? Yet, that means the unloved will receive less care and less justice, and how can that be right? I remember reading in some Taoist text that those on the Way provide vast compassion to the deserving. *And*, they provide vast compassion to the undeserving (and unloved).

At the most intimate level—Ed, me—I can see the temptation to rationalize. His care tires me and disrupts my sleep, he is often stinky with pee, I even think he may have gotten into the invalid role a bit more than his condition warrants (who knows?!), and he is rarely the satisfying companion of old. He disrupts camp life hugely. He can't possibly live much longer anyway, and his quality of life is so diminished, therefore... No one would challenge the decision. But it would be for me, not him, and that is the crucial decider. Still, this scale is precariously balanced, and it won't take much more debility to change the equation, rightly I think.

Another interesting aspect of this is that my location means that euthanasia must be both chosen and implemented by me. Probably a good thing in that it necessarily requires more certainty than handing the burden over to another might. (I have often wondered how many more vegetarians there would be if people had to personally slay and dismember all the animals they eat.)

Why do we claim to value life so highly? An odd question? Each individual existence is but a sub-nano-sized portion of the eternity of its nonexistence and about the same spatial portion of the Universe. Should its microscopic nature raise its value or lower it? In relation to human life, but far less so with other forms of life, we call it sacred, of ultimate value, etc., etc. But we don't usually act as if we believe this. War would hardly be so common or fetus-cherishing zealots so indifferent to conditions post- partum if life were really experienced, rather than merely conceptualized, as sacred. Prisons wouldn't be so full, vulnerable people so poor, hungry, and ill, racism so frequent, and on and on and on if we believed it. "Culture of life" bumper stickers coexist happily side-by-side with pro-war, pro-gun, and pro capital punishment messages. It's a meager sacrality, if any at all.

More suggestive, though, is the manner in which so many people actually lead their lives. How would people who truly considered their short span ultimately valuable be expected to use it? If more highly valued for its brevity wouldn't each precious moment be treasured and seen as opportunity to discern and live out the ultimate values that make it ultimately valuable? Where does one see people living with this kind of seriousness? What in our culture fosters it?

Caring for Ed is caring for life. Flawed as I am, and pessimistic, with Marcus I recognize where I am and what gives it importance and wish to honor that in all possible ways.

Ed remains much on my mind. Last evening, for the first time in years, I read a journal I kept on a long visit to Yosemite Valley five years ago. And there was Ed, younger and fitter, and I was touched at the reminder. I'm going to insert a few selections from that journal just because I like them and they enrich the memories of my fading old friend.

The first is from July in '04:

Ed and I just finished our evening walk. Each night the Valley walls present themselves differently, or so they appear to me. Mostly it's changes in the light but also I look upward from different spots, catch a new angle, form a different gestalt, combine into new unities, see aspects unnoticed before, or the same sight with new vision. I know there is an objective Valley, but the correspondence of that with my evolving experience of it is never certain.

Ed is about fourteen. Impossible to know for sure. He found me seven years ago, is heavily grizzled, and increasingly stiff of gait. Occasionally his front legs give way and he falls on his side or face in an embarrassment that he tries to hide behind a brave and seemingly unconcerned manner, as if he had just decided spontaneously that this was a good place to lie down and catch his breath. Once as he walked behind me I heard a "whump," the leash tightened, I looked back and he was down and immobile. I thought for a moment he'd dropped dead but it was just his stumble.

His disabilities seem about the same as Annie's when she was fourteen so I consider him about that age. Annie came with me on my first trip to Yosemite in '88; she was four years old and my great dog love, traveling with me almost everywhere for all of her 15+ years. Two years ago she died quietly while sleeping beside my reading chair. I had been away for several days and returned to find her pacing, as she had taken to doing, in the meadow beside the house. We greeted each other, I unpacked, reunited with L., settled down, and within the hour I looked up from a book and down at Annie, and she was dead. It was her time; she was in bad shape (incontinent, deaf, crippled) and had had a long good life but I miss her still and weep as I write about her even now. She jogged and hiked with me until she was twelve or thirteen when, try as she might, she couldn't keep up. She had always seemed indestructible— tireless, strong, full of good cheer. But none can avoid aging. She declined and she died. I buried her beneath a live oak in the meadow, a finely shaped stone at her head. Beloved Annie.

And now there's Ed, having his first Yosemite time, and he too is fading. At home he mostly sleeps, but it has been interesting to see what individual attention and new surroundings have done for him. A springy new step (when he isn't falling), spaniel nose browsing the air for scents. He, like Annie, is a "dog-dog," the best there is, a medley of multiple breeds. He must have his evening stroll. Considering the contrast with his sedentary home life, I realize how much adjusting dogs must do to live in homes and fenced yards. They mostly have experientially impoverished lives but with animal graciousness and adaptability seem to accept it. I believe animals are naturally spiritual, beyond humans who have to guide ourselves toward it. They are present-centered, receptive, minimal ego, apparently at one with being. Still, I often wonder if it wouldn't be better if the animals called "pets" went extinct. Their lives are not their own, their biology to a great extent artifactual, their presence encourages the human sense of dominance over the nonhuman world and it may substitute for a richer, more attentive relation with wildlife and Nature. We use them for our purposes and for every loved and well-cared for dog there are others who are abused, neglected, and finally killed by "humane" groups and animal control departments because they have no home—as often as not because their "owner" deserted them. A truly respectful relation between them and ourselves would have to be a very different one.

This is from a couple weeks later:

Bear trap was gone two days ago after only a short stay. I don't know if it successfully lured a victim. Then it was back, and yesterday morning at six while Ed enjoyed breakfast, I looked down the road toward the trap and just this side of it an adult bear meandered out of the bushes, ignored the trap, and continued on. Five minutes later the bear trap tender arrived, disconsolately released the open trap door, and cursed when I told him the news. When Ed and I walked, in the shadows of cedar and pine, there sat bear watching us. I wonder what was on his mind.

Ed is powerfully drawn to these traps. They contain food as bait and that attracts him. One morning large chunks lay outside the trap leading to its door and he munched them down promptly. But his curiosity seems more than gustatory. He sniffs the thing end to end, perhaps for food inside but not improbably at residual bear scent as well. He has a marvelously demonstrative form of sniffing—nose arches up above his head and seems to winnow the air, swinging up-and-down and back-and-forth. Often this goes on for 10-20 seconds or more before he lowers it to ground in the traditional posture. He seems to be inhaling the world, turning it over and over, massaging it in his olfactories and then classifying it. It reminds me of a person carefully scanning a mountainside with binoculars, looking for what's hidden. For some reason it affects me poignantly; it shows another way of knowing the world, knowing it well and in ways I never will. I would give a lot to live a day as a dog, to learn some of what they know that escapes me, and to experience Ed's evident pleasure in catching and following a scent.

We're at the end of the month now:

When you share a small camper with your dog and walk him several times a day on a leash, you unavoidably become familiar with his intimate habits. Among these, I notice that dogs and people have nearly opposite approaches to the intake of nutrients and outgo of waste products. Ed loves his morning meal and gobbles it down with relish, no delicacy whatsoever, augmenting it with random tidbits he finds as we walk, such as those around the bear trap. Humans, on the other hand, modern ones anyway, affect more concern with preparation, appearance, taste, and eating rituals, although the advent of "fast foods" and the growing practice of eating while engaged in other activities has diminished the salience of these niceties (and stimulated the emergence of an opposite approach, the "slow food" movement). Quality and healthfulness have receded before the fast food juggernaut and been replaced with artificially flavored, scented, colored, and textured food-like substitutes for genuine meals. But we still, on special occasions, go through the motions of preparing (or having prepared) and eating food with attention to what it is and a degree of recognition that it can be a kind of sacrament and that, in any event, as physical beings we require food and that it be somewhat nutritive. Ed is unconcerned with any of this.

On the other hand (other end, to be precise), Ed treats excretion, both types, ceremoniously. When I tend to this, it's down to business and finish as quickly and thoughtlessly as possible; Ed undertakes these functions as veritable missions. Urination never happens all at once, simply to empty the bladder. Urination is communication, but not at all like a lecture or after dinner speech. More like a series of statements, missives to unknown interlocutors, many of whom have left their own communiqués for him, as his excellent nose notices as we perambulate. If dogs wrote notes on paper, I picture bushes, trees, stumps, rocks, and tires all hung with sticky-notes like flowering plants in full bloom.

I'm not so sure about his larger goals with defecation but whether communicative or not it is artful, and not just any spot of ground will do. He prefers high grass, thick duff, pine needle piles. He searches until satisfied that landing conditions are to his liking, then it's bombs away, and he furiously and fastidiously scratches the ground with all four paws driving dirt and organic matter back in the general direction of ground zero, and then moves on with a gleam in his eyes and bounce in his step, leaving a few more sticky notes on our way back to camp.

I don't know what to make of these dog-human contrasts. But Ed's attentiveness to doing it right at the nether end adds to the mystery of animal variation and behavior. What do those guys have on their minds? What is the world like for them? We don't know half of what life feels like and what it means to dogs or to any of our other brethren species. But I assume they find it mostly good and are pleased at the time they are allowed to enjoy it.

I'll end with this, a week later:

Last evening as Ed and I went on his long walk—the one not merely to satisfy biological needs but that provides leisure for him to seine the air for intriguing scents (sniff-sniff-sniff, nose swings back and forth, up and down, purposeful and skilled as in scholarly exegesis of a text), to pee expressively and frequently, to drop down into the Creek and sip as he swims, to prance a bit in an old guy's way—I sensed that we were followed. It was a coyote fifty yards behind. We stopped and turned, coyote stopped, he and Ed stared and communicated obscure canid vibrations to one another, coyote slowly lowered himself to the ground on chest and belly, legs in front, head erect, and there we were, three immobilized curious creatures. I'm certain the coyote knows dogs from experience, but I don't know what Ed might have learned before wandering into my orbit years ago; as far as I know he's not previously encountered coyotes. Out of curiosity about coyote's intentions, I persuaded Ed to turn back in our initial direction and we walked forward a few paces; coyote did the same. And again. At this point we approached a stationary bicyclist with camera who wanted a picture but was afraid to move too close for fear he would be attacked. I assured him that he needn't worry. Now we were four, still immobile, alert, savoring the moment, wondering what might happen next. My curiosity about that will forever remain unsatisfied. In the distance behind coyote I espied a jogger coming our way. I hoped she too would stop and enjoy the scene. Coyotes are sometimes, but not commonly, seen in the Valley so this was a serendipitous encounter for us all. But she did not hesitate nor show a particle of interest, just kept running. Spell broken, coyote headed off into the brush. I wanted to accost the woman, to know of what dispirited stuff she was made. This little mystery meant nothing to her, so she missed it. But the other four of us enjoyed it while it lasted.

I have great admiration for coyotes. They are clever and appealing and durable as hell to have survived and flourished despite our cruelties and exterminative assaults. Like Ed, they march on entranced by life and adding their unique charm and definition to it.

I may risk my Stoic credentials with this blatant sentimentalizing about Ed back when we could still take walks together. So be it. This is our fifth time to come to the Valley and spend *a few months here. One of the ways I've marked his aging has been by the declining distance of those walks, from a couple miles to a few yards. The years will do that. But I recollect not to hold on to past or despair at present. These memories are satisfying. They are part of what binds us together and help prepare me for unbinding when the time comes.*

Ed is dead. He took his final breath yesterday morning between six and seven. I had expected it earlier and arose at five planning to bury him before I left camp. At five he looked dead, even smelled of early decomposition, but rattling breaths continued. This last stage of unconsciousness had persisted for two days and I blame myself.

Over recent days his decline accelerated. He showed less interest and ability to stand and incontinence became complete, but he had moments of looking around and focusing on me that led me to think he wasn't quite ready to go. Wasn't he, or was I not ready to help him over the hump? On Thursday evening he was uncomfortable; his pain relievers weren't relieving. I had the bottle of tranquilizers with which I planned to euthanize him if it became necessary. Thinking that one, a nonlethal dose, might make him more comfortable and allow a good night's sleep, I gave it to him. It worked, but 24 hours later he remained unconscious. The time had come. I gave him a half dozen more, expecting that this would swiftly ease him over the edge since one had had such an effect. But, no; Saturday I gave him the rest. His strong old soul hung on till Sunday.

Tranquilizers were not the preferred way, but under our circumstances in camp far from town, it was the only way. I don't believe he suffered, but he lingered unnecessarily. I spooned him water. I caressed and mourned. It took too long. I feel I failed him at the end.

I had identified an isolated spot where I could bury him,

likely without interruption, which was important since the Park Service does not approve such uses of the Park. An undisturbed mountainside, heavily forested, permanent shade, dry creek bed just below. The only impediment was hardened, rocky soil so I couldn't put him as deep as I would have liked. He is vulnerable to scavenging by mountain lion, coyote, or bear, which does not trouble me (though I worry that the drugs may still be potent), except that I want his peace finally to be complete. We are all eaten eventually by some array of creatures. Those endless transformations that so occupy Marcus...that is part of the majesty of it all. Ed as bear muscle and bear poop, pine nutrient and food for fungi, microbe, and insect, merging with soil and duff, dissolving, absorbed and sipped and carried around these mountains by jay and raven—a pleasing image and eventual reality.

Easy to say. A large space has been left empty, and I have been weepy. Ed seemed to me, from first encounter, an animal with uncommon dignity and interiority. Like me, he was essentially a loner. Even surrounded by other household dogs he maintained his separateness. When we all took off for a walk over the pastures, he moved out on a perimeter and as if connected by an invisible tie maintained a set distance, gliding through the tall grass with head high, nose scouting, in classic spaniel hunting style. He neither played nor competed with the others; he was in his own world. The only unprovoked aggression I ever witnessed in him, scant at that, was half-hearted chase of a hen that left her minus a few tail feathers and much dignity. I called him down and he halted, feathers floating from muzzle. He had forgotten himself.

We don't usually attribute a complicated inner world to dogs, but to Ed I did. He had gravitas, a solemn taking in of his surroundings, calm comprehension, an elevation not prideful. I can't resist thinking him the Marcus Aurelius of dogs.

I recall a long ago reading in Annie Dillard that I will

paraphrase to fit my feelings about this. The proper response to loss is first, "Thank you, Nature, for what you gave." And then, "I grieve the loss." But never, "How wrong this is. Can't I have more?" Creation blesses us with moments only. *It,* not *I,* matters most of all.

Rest in peace, old man. Travel the Sierra Nevada in plant, animal, and microbe. I loved you. I miss you. [A year later I visit his grave and find it untouched except by pine needles and snow melt, a bit of black fur revealed.]

A few days have passed since Ed died. I have found, since Ed's mountainside interment, that I have been sensitized, opened in some way to a deeper experience of love and loss than is normal for me. Toward absent wife, acquaintances in the Valley, Yosemite, Sierra Nevada and Ed's memory, even toward Marcus and my brotherhood with that fine, long dead kindred: the conjunction of events has informed me irrefutably that relations I learned years ago to think of as *Thou* are the center of existence, source of its joy and meaning. In his eighties, after his stroke, Bede Griffiths, the Catholic-Hindu monk,[3] said that his capacity for love was hugely strengthened as his cognitive propensities had been weakened. I feel something like that; loss and limitation and inspiration have awakened responsiveness.

I see this is the second time I have referenced stroke victims as people who experienced dramatic new insights and enhanced capacities as a result of their brain traumas. I recently happened upon a third. Lama Anagarika Govinda,[4] German born but devoted Tibetan Buddhist monk and scholar who died a quarter century ago. As described by a friend in his last years: "He assured me that the strokes

---

3. Shirley du Boulay, *Beyond the Darkness: A Biography of Bede Griffiths,* (O Books, 2003).
4. Richard Power (ed.), *The Lost Teachings of Lama Govinda: Living Wisdom from a Modern Tibetan Master* (Quest Books, 2007).

were the greatest of blessings, not a hardship at all. He said that he had previously thought he had achieved some understanding of emptiness, *shunyata,* the great void of blissful freedom at the core of Buddhist reality, only to realize *with each stroke,* how much more profound, how much more miraculous it was!" Disability surely isn't a preferred facilitator, but it is notable that these three people—a scientist, Catholic/Hindu monk, and a Buddhist—experienced strokes with such similar realizations. They tell us how much innate but suppressed ability we all may have in these realms—a talent for union housed right there in our brains. As recently taught me by Ed, grief too will instruct if I pay attention.

CHAPTER 9

SIERRA NEVADA
WATER & TREES

THE DAY BEGINS WITH HOURS beside flowing water. The walk starts near the confluence of Tenaya Creek and Merced River. Late June, and the high country snow is fast disappearing, but the watersheds of both these streams still send down a generous flow, a gift of water I always consider particularly pleasing. Whenever I leave Yosemite I do it with full jugs, which remind me of this place whenever I drink.

Today I carry a liter of it in my pack while its generous source sails past as I walk upstream along the Merced. The trail is dusty, shaded, littered with horse droppings. The flow is rapid in this stretch and frequently squeezed along even faster by bouldered constrictions. It is absolutely transparent to its rocky bed and beautifully reflective of its surroundings: Stream flowing over bed of rocks that came from elsewhere and are now settled in place, stabilized though immersed in change. Water astonishes with its protean, forgiving, implacable nature; its manifold generosity seems endless, though 21st century humanity sorely tests it.

As I sit watching, it reminds me of a film reel, scene changing slightly with each frame. The ancient notion that "you never step into the same river twice" seems true only in a limited sense. Coursing water molecules

are new every moment but they are only partial represen-
tation of river being. River begins in hidden notches at its
highest reaches, gathers, welcomes feeder streams and
meltwater all along the way, follows its bed (which persists
even when water has temporarily dried), and forms a braid
of continuity from beginning to end. It is whole with shifting aspects. I meet the same, though changed, River whenever I visit.

Zen master Shunryu Suzuki visited Yosemite Valley
several decades ago. In *Zen Mind, Beginner's Mind*,[1] he
speaks of Yosemite Falls and how it recalled to him other
streaming water in his Japanese homeland. The book is a
collection of his teachings, and one, "Nirvana, the Water-
fall," has had special meaning to me since I first read it. He
tells of his former monastery and of two practices there:
when Dogen-zenji dipped water from the river he always
returned the unused portion back to the river; and when
monks washed, they filled basins only partway and then
emptied the water towards rather than away from their
bodies.

> This expresses respect for the water. This kind of
> practice is not based on any idea of being econom-
> ical. It may be difficult to understand why Dogen
> returned half of the water he dipped to the river.
> This kind of practice is beyond our thinking. When
> we feel the beauty of the river, when we are one
> with the water, we intuitively do it in Dogen's way.
> It is our true nature to do so.
>
> ...When we see one whole river we do not feel the
> living activity of the water, but when we dip a part
> of the water into a dipper, we experience some
> feeling of the water, and we also feel the value of
> the person who uses the water. Feeling ourselves

---

1. Shunryu Suzuki, *Zen Mind, Beginner's Mind* (Weatherhill, Seventh
Printing, 2004).

and the water in this way, we cannot use it in just a material way. It is a living thing.

One knows: Water *is,* all that it is. I understand this response.

As I walk the two miles toward Vernal Fall the grade steepens, the bed narrows, and car-sized boulders become more common. Water is white with turbulence and alive with energy and grace as it surmounts and circles, bends to the rocks' demands. Pools, eddies, chutes, and then at the Fall, splash, spray, mist; I've traveled from silence to cacophony, from transparency to prismatic colors as the rising sun plays with floating droplets.

I don't remember when water began to affect me as it does now. It is difficult even to describe the effect. The material nature of water seems to manifest spirituality more than other substances, even when they assume the most striking forms. Valley wall formations, backcountry peaks and domes, forests and wildflower meadows: there is no resisting any of these, no doubt that they also speak clearly of invisible forces and realities (and of the water that has shaped or fed them). But there is something more in water that eludes me, something totemic.

Since I came upon it a couple decades ago, John Muir's account of raindrops has remained my favorite expression of enchantment with water.[2] He was enjoying his first time in the Sierra Nevada, in the high country north of Yosemite Valley; it was 1868. Thirty years old, he had recently arrived in California after a trip begun by train from his home in Indianapolis to Louisville, followed by a long walk across Kentucky, Tennessee, Georgia, and into Florida. Laid low with malaria, he delayed for recuperation, and then continued by boat to Cuba where he stayed several weeks. Then to New York to catch another boat which took him to Panama, crossed the isthmus by train,

---

2. John Muir, *My First Summer in the Sierra* (Penguin Books, 1987).

and then on to San Francisco. Altogether, about a seven-month journey.

Muir had been in the mountains six weeks, a time of daily rapture as he immersed in the landscape, when a rain storm thundered in just after noon. "How interesting to trace the history of a single raindrop!" Two pages of lyrical transport combined with immense attentiveness to raindrop travels then follow. He reflected that the first such drops, geologic ages ago, fell on barren granite, but now they have peaks and domes, forest and garden, to receive them. Some join streams and lakes, falls and cascades, while others merge with meadow and bog where they "... creep silently out of sight to the grass roots, hiding softly as in a nest, slipping, oozing hither, thither, seeking and finding their appointed work." Some sift downward through leaf and needle of tall trees while others attach to minerals and shine upon mates drumming through broad-leafed plants of countless varieties.

> Some happy drops fall straight into the cups of flowers, kissing the lips of lilies. How far they have to go, how many cups to fill, great and small, cells too small to be seen, cups holding half a drop as well as lake basins between the hills, each replenished with equal care, every drop in all the blessed throng a silvery newborn star with lake and river, garden and grove, valley and mountain, all that the landscape holds reflected in its crystal depths, God's messenger, angel of love sent on its way with majesty and pomp and display of power that make man's greatest shows ridiculous.

Then the storm ends, "...and where are the raindrops now—what has become of all the shining throng? In winged vapor rising some are already hastening back to the sky..." Others are nurturing plants, or if they fell in the highest mountain reaches have locked into ice crystals; and finally many, through spring, stream, and river, make their way to ocean. "From form to form, beauty to beauty, ever changing, never resting, all are speeding on with love's enthusiasm, singing with the stars the eternal song of creation."

No one but John Muir can talk like this and get away with it. This and much more in similar vein are found in his *My First Summer in the Sierra*, which was my earliest encounter with him and it. I was enchanted and have remained so. When Martin Buber speaks of "hallowing the everyday," this is one instance of what he means. When we speak of gifts and reciprocity, this exemplifies; mindful adoration is its highest expression. Water falls and flows, is drunk and absorbed, cleans and cools, moves in and out of countless forms and conditions, and yet, so far, it abides and continues to replenish. I sit by the Merced River, honoring the mystic flow.

Another time, another foray along the Merced River toward Vernal and Nevada Falls. Water soothes. As I walked, the sun rose over the Valley rim just southeast of Half Dome. Tall trees stood above the rim, backlit. The one directly between my line of sight and the sun became solid, gleaming white, those just to its sides had branches aglow, and the next ones out had whitened needles. Large birds, probably ravens, flying into or past the trees were unknowingly whitewashed as well. While the physics of this are straightforward that doesn't detract at all from the magical feel of it. How variously we can experience common things just by a shift of light or angle. Magic isn't the word I want for this. There is a hiddenness to things, and when we're fortunate it partially reveals itself; when attentive, we open it to view. My first memory of this light phenomenon was years ago hiking a valley in the Mojave Desert, slopes covered in cholla cactus. I looked up eastward toward the rising sun and suddenly thousands upon thousands of cactus spines were deeply illuminated, glowing. It astonished me. In both experiences light penetrates and fills, whether pine needle or cholla spine. Another way that Nature speaks—of marvels simple but inescapably mysterious. I wish I could be more articulate about this. I am moved—something speaks from out there, perceptible when I listen. Entwinement, the good of life, its need and right to abide unharmed.

Later, another fine touch. Walking down from Nevada Fall on the John Muir Trail I come to an area where trail descends with high granite wall rising almost vertically to one side and steep falling slope on the other. Water flows gently down the wall. A narrow lip transects the wall fifteen feet above me and drinking-straw-sized waterfalls arc out, descend a few feet through the air, strike granite, and shatter into bursts of droplets that spread gaily out, some in free fall and others back onto the wall. These too captured the sun and shone diamond-like. Even more enchanting, the granite wall had a multitude of tiny garden spots all the way down, anywhere there was moisture to nourish them. A slit here where purchase could be got, a hole there, and often moss and lichen had gathered sufficiently to lay down a welcoming bed. A bit of grass, a tiny flower—these were randomly scattered over the surface and all seemed to flourish in their precarious perches. Such liveliness... What happens in a few weeks, though, when the water dries, how long can they last? I suppose they get their work done quickly—sprout, seed, spread their energies around; enjoy their floral being and allotted time; bedazzle passersby with their courage and beauty and improbability. And then pass on.

If someone asked if trees and flowers could grow out of a granite bed, what would you answer? Obviously not, you'd probably say. But the Sierra Nevada proves otherwise. Look at domes high above and you see they have tree "follicles" where none would seem possible. Up close

I have seen 50' high trees sprouted out of what appeared inhospitable rock. All over these granite mountainsides and mountaintops I see exuberant growth. It astonishes. Again and again, look!

As with the physics of light, botanical and geological science can explain all this. The nature of these plants is to reproduce; birds and wind scatter seeds; water and minerals and sunlight do their jobs. I understand all that and appreciate what it has to teach me. But I hear more, for empiricism is only one party to the conversation. Why the exuberance, this clear determination to spread life and beauty to the four winds? Why does Nature bother? What is the point? I don't know for sure, probably life is its own purpose, but as I stand before that wall, water droplets falling on my face, eyeball to tiny leaf that homesteaded this granite wall, feeling (strange to say) a responsive love for that water, that rock, that sunlight and air, that adventurous, eager little plant, I do know that a lot goes on on this Earth that doesn't fit our categories, but for which I earnestly give thanks.

There are sometimes funny little paradoxes on the trail. I looked down toward the Merced and saw a placard on a stand in what appeared an odd location. So I diverted and made my way down. It looked as if it had been there a long while, a quote from John Muir posted on it: "...rocky strength and permanence combined with beauty of plants frail and fine...water descending in thunder, and the same water gliding through meadows and groves in gentlest beauty." A few feet away, on another stand planted on the riverbank (amidst boulder and steep slope and trees—a lovely spot, no wonder someone chose this place to put Muir's placard) was another: "CAUTION: Slippery rock surfaces." Someone feared that Muirian lyricism would make people careless.

At the top of Vernal Fall, a bush reaches out over the cliff and looks down 300 feet. Among the leaves and branches, foraging obliviously (and making me nervous) was one of the ubiquitous ground squirrels. After a few minutes he returned nonchalantly to rocky solidity. I want to know how he appraised the danger. Brave and agile, he may not think it worrisome.

I moved camp this morning and caught a ride to the intersection of Porcupine Creek and Tioga Road, several miles north of the Valley. Fourteen miles hiked and a late afternoon return to camp. I'd have stayed out longer but storms rolled in at noon. I was high up on North Dome preoccupied with seeing everything from an astonishing perspective thousands of feet above the Valley—far and near, way down to the forested bottom—when a booming thunderclap shook my composure. I moved back off the Dome into a rocky pocket with a perfect view of Half Dome, ate lunch and watched a hawk glide and circle between the two Domes, which seem about a mile apart, though estimating distance is uncertain at this scale. I think these birds often fly like this for the pleasure of it, just as I hike for pleasure, and we both do it as our response to the spirit of the place. I walked a little under five miles through forest to get here from my drop-off and then west through deeper forest about the same distance to Upper Yosemite Fall. The trail crossed several charming little streams in miniature valleys. One in particular made home for a host of ferns and delicate flowers. I stopped to take it in but thunder rolled loud and close, so I left sooner than I wanted. A mile before the Fall, rain whipped in carrying bits of sleet. I saw streak lightning to the north only a couple miles away and heading south so I donned rain jacket and hustled. Twice, dramatically, as I peered down for footholds on the trail, I saw flash of lightning reflected on the ground around me and in a split second thunder broke over me and brought a strange sense of exaltation and vulnerability. Ominous storms with dark, heavy clouds above and wispy white ones drifting among the trees through mountain and valley to the north. Gloomy and gray and cool. Then down the slippery path from Fall to Valley, once landing on rear rather than feet—fourteen miles and almost 4,000 feet of elevation change behind me.

How I love these mountains and their displays of Nature's artistry and power. I sometimes wonder that I'm not completely overcome by it, as if I'm missing something inside that prevents my bursting with ecstasy. I walk everywhere and see each time the same granite walls and surmounting domes, columns, spires, and waterfalls. I marvel and bow.

Today I walked again. I found much to marvel at and many interesting encounters along the way. I saw a parent quail with several newly hatched chicks and wondered where the other parent was. A parent of any species tending their young is always strangely engaging, regardless how often we see it. The faith of the youngsters in the parent, the parent's earnest caretaking, the promise of renewal and continuity, even the recognition that many of the young (and old) will be taken by predators—it always brings a smile. And sometimes a few tears, touched as we are by such trust and devotion and presentiments of loss. I am thankful for these things and the chance to share them.

Once I embraced a giant pine in order to sniff its bark. Jeffrey Pines are said to smell a bit like vanilla but I couldn't detect it. I did the same another time with an incense cedar, hugging and sniffing. Both times I noticed as I drew my face back an involuntary stroking of my hands on the tree, gently, as I would a loved person. It seemed simultaneously strange to find myself doing this and yet utterly appropriate. Strokes are for the doer as much as the recipient; I felt tender toward those trees and their silent, solemn aliveness.

I think it nearly impossible to pay close attention to trees, whether individually or as forests, and not be affected. So steadfast and graceful, they easily become companions. It seems a miracle they can stand so high, waver in the wind and remain upright. Were I the creator, I'd never have had the imagination to try something that seems so improbable. A freshly fallen, still living tree evokes sympathy and a frustrated wish to make it right again. While a long dead "nursery" tree supporting a linear stand of youngsters makes me smile and say thanks on their behalf.

As John Muir followed sheep up into the Sierra Nevada on his initial foray 141 years ago, he mentioned that "Another conifer was met today—incense cedar..." That "was met" tells that this was encounter with individual life and recognized as such. "I feel strangely attracted to this tree...It would be delightful to be storm-bound beneath one of these noble, hospitable, inviting old trees..."

Earlier than this, in the seventeenth century, an adolescent was converted and brought to God by a tree. He became Brother Lawrence of the Resurrection, a monk admired for his steady "practice of the presence of God" and his humility.[3] Almost four decades after his conversion he described the experience to his Abbe who recorded the conversation. "One winter's day he saw a tree stripped of its leaves, and considered that sometime afterwards these leaves would appear again, followed by flowers and fruit. He then received a lofty awareness of the providence and power of God which never left him." Well, of course. Who wouldn't tend to react that way if he really thought about it? Botany and theology become one.

---

3. Brother Lawrence (Robert J. Edmonson translation), *The Practice of the Presence of God* (Paraclete Press, 1985).

J. Krishnamurti seems once to have spent the entirety of several days entranced and enlightened by a tree. At sunrise it became golden leaves filled with life, and "... as the hours pass by, that tree whose name does not matter—what matters is that beautiful tree—an extraordinary quality begins to spread all over the land, over the river." Each hour reveals new tree qualities: brightness, liveliness, somberness, quietness, dignity. One may sit in the shade beneath it, "...never feeling lonely with the tree as your companion." At sunset finally the tree rests. "If you establish a relationship with it, then you have relationship with mankind. You are responsible then for that tree and for the trees of the world. But if you have no relationship with the living things on this earth, you may lose whatever relationship you have with humanity..." Later, ending a meditation on the human propensity to kill, he extends this thought: "If we could, and we must, establish a deep, long abiding relationship with nature—with the actual trees, the bushes, the flowers, the grass, and the fast moving clouds—then we would never slaughter another human being for any reason whatsoever." (My apology to the publisher from whose book I drew these thoughts; I have lost the reference.)

Even Martin Buber,[4] who recognized Nature as a distinct realm of Thou relatedness without being very comfortable there himself, spoke about trees. He knew they could be "It," a species, a botanical member of an ecosystem, just lumber. "In all this the tree remains my object...It can, however, also come about, if I have both will and grace, that in considering the tree I become bound up in relation to it." And more: "The tree is no impression, no play of my imagination, no value depending on my mood; but it is bodied over against me and has to do with me, as I with it—only in a different way."

---

4. Martin Buber, *I and Thou* (Second Edition, Robert Gregor Smith [trans.], Charles Scribner's Sons, 1958).

To paraphrase an old television commercial, "These are not your father's trees." (The vast majority of those have been clear-cut.) But they are real trees and possible relations. I have been to the forest, and with Muir and the others, I have met these trees.

ETHICS PERSPECTIVES

CHAPTER 10

WHAT GOOD IS MORALITY?

HERE WE ARE IN 2021. Despite all our learning, science, and internet-load of information, it turns out that honesty, evidence, and facts may no longer matter in the public sphere. (Who knows what may have happened in the billions of little private spheres?) Nor is it considered necessary or even desirable to listen to alternative points of view or to read and take seriously anything whose conclusions you don't already know and find agreeable and comforting. Denial, avoidance, confabulation...there are more ways to carry on with a placid and undisturbed mind than milligrams of cholesterol in a cheeseburger and with effects on the mind's good functioning analogous to the burger's on a healthy heart. They have even worse effects, considering that disregard of reality has swift and deadly consequences for perspicacious thinking and effective decision-making. Heart failure tends to take longer. A steady diet of self-deception and acceptance of others' deceptions renders the gift of an originally good mind almost pointless.

The failure to speak truth to oneself demeans and degrades the soul and poorly prepares one for navigation through reality. And it is immoral when aimed at others. Those of an opportunistic mind-set may imagine they keep the two realms separate—truth for me, falsehood for you—but this maneuver is never fully successful. They cannot know the truth while retailing its opposite, nor avoid truth-telling with themselves about deception of others and not pay a psychic price, a diminution of the self. The distinction between honesty and dishonesty, truth and falsity, sinks into darkness as if it did not matter. It grievously impairs the self's integrity, in both senses of the word: its unity and its uprightness.

What *are* morality and ethics? Why should one care about complying with their demands—as shown above, for example, the demand for honesty? What draws some people to value these qualities? How do they come to do so? These are ancient questions but always worth revisiting—unlike, say, theories of gravity, where research hopes for final answers, questions about goodness and truth never will have final answers. Each new person who comes along has to reopen and answer them for themself because they are intrinsic to fashioning a good life, and times change. Without occasional self-reflection, how would they know whether they might be going astray? I remember my first foray into graduate school where I entered a program called Ethics and Society, my purpose being to understand better what ethics and morality really meant and the role they could or should play in human life. (This was during the Vietnam War, and for reasons connected to the war, these concerns had particular salience.) The question has recurred over the years, especially now. I am perplexed at the tolerance for immorality in the form of dishonesty that we are seeing in unexpected places, as well as places less surprising, except for the degrees of deception that those who operate there have twisted themselves into accepting, assuming that twisting was required. To all appearances, a lot of people have moved dishonesty out of the moral sphere and made it acceptable as a tool judged only by its usefulness.

For example, consider white evangelicals, a large majority of whom believe that President Biden stole the 2020 election from Donald Trump and who still support

Trump after four years of his tumultuous and scandal-saturated tenure. I don't think it's unfair to say such people are adamant in their condemnation of what they consider the sins of abortion and homosexuality—obsessively so, it sometimes seems. They were scandalized by the sexual peccadilloes of a previous (and Democratic) president, whose lack of character was thus demonstrable in their eyes and clearly made him unfit for office. Their religiously based morality is unyieldingly righteous toward what they see as the evils endemic to these acts *in the abstract,* dependent apparently on the perpetrator. It is neither unfair nor inaccurate to assert that the president whom they hold in their tender embrace is almost certainly the most dishonest person ever to hold that office. I personally have never known of anyone as thoroughly, openly, unconcernedly, and crudely at odds with truthfulness. The truth seems no more germane to his thinking than the chemical composition of anthracite, for which he claims an affinity. I assume honesty is still considered a virtue in evangelical eyes, but apparently it is dispensable when violated by someone who says he shares their rejection of the two sins mentioned—even while known to participate with fathomless incontinence in other sins *not* mentioned. We all make compromises from time to time, but this one may be a challenge to explain on the judgment day they declare we all will face eventually: did their ends really justify this means? But then, some of them do not consider it a compromise; I read recently that one evangelical leader asserts that Trump has been chosen and made president by God—who apparently has the same elasticity of commitment to truthfulness (and who must have had a scant field of applicants for the job)—in order to carry out the expulsion of those sins and other dangers from our lives, the magnitude of his personal sins notwithstanding.

Morality may be one of those areas, like the weather, about which everybody talks but do nothing to alter. In its nineteenth-century origins, I imagine this adage was ironic and pointed to humans' inability to turn bad weather good despite all the attention they paid it. Now, unfortunately, our climatologic incompetence has turned ominous as we do a great deal about it by way of destabilization and turning good weather bad, a deeply unethical transformation because of its certain consequences and provenance in plutocratic, self-serving choice, one more demonstration of dishonesty in action on behalf this time of material self-interest. And for the multitudes whose interests will definitively not be served but who accept the deception, their failure is of another sort.

Although *morality* and *ethics* are sometimes used interchangeably, they don't always refer to the same thing, even though both describe notions of right and wrong, good and bad, excellence and its opposites. *Ethics* refers mainly to external standards and principles, sometimes of a general nature and even rising on occasion to the level of what makes for excellence of human character. We speak of professional ethics as the standards of proper conduct within a profession and virtue ethics as qualities of character such as temperance, prudence, justice, and courage. Morality more often refers to behavior based on personal or collective values pertaining to what's right and what's good. The concepts point in the same direction so there's no need to quibble about differential meanings.

I want to say a few words on behalf of morality's sources and importance. No single morality fits everyone everywhere at all times, so a certain degree of pluralism is fitting. We make different attributions of value and importance, and different interpretations of their meaning and our responsibilities, that are reasonable in certain areas of concern, especially complex ones such as, for example, abortion or the rights of animals. But pluralism is not relativism; morality is more substantial than taste or feeling and certainly more so than convenience. It will at times make demands that we experience as onerous—just ask someone whose sensibilities lead them to honor the rights of animals and thus forswear eating them. Morality's strong presence in a person's character is a vital part of what makes them worthy of our respect; it will be woven into a life well lived, reverent toward being, and often joyous about it—a good life and a meaningful one.

Humans have discussed the bases of ethical reasoning and conceptions for thousands of years; we don't need repetition here. I am more concerned with what seems to be present in people whom we would say are of firm, reliable moral character. It seems unlikely to me that humans are born either good or bad. I imagine that individuals have innate proclivities that are shaped and reinforced by very early experience and that time and inner strengths will turn habitually toward certain points on the moral compass. Human nature is something of a blank slate in ethical terms but contains and/or develops and comes to manifest traits that are fundamental to daily moral awareness and action.

As alluded to above, our moral exemplar will respect the otherness of other beings (for some this will include *all* other beings). That is, one will recognize that they have needs, aims, and courses of existence that are independent but parallel or analogous to one's own and that matter to them (or to the fabric of being) in some fashion and so must matter to our exemplar insofar as he or she affects them. Such a person will feel sympathetic toward their strivings and may decide to help, if necessary, or simply leave them undisturbed. To varying degrees this person *cares* what happens to them and even identifies with them, recognizing that we all derive from the same beginnings, evolve in response to similar contingencies, depend upon the same fabric of life for sustenance, and occupy the same good Earth in a sort of brotherhood and sisterhood of life.

Two terms in the preceding paragraph can seem contradictory or at least in tension with each other: *otherness* and *identification*. *Otherness* points to inherent separateness;

identification does not negate otherness but reaches across in caring recognition of commonality. As in a marriage, for example, the two beings involved respect their ineluctable individuation while being linked in mutuality of interests and care.[1] Morality is a key aspect of any relationship and shows itself in the interactive area *between* or *among* those who participate in it; mutual respect encompasses both separateness and recognition of shared existence. To put it more plainly, think of the common expression, "I identify with what she is feeling." This means, I know we are different people, but I recognize what she is experiencing, may have felt it myself, sympathize, and care that it will work out to her satisfaction; I will also help if needed. This is part of how morality expresses itself.

What this comes down to is that we will be moral to the extent that we allow ourselves to be affected by the being and the circumstances of the other. Both of us are vulnerable creatures, and both aim toward fulfillment. I will not lie to another because it damages both self-respect and the respect I owe the other, which makes it wrong, whereas truthfulness between us contributes to excellence of relation as well as to goodness of existence. These principles— respect, sympathy, care: any ethic from any tradition will rest comfortably in their embrace. They will not answer all questions or clarify every mystery or light every dark corner, but they imbue those who search with attitudes that bring reconciliation and the acceptance that mortal creatures never have all the wisdom they need.

I recently read an essay about farming, of all things, and saw that the author's description of what went into *good* farming was, as he intended, also a metaphor for what goes into making good lives and communities. It was

---

1. Although discussing marriage would take us away from what chiefly concerns me here, a similar dynamic of care operates even when one of the entities is a person and the other an animal or a forest; obviously, mutuality cannot operate in the same way on the part of the other, but for the human engaged in the relation it does.

written by Wendell Berry, who has a gift for seeing both particularities and wholeness and the ways they join. Metaphor, though, does not fully convey what he intended. He was describing an ideal of wholeness, of lives that include many parts, with each also an extension of the others and all together aspiring coherently toward the sort of excellence that Aristotle seems to have had in mind when he spoke of the virtues, forms of excellence composing a person's character. Berry, who is in his mid-eighties (in 2020), has made his living as a farmer and writer. I am sure he is a good farmer, but it is easier to measure his output as a poet, essayist, and novelist. He is prolific, with more than sixty books to his name and countless shorter pieces scattered around. I have a couple dozen of his books on my shelves, have been reading him for decades, and consider him uniquely wise, well spoken, and acute in his observations about the conditions of twenty-first-century economy and culture.

Both as writer and farmer, Berry is rooted on the land, with an emphasis as much on *rooted* (placed, situated, organically entwined) as on *land*. His philosophy is agrarianism, which implies more than good farming. Its opposite, industrialized agriculture, is more than just bad farming. Whatever the industrial mind-set touches, it diminishes and often destroys. Its god is quantity, which is attended by the demigods of efficiency, instrumentalism, power, and profit—there are no other stars in its sky. (In the following I interpret Berry, find inspiration and support, but speak for myself.)

"Imagination in Place" is an essay in his collection *The Way of Ignorance.* These are a few of his thoughts from this essay:

- The most insistent and formidable concern of agriculture, wherever it is taken seriously, is the distinct individuality of every farm, every field on every farm, every farm family, and every creature on every farm.

Farming becomes a high art when farmers know and respect in their work the distinct individuality of their place and the neighborhood of creatures that lives there. . . . Such *practical respect* is the true discipline of farming and the farmer must maintain it through the muddles, mistakes, disappointments, and frustrations as well as the satisfactions and exaltations, of every actual year on an actual farm. (italics mine)

• Hovering over nearly everything I have written is the question of how a human economy might be *conducted with reverence*, and therefore with due respect and kindness toward everything involved. This, if it ever happens, will be the maturation of American culture.[2] (italcs mine)

I have italicized *respect* and *reverence* because they are crucial to the agrarian (and the more than agrarian) philosophy I am suggesting to encompass the morality and ethics with which we began. I could have added another of Berry's observations about the "inherent sanctity" of landscapes (pp. 50–51) because it, too, is fitting. Or I could have added lines from one of his poems, cited in the collection *The Humane Vision of Wendell Berry*:

There are no unsacred places;
there are only sacred places
and desecrated places.[3]

In other writing, I have advocated a way of being and knowing that I refer to as *reverence for existence*, which is clearly of a piece with Berry's perspective. In my view it comprises ways of being that begin in honoring the soil, whose fecundity supports life, and proceeds all the way out from there—through crop and forest, stream and

2. Wendell Berry, "Imagination in Place," in *The Way of Ignorance* (Berkeley: Counterpoint Press, 2005), 45–46, 50.
3. Berry, "How to Be a Poet," in *Given: Poems* (Berkeley: Counterpoint Press, 2006), 18.

ocean, beetle, bear, and human—until one realizes that it is not this or that that is sacred but this *and* that and everything all around, the one creation. No theology is necessarily implied in this; rather, one finds himself surprisingly affected by what he opens to and with which he steps into mutuality of relatedness in caring identification, even if only imaginatively. It seems almost unfair, though admittedly natural, that words having the power to express the deep veneration and devotion one can feel toward existence are mostly religiously derived. For example, I could also use *piety* to express what reverence means. So I borrow the words and their power but omit the theology. To clarify, let me speak of some of the elements that make up the attitude and practice of reverence.

The *wholeness* of a life: this is a particularly rich notion that Berry frequently refers to. Such a life is attentive to means as well as ends and takes responsibility for whatever it affects in pursuing its aims. It fits itself to place, seeks proportionality and right scale in aspiration, finds its good continuous with the good of others. It knows what matters, small and large, immediate and remote. It seeks right relation with Nature, animals, and other humans and will have some form of engagement with fundamental mystery. Wholeness is a practice of goodness, of integrity in self and action. It provides a coherent response to the question, Why do you live?

Propriety is a virtue of belonging, of affirmation and engagement. Order and harmony are most likely to arise from knowing one's place (in both senses, relational and locational) and looking to its good, finding the best fit between and for oneself and the other. We are creatures of contexts, which bring gifts and impose obligations. We must respect limits, know freedom's boundaries, live consciously. The ecology of Nature, the society of humans, the communities of friends, the kingdoms of our fellow animals and plants: we live in all of these groups simultaneously. We will nurture all of them and do no unnecessary harm. Propriety honors what is called for by the setting or situation we find ourselves in.

Coincidentally, as I was writing, I came upon a related word, related not in its contemporary and rather pallid sense but in its origins two millennia ago: *decorum*. Cicero particularly relished this word and concept, which referred to fit, attunement, responsiveness, all referring to one's actions and words in ethical relation to one's situation and aims. For a virtuous Roman, failure in decorum brought shame.[4]

Wait, I hear the modern ear exclaiming: Propriety? Decorum? These sound like formal, stilted, rule-based strictures; what room do they leave for freedom and individuality? Plenty, I believe, but we first have to abandon the idea that freedom thrives with no limitations. If you've ever hiked up to ten thousand feet, found a small alpine lake, and spent some time in its presence, you know that not just anything is appropriate in that setting. You wouldn't leave food containers in or beside it, trample foliage along its banks, or relieve yourself (urinate, defecate) in its shallows. Rather, something tells you to tread attentively, speak quietly, honor the grace of the place. Constriction of freedom, yes, but for a higher purpose— for the kind of freedom that shows itself as self-mastery of the ego impulse combined with absorbing the beneficence of caring relatedness. The oldest tradition of freedom is just this—that one has freed oneself *from* ego and unconstrained appetite in order to free the self *for* deeper relation and deeper understanding of reality's offerings. Similarly, individuation does not arise undistorted so long as egoism is in charge; it flourishes when freed from that anchor so as to be free to respond to other and finer voices. Places, beings, situations, aims, and more—when

---

4. Rob Goodman, "Decorum Is an Unfashionable Word But It Has a Radical Core," Aeon, 2018, https://aeon.co/

called to some form of action or inaction, we listen for what is most right, now and here—an ethic for being alive and responsible.

Seek truths: The idea that humans are born wanting to know reality in ways unbent by bias goes back to Plato and assuredly beyond. You awaken to the world and want to make a place within it. How else but to know its warp and weft, its realities? The notion of free will is hard to sustain, but implementing your truth-seeking vision through ethical practice will draw you out of the immediacies of desire, attachment, and deterministic contingencies into a relative freedom *of* will as you raise questions. What is the place of money in a well-lived life? What work offers the most meaning for me with my values and abilities? What *are* my values? What do I owe family, community, nation, the natural world? Am I right about...? How should I...?

Non-egoistic freedom also involves making porous the integumental binding or cocooning of ego, so that self-interest does not dominate but takes its place alongside other interests. Morality/ethics does not thrive until one realizes that one is not, cannot, and ought not be a "free" individual, unencumbered by ties that bind. We receive and must reciprocate. Ego constricts vision, whereas self-forgetting frees us to know the world as it is. Similarly, spiritual awareness can rise only with the decline of ego. Our culture glorifies the individual self. In its extreme version, this is wrong; put differently, it is partial, disproportionate, noncontextual, value free ethically.

Each of these ways and characteristics, and more that could be added, are how the attitude of reverence—of responding to our world with due respect and gratitude—becomes normal and does not depend on but may incorporate what might appear to be its mystical harmonic. The moralism with which this essay began can now be seen in the light of a way rather than a rule, a way that is essential to one's meaning, one's wholeness. I think about Wendell

Berry's kind of farming—he wants a productive field and pasture but within a landscape that is healthy, that takes no more than it preserves and returns, that knows its neighbors and knows that downstream and upstream are one stream. We cultivate a right piece of Earth in ways harmonious with the context, just as we cultivate our lives.

CHAPTER 11

DOES HUMANITY DESERVE TO SURVIVE?

IT'S A QUESTION I CANNOT help asking. With our record of heedless endangerment of the biosphere, would even God defend the human tenure, or if we bring it to premature termination, grieve our passing?

As a thought experiment, I imagine that the Creator Universe (slightly anthropomorphized), whose transcendent view I aspire toward on a matter such as this one, decides to size up what has become of its creative endeavors. Although Earth is but a nanoparticle in the immensity of space, the Universe may have known 4.6 billion years ago, as our solar system took shape, that Earth had unique potential for a planet in its cosmic region. Now it asks, How has that potential turned out?

Life appeared 3.7 billion years before today in the form of microbes. Since then, it has developed increased diversity, complexity, and fascination. It even endured setbacks that wiped out most creatures but bounced back and moved on. If the focus were on how Nature evolved and the incredible mixes of life, landscape, and beauty it birthed, the Universe would surely announce success: "It was good," I seem to hear it say.

Recently, however, relatively speaking, two to three hundred thousand years ago, the species *Homo sapiens* appeared, earlier hominids having emerged around six million years ago. The Universe may have suspected early on that a species with such a brain, consciousness, and range of capacities was an evolutionary gamble, although it may not have appreciated the extent of the risk it was taking, but it does now.

Scattered over the Earth—a result of risks taken—there are, and have long been, groups with various ideological and religious convictions slaughtering other groups with different convictions, killing children and other noncombatants as remorselessly as those wielding weapons. Intra-species violence presumably has been going on for a very long time, with Homo "sapiens" never having effectively realized its futility and with evident, perhaps innate, impetus toward repetition. It may just be who we are. Along with our depredations on each other, we behaved toward the natural world in the same manner, taking and taking and taking with hardly a thought of what was left behind or its condition. Materialist humanity does not much care, as long as it gets what it wants.

The Universe learned that humans are vulnerable to self-centeredness (as a species relative to other species and as individuals and groups relative to other individuals and groups), to anxieties over real and imagined prospects of loss or threat, and to a low threshold for aggression when either desire or fear are evoked. Humans might have learned to control and redirect these often fatal inadequacies, to supersede them through better judgment and measures less exclusively self-interested. But, alas, it has not turned out that way.

So, in light of the serious harms we cause to ourselves and other life, including present ones of such monumental eventual impact that the question now has unique poignance and relevance, does humanity deserve to survive? To put it more clearly, if we manage our extinction, or its near fulfillment, and the collapse of civilization as we've known it, through the predictable consequences of our own choices and actions, would that be any great loss to the continuation, to the being and value, of Earth? Would it be a tragedy or an injustice? Losses there would certainly be, instances of selfless love, compassion, art and other creative expression, community engagement, many meaningful endeavors, the joy of being alive for those who paused to notice it. But are these enough to justify our habituated forms of life negation, our willingness to risk it all for foolish pride and ultimately trivial yearnings, our willingness to gamble with the good Earth's future by way of nuclear annihilation, catastrophic anthropogenic climate disruption, and/or massive extinguishment of biodiversity and ecosystems?

We live as if oblivious, and we allow corporations and governments to act as if that were a permanent condition. It is remarkable; one imagines the last looks we will give each other as our denouement implacably sweeps over us, looks of spurious surprise and disbelief, as if to say in all innocence, Who could have known?

The question again: Would human extinction be a great tragedy and loss to existence? Does humanity deserve to survive the Earth-altering consequences of its own behavior?[1]

The affirmative:

- Evolution led in humans to unique forms of consciousness and reasoning abilities. These are distinctive and perhaps irreplaceable.

- None but humans has the capacity for artistic, scientific, and intellectual creation. Aided by our technological ingenuity, we have investigated the quantum and

---

1. My initial thinking about this was inspired thirty years ago by Robert Nozick's essay "The Holocaust" in his book *The Examined Life: Philosophical Meditations* (Simon & Schuster, 1989), which brought the scrutinizing eye of a brilliant philosopher to the question. For him, it was provoked by the Nazi effort to exterminate Jews, but similar considerations apply to these other forms of world-rending myopia and evil.

the Cosmos and developed a vast array of methods and devices that support our health and well-being and deepen our understanding.

• We have the potential to remedy every problem we have created. Even the vastly life-altering, life-ending prospects of nuclear weaponry and environmental destruction will yield to human cleverness, ingenuity, and that virtue at the summit of all capitalist virtues, innovation (that leads to a profit).

• With our intelligence and associated abilities, peace, justice, prudence, and better ways of life may in time emerge.

• If humans died out, all of the unique and special experiences and possibilities that only we have would never be realized again.

• God loves us despite our flaws.

The negative:

• Yes, the level of human consciousness and reasoning is unique and, one might have hoped, conducive to good lives in good societies. But it has not had that effect. Those capacities are double-edged swords, dramatically so or the question before us would not arise. Reason in the twenty-first century appears degraded, turned chiefly to materialist and ego-driven gratifications, which themselves feed the risks that underlie this discussion.

• Indeed, humans have much to be proud of. We have learned a lot about physical reality and have generated music, literature, and arts that are admirable and occasionally ethereal. But the technological virtuosity that produced computers also developed nuclear weapons along with an ever-growing array of new versions and new ways to kill each other more efficiently. Even nonviolent civilian electronic devices pass the point of genuine usefulness and become trivializing obsessions at the service of moneyed interests and citizen complacence. Technology that might open the world instead shrinks and distorts it.

• Regarding the matter of nuclear weapons targeted on people around the world, there is no evidence we will find a remedy and little indication so far that existing efforts can alter the fixation on their possession and continual upgrading. As for climate and biodiversity, it may already be too late. Those with money and power and no obvious interest in much else choose to deceive and obfuscate. Citizens who could challenge and hold them accountable choose complicity and the easy way of not thinking critically and acting collectively and decisively.

• There is, again, no evidence that humanity will ever use its intelligence in a sustained and perceptive manner to make and maintain a good world. To accomplish this we would, among much else, need to face human nature straight on, identify its dangerous proclivities (such as a generalized inability to handle wealth and power responsibly, aggressive tendencies, egoism, and speciesism), establish ironclad controls, remain alert and informed, forbid backsliding—and do all this forever since these vulnerabilities are unlikely ever to go away. Protection of a better world is a never-ending struggle against those who wish to dominate it and expropriate more than their fair share.

• It is true that human extinction would mean the end of those experiences that only humans can have, a sad and unfortunate consequence. Of course, none but humans put the biome at risk either (before humans, in fact, it was only lifeless matter and energy that threatened the Earth so dramatically). Those cherished experiences have not penetrated denial of the risks and costs of other unique human capacities, those rooted in desire, anxiety, and ignorance of humans' true good.

- Assuming that God and Universe are closely associated, even identified with one other, its love of humans must be sorely tested by now and balanced against love for Earth and its other life forms, none of which threatens the whole. The common assumption that Universe/God created everything merely to serve as resource for humanity is yet another belief without foundation and symptomatic of a profound and self-defeating misconstrual of reality.

To repeat: The inquiry concerns whether the human species deserves to survive the consequences of its intentional actions, a question that would only arise in the presence of clear anthropogenic threats to Earth's life, including our own. For over seventy years it has held a Damoclean sword over being, one that hangs from a startlingly tenuous thread considering the possible losses. Amazingly, with all this time to reflect upon what it has wrought, rather than stepping back it chooses to magnify the threat, to expand its armamentarium. To this danger humanity has added climate change and associated ecosystem disruptions that on the present course will reduce the diversity of life by well over half, its absolute numbers by far more, and our own by perhaps hundreds of millions, maybe billions. It does this knowingly and with remedies at hand but largely disregarded, owing to inertia, habitual ways and attitudes, the short-sighted greed of those who profit from inaction, and feckless leadership. The risks that have been willingly incurred are momentous and inexorable. We were granted an Earth of astounding beauty and richness, we have treated it with disdain, and we may lose it all—based on the evidence, deservedly.

I ask a moral question: Does one species that puts itself and all other species at great peril have a moral right to survival? How can we not be disturbed, even changed, by the knowledge that humanity constitutes a moral pariah among other forms of life?

We recognize that these apocalyptic prospects are only more extreme and dramatic versions of daily practice under presently accepted assumptions and aspirations. We live for chimerical purposes, too often unaffected by higher-order values, and take existence for granted.

There have been times and places (pre-Socratic Greece and traditional cultures scattered around the Earth, for example) in which humans appear to have marveled at life and to have sought understanding of its ways and meanings out of wonder more than utility. To this, many added a wish to live appropriately in relation to existence as they came to understand and experience it. The Cosmos was sensed as orderly, purposeful, and meaningful, and humans as part of that could thrive insofar as they rightfully interpreted their role. Life was good but serious (deep, nontrivial). One view of how this organic sense of human engagement with life declined has it that the more humans presumed to control the conditions of their existence and became preoccupied with its material aspects, the less they experienced the beatitude of pure, mysterious being and its inherent joys and satisfactions. The less there became of conscious mystery and wonder as humans turned toward immediate gratifications, the less there was of respect and reverence.

How should a person live if he would achieve a good and honorable life? That is the ancient, most vital philosophical question of all. It seems to have little contemporary purchase. If humans survive, what will they survive *for*? The answer is clear. If humanity became extinct, all the rest of life would figuratively applaud and breathe sighs of relief. Even those of us who love life and mourn human failure would, as our last, impotent gesture, feel compelled resignedly to join the applause and wish Earth a better future without us.

- POSTSCRIPT -

Ninety-nine percent of all species that every existed have become extinct. To ask, in seriousness, whether humans deserve to survive, and why or how it would matter to existence if we too become extinct—would the Universe grieve?—will sound bizarre to many. The asking does not arise out of misanthropy or nihilism. Present circumstance renders it utterly appropriate, a natural question, even if only in the form of a thought experiment.

The question's appropriateness derives from this: Humans could become virtually extinct under present conditions in a day or a century, not from an uncontrollable event (asteroid collision, megavolcanic cataclysm) but from our own conscious, deliberate actions. Rather than suicide of only one species, it would more closely resemble ecocide, the killing on a vast scale of entire ecosystems and classes and orders and families of life. It would be a sixth great extinction, differing from the first five in its conscious perpetration.

If you were the Universe, what would you think best from the higher perspective? You might wish for a more selective, targeted way to brush humans off the Earth than generalized destruction by nuclear conflict or climate change—human infertility, perhaps. But this is idle (although maybe not entirely since evidence suggests that sperm counts may have fallen by over half and the quality of sperm and eggs declined over the last half century, all presumably due to environmental contaminants, another problem of our own making). In all probability when we go we will take multitudes with us. It will be by our hand and none other. When we go we cannot blame fate and we cannot honestly imagine it tragic. We can recognize that the Earth will be a better, more flourishing place with nothing left to sorrow over. We would not have deserved anything better.

What does it mean to "deserve" something? We know that humans are infused and shaped by genes and experience, conditioning and circumstance. Some scientists and philosophers believe free will and autonomy are mostly fantasy, and I agree. But we are not automatons; a measure of freedom exists with which we can exercise reason, moral character, and quasi-objectivity. Desert, then, lies in how we use this freedom, in what we demand of ourselves and what moral imperatives we honor. Choices made by modern humanity are evident, as are the results. Alternative choices that made better use of our measure of freedom and based on humility, moderation, respect, and gratitude would have led to a very different present—one in which the question of humanity's desert would never arise since the answer would be implicit in its more virtuous ways of life.

The common response to this discussion will be consistent with the dysfunctionality under discussion—it will say that humanity has no need or obligation to justify itself. It is, after all, atop the great chain of being and dominion over Earth is its birthright. Mistakes will be made, have been made, it will say, but human exceptionalness is such that they will be overcome and progress lead unceasingly toward a better world tomorrow. But who can believe it?

CHAPTER 12

LIVING IN ACCORD
WITH NATURE

IF YOU SPEND ANY TIME reading the Roman Stoics of the first two centuries CE, principally Marcus Aurelius, Epictetus, and Seneca, you will encounter variations of the phrase "living in accord with nature" (as you will among many who did not identify as Stoics but for whom a nondoctrinal version of the idea was still meaningful). I was attracted to the phrase when I first encountered it and sensed intuitively that those five plain words intimated something worth investigation, that they portended insights about human existence and ethics. I could not explain the source of the attraction or the content of the anticipated insights any more than I could adequately describe quantum paradoxes, which were also intriguing notions. Continued time in the presence of these ideas, listening to their voices, have helped but not to my full satisfaction, which is why I decided to write about the notion on the principle that there's no better way to clarify thinking than to prepare to explain it to others. I hope to capture the meaning and to find that my attraction to the concept is well founded. I will spend no more time than necessary on the ancient philosophical background and focus on illustrating how aiming for "accord with nature" can have value today. I consider it a promising path for approaching the most crucial question, the eternal question: How should I live?

Still, one could reasonably ask: Why bother with this particular path? Who needs this eccentric diversion into obscure worldviews? My answer is that those who reflect on the serious questions of existence inevitably seek a base, a few foundational understandings about the kind of creatures we are and the kind of world we inhabit and the sort of thinking that's been done about these matters over the ages. They ask about what's reasonably and rightly encompassed within that self:world relationship, which birthed and sustains us and that might justly have some claims to our focused attention and respect. Such queries and understandings would also provide a context in which to elaborate beliefs to live by and that supports their plausibility and suggests a range of related beliefs that offer completeness and consistency. The old Stoics, along with followers of other ancient schools, thought deeply enough about these matters to offer insights that those who spend time with them even today recognize as uniquely valuable; there are good reasons for their having endured so long.

Serious ethical commitments, above all, interpenetrate other values and beliefs; they affect the shape they take and will be seen as rational and utterly essential to their affirmation—the best foundation to build on, using the best blueprint for this person at this time in this place. Religious affiliation does this job for some, although it isn't clear to me that this arena is exactly flourishing these days. Much of it quiescent, focused on internal or otherworldly matters, or having offered itself up for sacrifice on the altar of political partisanship. Other group memberships can be foundational as well but as with religion can present problems of inclusion, anthropocentrism, partiality, and intolerance of divergence from the established belief system. The advantage of the Stoic-based notion that I want to describe is that it values not merely certain ways of understanding how the world is built and operates but insists that a large part of what makes it vital and meaningful to humans consists in deep thinking about its nature and our nature and how they entwine. Stoicism affirms lifeways that reflect human diversity but within a unifying wholeness.

Taking "Why bother?" a step further, I expect the person who chooses to be bothered will already have a preoccupation with existential and ethical questions; they will be concerned about authenticity (being *real*, genuinely themself); with fashioning meaningful attitudes, endeavors, and well-founded happiness; and about the nature and condition of their communities (personal/social, living and workspaces, nation) in the awareness that they may be weak on justice, peaceableness, or common purpose and so require attention. In light of these personal qualities they may be attracted to the prospect of learning how some of the best people in antiquity grappled with such matters and intrigued that they were so focused on them (as they themselves are all these centuries later) and self-critical about living the philosophy those originals had worked out. How could one not respect the integrity and seriousness of such reflective and courageous people and feel drawn toward living in similar ways, albeit shaped for a vastly altered world?

Furthermore, the subject matter of their concerns will feel remarkably current: interpreting and managing emotions, fulfilling commitments, participating in the community, detaching from matters beyond one's control as well as from materialist and other secondary desires, seeking truths within a world of diversity and competing values and often one of ignorance and dissembling, caring for the "soul" (character, conscience, mind: one's center). They will be intrigued by the notion that life takes place within a framework of wholeness in which their nature, other humans, other life, and, in some hard-to-define manner, the Universe are all aspects of *one nature.* And Earth Nature itself (plants and animals, mountains and rivers, air and water) reveals a profundity and beneficence that could be a model as they interpret and respond to existence and the choices it offers. They will want to grow wiser and better rather than richer, because they intuit with increasing clarity the ancient truth that the only vital question pertains to the state of one's soul and the life chosen.

An analogy helps to define living in accord more pragmatically. Whereas many modern humans live seemingly unrooted to any particular place, one of the chief characteristics of traditional people was their adaptive fit to the places they made homes. Think of Inuit in the Arctic, Bedouins in the desert, early Polynesians plying the ocean, indigenes of the rain forests, and Native Americans scattered among tribal niches across the Western Hemisphere. It is almost impossible to picture these peoples without picturing their place-based ways of life. I think of this rootedness as one aspect of living in accord with nature. Step it up a level to situate people and place on Earth-within-Universe and imaginatively portray for yourself what that offers and what adaptive reciprocity could mean. The Universe is wild and improbable, but who can doubt its beneficence, especially in its creation of Earth with the potentials that transported it across eons to now? Humans awoke as a species within providential plentitude; it may have seemed veritably Edenic as they found their places within it. I surmise that it felt of a piece to them, a unified whole that gave what was needed; in return for such largesse, accountable souls must have felt a wish to comport themselves toward life and landscape with appropriate gratitude, humility, respect, and reciprocity. Of course, humans being human, such prelapsarian bliss couldn't have survived unimpaired for long, but few traditional survivors of the first couple of hundred millennia whom we know anything about lost it entirely. Despite the impairments, is it so hard to imagine that living in accord suggested forms of piety and virtue consistent with the beneficent order of existence: to live in proportion, with care, toward justice as an honoring of all beings who shared the good fortune of living their assigned ways and duration. I imagine that something like this follows from a conscientious apprehension of gifts received from "nature," from being.

And so, *living in accord with nature*: as suggested, the first thing to understand about this mysterious notion is that for the Roman Stoics it was a succinct statement of their fundamental conviction about the right way to conduct a human life, it was the cornerstone. It reflected religious commitment, for Stoicism was a religious philosophy that had its beginnings in Greece three hundred years before these Roman Stoics made their marks. By *nature* the Romans meant Universe, Jupiter, Universal Reason, the life force, or simply the way the world is under guidance by providential *being*. Jupiter/Universe ensured that humans have available all they need to live a good life, which would become apparent as they worked to guide their lives compatibly with what nature intended for *Homo sapiens* as a species and for each individual. One's personal nature as a derivative of Universal nature needed only to be shaped into a form consistent with the universal. As with clay and other raw materials, many shapes are possible but only when the material's distinct characteristics and limitations are honored.

The severing of this dependence on belief in a providential god (Jupiter) and gods as composers of the Universe's structures and purposes, but not from recognition that such structures and purposes exist, is part of my intention in showing that "living in accord" can still help us shape meaningful, ethical ways of life. Of course we recognize that whenever a philosophy draws a god or gods into its realm, it prompts a compulsion to comply, but Stoicism without a god is happy to give up compulsion, which does not seem all that effective anyway: how many "sinners" are willing to risk perdition for immediate gratifications? It also will not claim logical entailment. What it relies on is experience of existence as deeply fascinating and lit up with meaningful prospects that draw one to desire and engage with them. They naturally appear to link a good life with seeking truths of existence and caring for ethical excellence in whatever area you settle into. You are drawn by its feel of definitive rightness, not by necessity, logic, or doctrine.

I will begin with a few citations that demonstrate how the Stoics used the term. Epictetus first, from his *Discourses*. (The provenance of each citation is indicated by numbers corresponding with book, chapter, and sentence in the text.)

- The most important goal of education is "to bring our preconceptions of what is reasonable and unreasonable in alignment with nature." (I.2.6) Epictetus taught in a school he founded in Nicopolis, Greece after the emperor Domitian expelled all philosophers from Italy in CE 95; he doubted their loyalty and evidently lacked philosophical principles or sympathies of his own.

- In measuring his students' progress, Epictetus told them that it wasn't their book learning that mattered but how they used that learning and conducted themselves out in the world, beginning with good judgment and self-control: "I want to know how you apply and prepare yourself, and how you practice attention, so that I can decide whether with you these functions operate in harmony with nature." (I.4.14)

- One's ultimate achievement: "Understanding the will of nature." (I. 17.14)

- The "law of life" is "that [which] obliges us to act in accordance with nature." (I.26.1)

- The "goal of life": "To follow God." (I.30.4)

- God, nature as universal being and process, reason: think of these as different forms of expression for

one *presence* entwining the diversity of existence: "...
all things are united as one." "...there is interaction
between things on earth and the things in heaven." "...
our minds are so intimately connected with God as to
be divine sparks of his being." (I. 14.1,2, & 6)

As you read Epictetus, you enter the mind of a hard-nosed
philosopher and demanding teacher. Life had convinced
him beyond doubt that self-mastery, equanimity, detachment, acute awareness of what did and did not matter
and what was and was not under one's control, all under
guidance of reason (how else to know what was real?) and
virtue (how else to do what was right?), and most of all,
as informed by steady accord with the divine plan: all of
these he knew to be utterly essential to fashioning a good
way of being. Having been born into slavery and required
by his owner to serve in indeterminate ways in or around
the emperor Nero's insane court undoubtedly influenced
the acuteness of his reality perceptions. His owner permit-
ted him to study under Musonius Rufus, the foremost
Stoic philosopher at the time, and eventually freed him.
These experiences were surely a large part of his emphasis on real freedom versus enslavement to conventional
ways of thinking and acting. He believed that the ways and
perspectives just described were the only means of achieving real happiness.

By way of comparison, let's hear from Marcus Aurelius,
a Roman emperor for close to twenty years until dying in
CE 180. He had read Epictetus but never met him, since
Epictetus died in CE 135 in Greece, when Marcus was only
fourteen and in Rome. Their places in life, externally, could
hardly have differed more. Their presentations of Stoic
belief reflected their personalities and circumstances, but
both were committed to "living in accord with nature."
(Citations from Marcus Aurelius's *Meditations* are indicated
by book and chapter numbers, both of which are always
briefer than those labels would suggest.)

- On keeping perspective in dealing with aggravations by other people, which were many: "[A]ll of them [are] due to the offenders' ignorance of what is good or evil... but as a fellow creature [they are] similarly endowed with reason and a share of the divine...; for he and I were born to work together,...To obstruct each other is against Nature's law." (II.1)

- The way things are: "Remembering always what the World-Nature is, and what my own nature is, and how the one stands in respect to the other—so small a fraction of so vast a Whole—bear in mind that no man can hinder you from conforming each word and deed to that Nature of which you are a part." (II.9)

- Shaping a good life: "[A]lways adhering to strict reason...yet with humanity, disregarding all lesser ends and keeping the divinity within you pure and upright...only seeking in each passing action a conformity with nature and in each word and utterance a fearless truthfulness, then shall the good life be yours." (III.12)

- The nature of reality: "Always think of the universe as one living organism, with a single substance and a single soul." (IV.40)

- Authenticity in the midst of turmoil: "Does this thing which has happened hinder you from being just, magnanimous, temperate, judicious, discreet, truthful, self-respecting, independent, and all else by which a man's nature comes to its fulfillment?" (IV.49)

- When confronted with criticism: "Reserve your right to any deed or utterance that accords with nature. . . keep a straight course and follow your own nature and the World-Nature (and the way of these two is one)." (V.3)

- Humans are troublesome, but "...what I choose is to live the life that nature enjoins for a reasonable member of a social community." (V.29) "The mind of the Universe is social." (V.30)

• Lastly: "All things come to their fulfillment as the one universal Nature directs." (VI.9) "[W]hat is there left to be prized? In my judgment, this: to work out, in action and inaction alike, the purpose of our natural constitutions." (VI.16) "Universal Nature's impulse was to create an orderly world. It follows, then, that everything now happening must follow a logical sequence." (VII.75)

Marcus's *Meditations* are aimed exclusively at himself (he most commonly uses the pronoun "you" in his dialog with self) and written much like a journal, whereas Epictetus was teaching students (one of whom transcribed his lectures; he wrote nothing himself), but also, in the course of teaching, certainly speaking to himself. Self-awareness and self-criticism were essential to Stoics. One regarded one's life with great seriousness, as would be expected for people who considered their lives part of a universal design that entailed responsibilities along with beneficences. When you received the gift of a life, in their way of thinking, you would want to fathom where it came from and what purposes it should serve. This they did, aiming the response both upward toward the Universe and outward toward humanity. One's gifts were freely given and received; who would want to fail at reciprocity?

I hope these few citations provide an adequate flavor of what these old Stoics had in mind as they strove to live in accord with nature. Can the substance it had for them two millennia ago be retained through translation into ways of thinking in the present? In other words, can we still experience ourselves as living within a meaningful context that extends well beyond, while still inclusive of, our individual selves? Do the *nature* of objective reality and the *nature* of a self entwine in ways that are congruent, that carry insights from the larger to the smaller reality about good ways of life, that imply preferred ways of being for creatures such as us who want to create meaningful and ethical lives?

To be clear, I want to do with that part of Stoic philosophy expressed as "living in accord with nature" something similar to what is done with other wise old doctrines that have proved their value but grown dated. Take constitutional, jurisprudential, and theological reinterpretations, for example. Times change. Although the commitment to old wisdom remains strong, new needs, new perspectives, and new learning must be incorporated, and the old must adapt if original insights are to be preserved with vibrant continuity. In short, pitch out the bathwater while maintaining the growing baby—clean, recognizable, and wearing new clothing that fits.

Let me begin at the top, so to speak: what do we know from science about the Universe and Earth that may intersect with what we've seen in the citations that conceived existence as providential, determinative, and under guidance from the gods or reason? Is Earth merely matter mutely doing what it will owing to physical laws? Or does it also speak to us about things and ways that are *good* and that are relevant to human choices for doing what we will, insofar as we too care about goodness?

It is said that of all species that ever existed of plants, animals, and other life forms, 99 percent have become extinct. This means that a billion, more or less, have come and gone, carrying with them trillions upon trillions, maybe trillions of trillions, of individuals. A winnowing on this scale is almost unimaginable but still leaves us today with perhaps 10 million species, the majority of which (about 80 percent) have yet to be identified and named.

With this history and what we know of evolution in action, one thing stands out: Nature (the natural world) cares far less about individuals than about the whole. Both individuals and species come and go. A cosmic blink can pass over multitudes in blithe ignorance of their imminent passing, but Earth has always persisted. Even after the worst mass extinctions, a measure of life has remained. Replenishing the stockpile takes perhaps 10 million years at times, but it happens. We have learned that life branches out in a profusion of forms, often with little resemblance to what and where they came from. And not in isolation. Interactions are everywhere. Ecosystems form and intersect with other ecosystems until this busy fecundity forms one large inclusive Ecosystem of the Whole. It looks like a unity of Earth existence; I cannot avoid seeing that it also looks like the spiritual union that mystics strain to describe. I suspect all beings are so deeply immersed *in*, and over time *as*, one another that separation is impossible except superficially. And why try? What would be gained? The Ecosystem of the Whole also fits pretty well with the Stoics' World-Nature, leaving aside Jupiter and anthropocentrism. As much as I admire the Stoic philosophic accomplishment, its assertion of human preeminence, the Universe's unceasing concern for human welfare above all else, leaves me cold. More realistic is the scientific and philosophic view (not the prejudiced, self-serving conventional view) that humans are just one species among many and count no more than any of the others except possibly as a force for destruction.

These views see an orderly Universe that can be described as rational in providing physical constants of a sort that allowed life to emerge and survive, the premise being that a Universe permitting, or enabling, life is better than one without. This Universe is beneficent in its provision of life potentials and need satisfactions (not the least being [who would have predicted?] beauty and our ability to appreciate it). As a Whole, it stands above and subsumes the partial. The Earth is a well-designed, well-functioning unity, and it is good.

I noted that living in accord with nature reflects a Stoic religious commitment, which I set aside in order to recognize a still authentic and encompassing ethical commitment that we can see as linked to existence and human emergence and human receptivity and care. Marcus and Epictetus were fundamentally moralists, or ethicists, unrelenting in their commitment to doing what they could to promote an ethically astute community and to live the philosophy conceived in Stoic thought—to live it as if belief, perception, choice, and action were united.

The modernized Stoicism that I want to depict and promote has these characteristics, shared to one degree or another with the ancient version—

Earth is a unified Whole that incorporates individuals as subsidiary elements of its unity.

Because we have been given so much we owe in return caretaking, respect, and balance in asserting our needs alongside those of other existences—a basic reciprocity combined with gratitude. It helps to remember that what may be a *means* for us is assuredly some other creature's *end*.

If we wish to have satisfying and meaningful lives, we will connect our search for truth and wisdom with virtue practices, such as promoting justice, responding compassionately to the needs of others, sharing, and generosity. This way of life does not make you happy; it is happiness itself.

Care of the soul, of one's intellectual and ethical center, is crucial to the best kind of care for the self. Humans are essentially rational and social beings; the egoistical denial or distortion of the fittingly responsive expression of these characteristics subverts integrity, character, and one's relation to the whole.

Since wholes are superior to parts, then insofar as we act according to the whole within which we are embedded, we engage our highest selves. The good of the whole becomes our good. Nonhuman life forms appear generally to do their part in creating a coherent world order; we can do the same, beginning with attention to our human communities and our effects on natural-world communities and offering them the respect and accommodation they are due.

Revere what is highest in the Whole and in yourself, and revere existence *per se*. Not obedience to god; rather, responsiveness to the needs of others (any others) and the call of virtue.

Last, a proposition: The surest mark of a person with greatness of mind, one who is honorable, worthy, virtuous, good (choose your adjectives), is that they care more about the non-self parts of existence and the higher values than they do about their own benefits. They recognize that what is good for the whole is good for them as well, but the latter is not their chief concern.

What is the point of all this parsing? For me personally, it shows continuity between an ancient philosophic, and especially ethical, conception of how to live that I have found compelling and consistent with what seems to me in the twenty-first century an equally compelling approach that draws on its insights and intuitions. It is a framework and foundation, and intellectually reinforcing, that long-dead thinkers and doers whom I greatly respect shared, even conceived, many of these views. We live in a time of ethical incoherence bordering on nihilism, a time that does not encourage deep thinking about truth and goodness and ways of life that embody them. Those who earnestly seek may find satisfaction and tranquility in views like these. In Marcus' words: "[R]emember that the needs of a happy life are few. Mastery of dialectics or physics may have eluded you, but that is no reason to despair of achieving freedom, self-respect, unselfishness, and obedience to the [call of truth and goodness]. (VII.67) (In the original, the bracketed conclusion reads "obedience to the will of God.")

There's more. How much do we care about beauty? What is its place in worldviews and daily lived experience? Considerably less than it should be, it seems to me. How else would forests get clear-cut or mountaintops mined? Nature creates beautiful landscapes, unique features, dramatic settings as if it were easy, as if their existence were as much for beauty as for anything else. And maybe it is. So much beauty in so many forms and places does not feel like an accident. I wonder if something innate to matter/energy made it prefer beauty as it came into existence in all its ways. It is becoming less preposterous for me, as for some scientists and philosophers, to imagine that, mysteriously, matter/energy may be conscious in some elementary form all the way down. It's as if consciousness, beauty, and life all lay nested in the atoms of existence just waiting to come out.

Whatever its story, Nature does like beauty. Whenever we humans create our own versions of beauty, in music and art, theorem and story, in loving union, it brings with it an enchantment that seems to me to be one with our response to Nature's beauty. This should not surprise since Nature is our model and original stimulus. When we pay attention, we become engaged with beauty, hear it speak to us, flow in and out of union and communion with it. We know indubitably that, as with life and consciousness, truth and goodness, beauty is inherently valuable. It is one of the keys to higher and better awareness, one that asks something of us: to delight that existence brought it along, to protect and share it, to make beauty ourselves at every opportunity—and to resist the blindness and deafness that have come to seem needful if a certain idea of progress and prosperity is not to be impeded by "sentiment."

The upshot of caring to live in accord with beauty is that we affirm its presence and recognize that *accord* speaks of harmony, balance, mutuality. We owe it to the flow of existence, which brought us forth as an expressive part of itself, to reciprocate. We can never give as much as we receive but as much as we can in accord with our capacities, which themselves are continuous with their source and do their part to hold it all together in unity.

I use the word *nature* in this essay in three ways that I want to distinguish. There is the nature of the Whole, what some Stoics called Universal Nature, which refers to *the way things are* in the Universe and in our part of it here on Earth. Material substance, energy, and physical laws are part of it, although in this the ancients were still at a rudimentary stage. Even so, what they called *physics* was one of the three areas of Stoic philosophy. From their sensible perspective, the more we know of reality, all of it, the better positioned we are to discern what it has to tell us and how we should comport ourselves as part of it. The other two areas of Stoicism were logic and ethics, but it was the latter that received their deepest investigation. Since their chief concern was to understand and describe the best life for humans, it made sense that ethics would be central. In this pursuit they moved beyond physical laws toward noting what the Universe revealed about the human place therein. Since it was well designed for life, fully equipped with everything necessary for all forms of life to sustain themselves, the Universe was clearly generous and sensitive; it manifested reason in its construction along with goodness and beauty and openness to being. The ancient Stoics surmised that the lives of humans in particular—conscious, reasoning beings whose breadth of capacities exceeded those of other life forms—were superior to the others, which existed to serve humans.[1]

---

1. This anthropocentrism is unacceptable today, but the truths in Stoicism are not affected by setting it aside. Too bad it is so thoughtlessly assumed by virtually all other belief systems and religions still and not fully and

The second use of the word *nature* refers to the nature of *Homo sapiens* collectively and individually. As above, human nature also seeks to know *the way things are*, only this time for people. What are our defining characteristics and aims and limitations as a species? How does a person tailor them for his distinctive expression? We are one species containing much diversity. For each individual, the question is how to live the life that best fits him or her while remaining within the species blueprint provided by the nature of the Whole. We are free to violate the blueprint and often do out of ignorance and self-centeredness, but at our ethical peril and at the cost of true flourishing.

The third use of *nature* will form the remainder of this essay, which has now arrived at Nature as the life and life spaces that evolved on Earth over the past 3.8 billion years, more or less. *That* Nature is the most astonishing, enchanting, beguiling. If it had merely produced unicellular life and stopped. it would have deserved credit. That alone was no minor feat, but Nature didn't stop there. Its plenitude is an everyday smack in the face of complacency for those who notice. Oh beatific Earth, we cannot love you enough! But we have some explaining to do. All those billions of years of evolutionary work, with life reviving itself after massive extinction calamities, life surviving to the present—and now one species has embarked on a massive fouling of its nest that may terminate in calamity as colossal as did the earlier ones. My purpose is not to rehearse what we already know about this shameful business. Rather, I'm interested in seeing if *living in accord with Nature* in this third sense of the word is a meaningful notion, one that could preclude anthropogenic calamity if it were heeded.

Here is some of what we know about Nature. All of its multitudinous parts work together, even in conflict, with each filling its proper niche and each receiving what

---

finally set aside. This pernicious doctrine has contributed to vast destruction and suffering.

it needs by way of shelter, food, and reproductive and self-protective and self-maintaining qualities. Humans, too, receive what we need of the basics as well as models for carrying out distinctively human activities (biomimetic processes that we are usually too busy and impatient to heed). Not satisfied to stop there, Nature adds inspiration for art, music, poetry, and other of our nonmaterial and even spiritual practices. These speak to us through Nature's beauty and unity and wholeness: ecology and spirituality may be different voices for one reality.

Earth's Nature lets us know that we belong here, as the Universe reveals also on star-filled nights, even though we are typically not the most courteous of guests. Nature provides a powerful reminder that although individuals pass on, the Whole does not. Violating its code of harmony and accommodation, conflict and resolution, acting disrespectfully and egoistically puts individuals out of balance and may threaten their survival. (Putting self before community is an affront to what sustains us and results in unethical behavior more generally.)

Earth's rhythms of cooperation and conflict resolve to a balance that works and benefits the Whole—predators are "above" prey and prey "above" plants within the who-eats-whom hierarchy, but tyranny of the human sort does not appear. Whether wisely or not (and who am I to question?), Nature's evolution set the table for humans to appear and thrive; we owe it respect and caretaking in return, as well as an explanation for how we got so fucked up and how we intend to change.

Nature is a vast society of life and landscapes. We humans form our own societies that rely on Nature, but we forget that we are essentially social and dependent, and we forget the behaviors that should follow from that. We fail to *live in accord* with nature in any of the senses described.

There is intuitive truth in the notion of lived accordance; I don't doubt its value, which is validated as it fosters

nontheistic reverence. But I concede that this will not reso-
nate literally for everyone. Maybe I should offer it as metaphor instead. Little worlds engage with bigger ones that
do the same with even bigger worlds; meaning is found
and created in that engagement. Experience (including the
present experience of ignoring reality) tells us that caring
participation seems to be what we were born for. Caring
participation would be a guide for what we know as both
the way things are and the way we need them to be. When
I let my mind wander imaginatively over the 13.8 billion
years that the Universe as we understand it has evolved,
and over the most recent 4.5 billion years of that period
in which the Earth formed, and over the 3.8 billion years
of that period in which life emerged and survived against
the odds, and look around today... It may have been pure
contingency, sheer accident; I don't know and don't find
that it matters. I am humbled by it and grateful. It's clear
that the uncountable parts of that long process somehow
worked together—each in accordance with the others—
toward the present reality, which is good regardless of how
humans misuse it.

I recently read about what's called the end-Perm-
ian extinction event of 252 million years ago, which was
the most devastating of them all, with life virtually wiped
out. Earth became a cauldron of heat, toxic air, and dead
oceans, but the remnants carried on, and in 10 million years
or so restored a new Earth and new diversity of life. I see
in that an implicit intentionality; although I don't suppose
Earth was headed toward specific kinds of life (it couldn't
care less what those were or whether they included *Homo
sapiens*), it is prima facie evident that Nature aimed for
abundance, variety, and ways of being that enabled life
to continue in *being*, allowing for vast time spans during
which old were replaced by new in response to changing
conditions: the cast of characters changed, but the leit-
motif endured.

Then a few hundred thousand years ago, the specifically hominid form of consciousness came along. It allowed a new kind of awareness and understanding of time and change. At humanity's best, it stuns us with the grand procession and elicits the desire to join in reverent and harmonious ways. Our best, though, is rare. Humanity became beguiled by materialism. It allowed itself to be led by those who were most preoccupied with running wild in the material domain and exploiting it for egoistic gratification and heedless desire. Materialism has captured humanity so completely that it now seems willing to risk a modified but still apocalyptic version of that Permian disaster via anthropogenic climate catastrophe.

Living in accord—metaphor and reality—arises in the souls of those who love existence and do not want to dominate and plunder it. It brings harmony and equanimity, aiming toward truth and care, and the satisfaction of belonging. Much has been given, and accordingly and in justice, much is owed in return.

CHAPTER 13

TWO SOURCES OF
MORAL ESTEEM

WHAT IS IT ABOUT ANYTHING that exists, anything that *is,* that evokes—or should evoke—my moral consideration and respect? Do certain qualities demand, or at least suggest, that one who has anything to do with some *other* becomes morally accountable for how he relates to that other because of its manifestation of those qualities? Is one not accountable if the other lacks those qualities, with *other* including humans, plants, and animals? You might ask why a person should care about plants or animals, but to me that question seems based on constricting assumptions that threaten to place those beings outside the wider moral realm, which I conceive as robust and inclusive. I write as one inside to others either inside that realm or on the margins who generally intend the good, to do what's right, toward others. Yet they also recognize that common practice assigns different levels of moral concern toward other beings on account of certain qualities and are sometimes made uncomfortable by this, even if not sure why.

Over the ages most people who have thought about this discovered that—such a coincidence!—only humans are morally worthy, owing to their high intelligence and reason (however poorly employed) and moral agency (disregarding the moral responsibility implicit in agency).

Other qualities have been added to the list, such as an orientation toward the future, subjective consciousness, range of capacities and experiences, and being the apple of God's eye. The effort aims to enwrap humans and exclude nonhumans, and on its own terms it has carried the day. Experience and research have found more "humanlike" qualities in some species of animals, the boundaries have inched outward, but typically it seems grudgingly and with exceptions and limitations. Think of chimpanzees in zoo cages or research labs, octopuses on exhibit in aquaria, and cetaceans doing tricks at aquatic amusement parks.

One objection to the approach just described might be to posit that existence per se is sufficient grounds for moral respect, a view I am comfortable with but realize will need justification.

A second approach to the question of when moral esteem is called for starts at the other end, the closer end. It starts with wondering if the more relevant variables may relate to the attitude of the person asking the question. Is there a morally imbued attitude or mind-set that guides the one who has it and that would include all that she beholds in its vision? She doesn't ask what characteristics possessed by the other create moral accountability. Instead, what do her moral sensitivity and vision tell her the other deserves from her? Or to put it in other terms, what does her open-hearted encounter with the other arouse in the relation between them? That her actions will be morally infused or informed goes without saying; she aims to offer the other what it is due or what it needs that she can give. Would this be a morally self-righteous person, priggish, moralistic in the tight-lipped, hyper-judgmental sense? Not likely. As she sees different colors without effort, so she sees different beings with different needs and vulnerabilities through eyes of respect and acts accordingly and without effort. Most of the time she goes her way, guided by a mandate of simple nonharm and noninterference. Or she

is merely present to the other: mindful, engaged, affirming. Other times, she sees the need for a caring response;
this is within her purview, and she gives it. She feeds the
hungry and clothes the naked, so to speak. And since there
are many needs in our world, she supports the formation
of agents—nonprofit organizations or government departments, for example—whose responsibility is to meet such
needs, even when she is unaware or unable. She does not
ask if they deserve her care; she asks what is needed and
who can respond to it best; this implies the kind of society
she wants to live in and the kind of person she wants to be.

It should be apparent, as already suggested, that in
the second approach nothing that exists is excluded. One
offers either passive noninterference toward the being
and course of the other—any other—or actively seeks to
protect it or provide for its need. The premise is simple:
one cares. One cares in the manner that one breathes—in
silent, automatic rhythm mostly, but sometimes heavily and rapidly, when one exerts oneself with unspoken
moral intent.

I consider the second approach the more vital one, the
one that fits the insights and feelings we have in deepest
reflection and mindful encounter, but the first is sometimes helpful as well: in making necessary discriminations
as in triage type situations, for example, or in distinguishing
between proximate obligations and those more remote.
And in deciding, as we do several times every day, what
to eat. Even so, the making of discriminations occurs in a
very different atmosphere when done under a caring gaze
rather than the gimlet eyes of hard, egoistic reason.

It is also true that the more we increase knowledge
and open our perception to the often quite remarkable
qualities of creatures whom we thought we knew, such as
animals (usually in ways that discounted them), and whose
lives will always remain somewhat mysterious, the more
we will encounter qualities that reveal more is going on in

and out there than we knew. Processes and experiences reveal lives with their own distinctive goods and therefore the distinctive harms that can be done to them. A little learning, taken seriously, can lead to wondrous results.

To avoid confusion, I will refer to the first and second approaches as, respectively, externally and internally oriented, with the proviso that exteriors and interiors are never divided by impenetrable boundaries. (Boundaries, in fact, are often distinguished by the ways in which they are penetrated.) Also, interiors invariably reach out to encompass exteriors; they can never remain isolated. My goal is to advocate for the approach that begins internally (accepting the caveats) and to explore what it means, how it comes to be, its ramifications, how it relates to what we know or assume about "human nature," what it has in common with some spiritual practices and the tradition of virtue ethics. Also, how it necessarily eventuates in the premise I mentioned above about becoming one who cares. I make no pretense of tying up an airtight philosophical case or of trying to. Rather, I aim to present an alternative way of knowing and being and to portray what makes it appealing and even reasonable.

The conscious, albeit inchoate, beginning of the ethical trip that brought me here was my discovery many years ago of Martin Buber's mysterious little book *I and Thou*.[1] It wasn't that I was bowled over by a revelation or even had a good initial understanding of what he was saying, but something was there that spoke to me, and I would spend parts of the next two decades and beyond figuring out what that was and what it meant for a way of life. The

---

1. I do not know what it suggests about the *zeitgeist* or cultural change but I'm informed by my spellchecker as I type that it would prefer I change "I and Thou" to "me and you." Is it through such baby steps that the downward slide is distinguished?

book describes what Buber considered the two fundamental ways a person may relate to the world, as Thou or as It. "Thou" comes from a place of respect, inclusion, identification with the other, engagement and affirmation, the place where love is sometimes born. "It" relates to the other in instrumental terms; one has a purpose to accomplish, and the It is useful. Although I–It may sound debased in some manner, much of the time it is a necessary posture for all of us as we make a way through life using and doing. We live out existence on a continuum between brazen, exploitive instrumentalism on one end, and relations of mutuality, respect, and care on the other. When Thou is fully manifested, it builds forms of union or solidarity, trust, and at times spiritual realization. Pure Thou-ness is always transient, but as an intentional attitude within daily living, it informs the conduct of all one's relations and endeavors. When It-orientation teeters at its extremity, it becomes definitively immoral, ego-centered.

This is brief but I hope clear. The book is still in print for those who want to go to the source, which I recommend.[2] In any event, my present focus is on questions Buber addressed but did not resolve as completely as he might have: those having to do with how the relational Thou with its emphasis on mutuality could apply in relations that weren't those of freely interacting, equal human individuals or of doctor to patient, teacher to student, parent to child. More challenging, what could it mean in relations with Nature, with trees and animals, or with a workplace or institution? Is Thou possible without full mutuality? Or could it be defined more broadly or perhaps be replaced by other postures or attitudes without losing its meaning?

---

2. There have been two translations. The first, by Ronald Gregor Smith, is my preferred version and has been reissued in paperback; the second is by Walter Kauffman. Kauffman translates Thou as You, feeling that the former sounded too religious, but to my ear "You" sounds too mundane.

A full response to these questions is beyond my present purpose, but I want to address what the responses to each have in common. Mutuality, or reciprocity, expresses itself in different ways; in a particular relation, it may give back in a currency different from the one offered. My special interest is the human relation with Nature, with landscapes, ecosystems, and individual plants and animals. It is no exaggeration to say that in our culture, and particularly in its domination by economic interests and values, the prevailing attitude toward the natural world is decisively instrumental, far out on the continuum of It-relations. Were it not, we would not be faced with industrialized forms of cruel conversion of living animals into dead body parts for food, or clear-cut forests, or the alarming decline in wildlife numbers and in species of both plants and animals, or anthropogenic climate disruption. In these domains, it feels almost laughably irrelevant, because so sadly obvious, to point out the absence of mutuality and esteem for the being of those killed or impaired. But for those who care enough to want to step outside of these practices, the question of esteem for others is central, and they will want to know how the need for, say, food or lumber can be morally met. This takes me back to the internally modulated approach to building lives having what I will call moral tone. One comes to care about how one affects others around oneself, all others, and acts responsibly—that is, in response to one's morally intoned spirit as it is addressed by the being of the other that is present before him.

The crux of I–Thou relations and of the internally generated approach to expressing moral esteem is just this: with its focus on the character of the *relation*, it is not what or who is "other" to "I" that relation is morally contingent upon, but what I offer, how I respond to the other. The relation *between* us arises as It or Thou through our attitude, sometimes through what we take or refuse to take and crucially how we take it. I am free to offer inclusion and care whether with a person or a pinyon pine or the raven on its branch. I may or may not speak words, and the pine and raven may simply be silently present in the beauty of their existence. Relational intonation arises with the measure of Thou we intend or spontaneously experience, and comes to expression in whatever distinctive fashion we choose. Bare existence, I believe, is enough to evoke morally infused attentiveness.

I vaguely remember a story about a spiritual devotee long ago traveling on foot for a day and discovering when he stopped that ants from his prior stayover had climbed aboard his baggage, whereupon he turned to take them home—an exaggerated demonstration of moral concern even for me, but the intention expressed, the care for the others' well-being, is of the type I advocate.

Many spiritual traditions and practices reflect this sensibility. Buddhism's Four Noble Truths recognize that suffering is endemic to human life, owing to ignorance and desire, but can be surmounted through following the Eightfold Path that can relieve the suffering of self and others through mindful, ethical, and wise living. Nonharm is a key aspect of the Eightfold Path. In the *Upanishads*, ancient Hinduism reflected on the unified experience of being and concluded: That art Thou, Brahma is present in all. Mystics from every tradition I am aware of encounter with certainty the unity of self with other and with God. Most traditions include versions of the Golden Rule; for some adherents, "treating others as they themselves want to be treated" receives a widely inclusive interpretation. Even in Immanuel Kant, the sober-minded eighteenth-century philosopher, I can find support for these ideas. If I take liberties with one version of his Categorical Imperative, others (only humans in his formulation) are to be treated "never merely as a means to an end, but always at the same time as an end." In other words, instrumentalism is a necessary component of human action but never without allowing for the dignity of the other whose benefits are sought.

Considerable research demonstrates many facets of plant sentience, reveals their ways of registering what's going on in their environment, how they communicate with and assist each other, how they learn and remember, how they resist predation and signal cohorts about threats, and so on. Similarly with fish, those morally forgotten creatures of the water realm. In *What a Fish Knows*, Jonathan Balcombe writes, "[E]ach has a one-of-a-kind life on the inside, too. And therein lies the locus of change in human-fish relations."[3] Well, yes, it makes a difference to discover that plants and fish have lives with trajectories that may flourish or wither, and that it matters to them. Knowledge reveals some mysteries, enriches others, adds interest, sometimes fosters awe, and may make disregarding moral respect harder. But plants and fishes, mountaintops in West Virginia, and undammed rivers everywhere make a claim—by dint of their very existence—to be left alone. If necessity rightly overrides that claim, they make another: to intrude nonviolently, thoughtfully, with care about the effects.

I mentioned human nature earlier. Attempts to attribute this or that human quality to nature rather than nurture, or to sheer contingency rather than resolute choice, are usually controversial, but in broad terms I assume we all recognize that humans are by nature and desire social creatures. Individuation is above all something that happens within community, without whose caring support it becomes stunted or deformed.[4] And community

3. A blurb on the book's back was provided by the Dalai Lama: "Jonathan Balcombe vividly shows that fish have feelings and deserve consideration and protection like other sentient beings."
4. Individuation does not imply a separation from relatedness, rather, a distinguishing of self from others, a self-awareness within a social ecosystem in which one remains embedded: oneself-in-relation.

welfare precedes individual needs in the few cases where the needs of both do not coincide or comfortably reside alongside each other. Thus, non-stunted humans move about the world looking out for each other. We are born with that predisposition as central to our nature and have learned solidarity with and within caring communities. Stunted, we may live with mostly egoistic intent. I propose that an emotionally and spiritually healthy person doesn't want to harm the other, whatever sort of being the other is, and tends to respond with concern when the other's welfare is at stake. It seems reasonable to imagine that most of us are predisposed to interrelate with a tendency to care and a readiness to feel morally responsible for doing so. Marcus Aurelius, that unique second-century Roman emperor and Stoic, said in his *Meditations* repeatedly and in various ways that "We are made for each other." If this is so—and I believe it is—it suggests that modern American society has been designed as, or been allowed to become, an environment inimical to fundamental human needs and even to human nature, that it diverts basic aspirations for happiness and meaning into channels that serve other ends. This may help explain a lot of what so many of us find unacceptable, sometimes even abhorrent, about its society as presently oriented.

Along with sociality, human nature appears designed to seek meaning: one wants to live engaged with groups, purposes, and activities that are worthy of commitment because valuable in themselves and therefore add to one's meaning. Many people find what has been called *caring for creation* an essential aspect of these commitments. Implicitly imbued with thou-centeredness, they ethicize their being and endeavors, discovering meaning entwined along the way. The attitude of veneration does this.[5]

---

5. I have participated in Buddhist retreats that taught me the Gassho: a bow with hands pressed together at my chest when meeting or departing from someone, when entering or leaving a room, and so forth, as a way to express grateful awareness to the things and beings I depend on.

What I want to suggest is that humans are necessarily formed internally to look outward in ways that may be mostly instrumental or mostly imbued with care. The premise that *one cares* builds on the base of innate tendencies to look outward with nonharming instrumentalism and the solidarity of morally infused identification with others and their well-being. I can imagine an origin myth similar to Adam, Eve, and the Garden, and also to what happens anytime one is born. The first thing to notice is its gratuitousness; birth is no one's right; it is unearned but freely given, as great a gift as ever one receives. Whether born into a school of hard knocks or by good fortune to a more nurturing environment, whether physically well-formed or impaired, she looks around and can't miss her dependence on others, for good or ill. Crucial experiences and encounters will form her "soul" and she can hope to find ways to thrive, remember the gifts, and aim to pass them on in suitable ways. Unless hopelessly distorted by destructive experiences, she will recognize her kinship with other beings and want to flourish within the flourishing of the inclusive community.

I recur to Kant again, this time without taking liberties. From his *Critique of Practical Reason:* "Two things fill the mind with ever new and increasing admiration and awe, the oftener and the more steadily we reflect on them: the starry heavens above and the moral law within...I see them before me and connect them directly with the consciousness of my existence." From this he derived humble identification with the Universe along with duty, and less personally, the unity of beauty with ethics.

Do I imagine that people are basically good? Is that how this story goes? Emphatically, no! Most are born with the equipment to move in any direction, depending on their history, circumstance, and choice, but close observation makes clear that humans are weak reeds in the currents of time and experience. Confronted by perceived threat, we become anxious and unpredictable; in the face of temptation, we yield to desire. Still, our social nature, combined with a mostly salubrious life course and good decisions, will often lead us to a minimal identification with the common good. Many will find Thou or learn reverence for being, and the minimal will expand. As it does, we remember that we did not earn our birth and that the gift of it comes with duties of reciprocity: to care for our birthplace, the Earth, and for our fellow sojourners of all species.

I have found that what is called virtue ethics, whose tradition goes back at least to Aristotle, fits comfortably with the source of moral esteem that I wish to speak for. Moral rules—whether for contract, consequence, or something else—are helpful as we frame and elaborate our values, but virtue ethics looks at a person's character, his moral makeup, to understand his spirit and action. Is he courageous and wise, just and temperate, aimed at truth and truthfulness? Or...not? Two of the chief virtues get too little attention: humility and generosity, both of which underlie and infuse, it seems to me, a robust commitment to justice, perhaps the most potent virtue of all. Together, these qualities help rein in the demon of ego and shape a path toward care for being. Altogether, they help to inscribe a cartography of the soul, something to illuminate what a life is for and where it might lead.

I can't finish without recognizing that my earlier assertion about the sufficiency of mere existence as a source of moral esteem might still sound bizarre. It is difficult enough for some to imagine incorporating both human and nonhuman animals when they conceive rightful recipients of moral respect. I hear them still asking—Can it be that simply by existing, nonhuman animals deserve moral respect? I return to that origin story: One becomes conscious and surveys the Earth with its landscape of other beings and finds, as creator God is reported to have said six times in the first chapter of Genesis, it is good. A presumption of gratitude and respect arises, as may wonder and reverence in receptive souls: I will have to turn some of what I behold to legitimate uses, but with this attitude I can see there are better and worse ways to do that.

But still, the skeptic continues, doesn't this go too far? Isn't the notion too commodious? Must one become an extremist and immobilize himself out of fear of causing harm? I know there is no place of utter purity in this world, no above-it-all posture that precludes the necessity of conscientious choice as to what and how to use or affect. We eat, we build shelters, we move about. We are all in this together, mountains and rivers, plants and animals, including human ones. Life feeds on life. Harms are unavoidable. But so should be restraint and care for one's effects on Earth and the common good.

In *I and Thou* and other essays and books, Buber depicted three realms of human existence: the human world, the natural world, and the realm of forms of the spirit (wherein are found art and other ways of giving expression to deep mysteries and responses to them). Although he did not speak of it as such, he too was drawing a vast circle around occasions of humans' encounters with their worlds. A later commentator spoke of his seemingly seeking to *ethicize existence*. When I first read that phrase some thirty years ago, I found it astonishingly accurate for both his intent and desired reality. It took more years to see where it led. I have been speaking on behalf of an internal turning toward reverence for existence that does not discriminate, except when it has to, and that finds the Universe and Earth good and worthy in themselves of deep engagement and care.

I finish with a few reflections on what the ramifications of this view could be. Maybe I should start by naming it.

I've spoken of it as reverence for existence and Thou-re-latedness, which are fine except a bit clunkily abstract and redolent of religious language. They surely imply spiritual experience, as I intend them to, but not of the theistic or conventionally religious sort. It seems that religion has more or less captured all the most powerful words for ultimate realities, so I try to borrow that power while wishing to decouple the words from their associations with pew and prayer. But there's no controlling the associations they carry, so I'm left frustrated by the effort.

In response, I've chosen a new way to portray the way of mind I describe, perhaps a better way than terms with religious freight and one that allows for the range of depth or commitment that people bring to their encounters with and conceptions of reality. What I've described in this essay is a *way of affirmation*, a way that begins with the goodness of sheer being and lets that shape what follows. It begins in mindfulness, attentiveness, or simply being caught unawares by a starry sky, a natural landscape, or love upsurged, and struck by the sense of there being more here than meets the eye and remaining present to the images and feelings that pass through the mind/body in the moment. The experience appears to confirm that, yes, there really is more than meets the eye, and it has something to tell me. It can be sparked by exchanging a look with another person, the beauty of Nature, offering or receiving compassionate support, realization of the value of a piece or a body of one's work. It's not predictable and, like happiness, cannot be deliberately sought, only facilitated by a way of living. And along with the sense that the experience and its provocation are intrinsically meaningful, it predisposes one to move about with humility and care for the *others* with which and with whom one shares or crosses paths.

In short, a way of affirmation sets ego aside, freeing us to fully engage with another, unencumbered by cravings, desiring only a shared good. It becomes a way of life with all that that implies. One of the people living and writing and, as it happens, farming today whom I greatly respect is Wendell Berry. In dozens of books and essays, he speaks of the importance of affection in relation to landscapes and your uses of them, of spinning out moral filaments that aim to leave or create more good than you take whenever you act. I envision the same goals as he does. He is sometimes criticized, however, by people who don't challenge his values but consider them insufficient to meet the moral calamities produced by modern capitalism, militarism, forms of oppression, and the atomization (called individualism) that subverts community and common purpose, common life, and the common good. I consider some of this criticism legitimate and the way I've described as equally subject to it, if I stop with individual perspectives and ways of being. As I've said above, there is intrinsic good in the ways Berry and I describe. Those who subscribe to them will be that many fewer candidates for enabling or complacently passing by injustice. But at this point in what appears to be our growing societal debacle, it seems to me hard to find hope and hard to imagine any conventional means of combatting the poisons of intolerance, misdirected fear, and greed. Corruption and concentrated wealth and power increasingly negate hopefulness. Living rightly is the necessary beginning and is essential, I believe, to anyone's cultivation of integrity, regardless of its proximate effects on society. From there I am drawn to what I know about those who are seeking communities of shared value that will unavoidably turn inward for their shared good, whether bound by geography or common commitments. At the same time, there continue to be people, particularly the young and those exposed to bigotry and other harms, and many others as well who simply reject injustice in all its forms, who struggle to make change, whether through political mobilization or civil disobedience, or through creation of alternatives to money-centered, exploitive commercial enterprise. Communities of shared value must support these endeavors in whatever ways they can, but for now I believe their priority will be sustaining communities in which moral esteem is normalized.

It would be naive to assume that good will necessarily prevail, or that even if it did, we could rest easy that it would survive. Corruption and self-centeredness have seriously damaged trust. For many, a commitment to truth and goodness is weakened by the will to power and the fears, dishonesty, and rampant cynicism that are part of its fuel. Still, I believe that even in the present catastrophe, people can shelter within their communities, remain faithful to their values, recognize the goodness of being even if it is unacknowledged by many beings, and find meaning. We can hope that these will be the seeds of better times.

CHAPTER 14

MAKING IT IN AMERICA

TO THE EXTENT THAT "HISTORY is written by the victors," it may also be true that cultural mythologies are maintained by those who are flattered by their themes—for instance, those who are socioeconomically privileged and whose class position is supported by mythology. Accounts of reality are malleable, especially early as they emerge and seek acceptance. Their durability as cultural myth depends on repetition, which beneficiaries of success mythologies tend to be well positioned to provide, as well as highly motivated and well financed.

The "self-made man," whom I will refer to here as the "putative self-made man," or PSM, is one of the most enduring of these tales, going back a couple of hundred years to Henry Clay. For a few it is a self-serving rationale for tax-avoidant and system-rigging stratagems for accumulation and retention of unjust levels of wealth. For others it is an accolade for having started small and finished large when the odds seemed against them. Surprisingly, perhaps, the myth of the PSM seems to enjoy passive acceptance by a large number of people whom it does not serve at all well and who might intuitively reject the concept if they thought much about it. Many of them, after all, have also worked hard, starting at or near the bottom, but never traveled far above it despite evident ability and effort. Challenging the PSM depiction seems almost anti-American or worse: as class consciousness and excuse making for the ne'er-do-well "takers" who we were told in the 2012 presidential election constitute almost half the country (a paradoxical claim by those who also no doubt assert that we are a great and exceptional nation). Who wants to suggest that anyone who really tries could not make it in America?

I've never found the notion of the self-made man convincing. For one thing, consider the words: self...made... man. They tell us that a "self" has "made" a "man." Within this frame, the self cannot be separate from the man (is actually another word for the man), so the postulate must be that a self makes itself. But where was this originating self to begin with? What were its man-making materials? Where did those materials come from? What was the self before it was made? For a self to make itself, it must have already existed as something. Who made that earlier self? At what point does that self have the wherewithal to make a new version? And which gets the credit? Selves are more complicated notions that commonly realized.

For reasons now obvious, PSM typically refers to the end product: a successful self (in business, almost always, and a possessor of wealth) who over time and from more or less humble beginnings has, we are led to believe, all by himself made the man. This myth does not identify a PSM's beginning but I think by implication his ascent is presumed to start when he first stares forward with steely-eyed intensity at the glittering Valhalla that he will surely achieve on a foundation of limited means forged into glorious ends by unlimited perseverance combined with native ability.

But of course, at the point where ambition seizes and directs consciousness, he was already halfway toward putative self-made manhood. His true beginning—or to use the term that may later describe his business development, his first merger—was of sperm with egg, which with time and luck became his infant self. Thenceforward, the eventual PSM was the medium in which a genetic inheritance combined with innumerable contingencies and learning experiences. An evolving self progressively unfolded of its own accord within this crucible, an ontogeny in which the self is mostly the spectator of its own development but becomes an active agent in limited ways owing to its evolved resources and traits. I can see no justification for claiming that the PSM autonomously asserts self to make man via qualities that are not themselves innate and/or exogenously shaped along with the talents whose potential they maximize. In other words, the diligence with which talent is used is no more self-made than the talent itself. Seizing opportunity depends on opportunity-seizing qualities that come with the ontogenetic package. By the time our PSM begins to think of himself in that way consciously, he has already been largely made by other-than-self factors working with intrinsic-to-self materials, largely unconscious of the assembly processes, which are no less effective for that.

This discussion overlaps with one we could have about putative free will. Free will does not exist; it isn't even clear what it would look like if we could imagine it in pure form. But I think we can posit, based on observation and intro-spection, a measure of freedom *of will*. I picture this will as analogous to a submarine's periscope rising to the surface, a periscope whose usefulness is only as good as the vessel from which it arises, the materials of which it is made, and the subsurface sailor peering through it. He looks, he assesses, he decides on a direction based on what appears real and right for his crew and his mission in the vision allowed, and then he acts. He can't fly, drive, or run because he's in an underwater capsule, but he does the best he can with what he has. And if honest with himself, he knows that those capacities for assessing, deciding, and so on all came with the package that is he. He did not "make" or earn them but mostly received them as gifts and accidents of life for better and worse. This does not diminish the importance of his measure of freedom, a freedom shaped by his life, through which intelligence and conscience and reason may exert themselves as he reaches toward a true grasp of reality and right pathways through it.

Like free will, the PSM does not exist. There's no shame in that—it is logically and as a practical matter impossible for a self to make itself *ex nihilo*. He still merits credit for the honor and ethics that he chose to guide his path, even if they and his talents weren't entirely self-made. But no validity goes with the notion that our self/man deserves all the credit for how he has come to be made, for what he has accomplished or even for who he is. We are not fleshy bots, but neither are we Promethean. We are creatures of fate adrift in vessels of variable quality and maneuverability, and we are most true to reality as well as most humane when we realize this in ourselves and see it as well in others.

Sometimes the PSM who claims genuine self-made manhood elicits our scorn. Other times we just smile indulgently, knowing that he needs to feel that way. But the PSM mythology is not harmless. It is an implicit justification for America's obvious lack of sympathy for the poor, the vulnerable, and the lower classes. (Should we call them self-unmade men?) America wants to believe that those who make it deserve all the credit, and those who don't deserve all the blame. Therefore, they are undeserving of our compassion, which would only tend to undermine what little gumption they are assumed to have, or else they wouldn't need our help. These thoughts lead us to another popular myth, which sometimes overlaps but does not depend on the PSM character.

We can't talk about PSMs without thinking about their relation to what is called *meritocracy*. The two notions have in common that they provide a seemingly objective and rational depiction of how those at the top got there (along with a congratulatory slap on the back), combined with a helpful rationale for disregarding those who, owing to the inexorable logic of existence, did not get there. Meritocracy's members have merit, that is, ability plus its steady application to tasks at hand, and thus they get ahead. Obviously it isn't necessary that a meritocrat (MC) also be a PSM. However he got his start, even if born into the lap of privilege, which can't be held against him, he became an MC due to his application of meritorious qualities. We are led to understand that he certainly deserves meritocracy's rewards. But the credit for his merit is as vulnerable to the same analysis as was the PSM's. Being born to privilege is doubly problematic. He was the fortunate recipient of some of life's useful gifts and was able to express them in appropriate ways. Society's good functioning depends on having such people available to get necessary things done with skill. It is grateful for their presence and should generously but not excessively reward them for their contribution to the common good. But those who don't have the good fortune to receive these useful gifts do not deserve scorn or indifference. Meritocrats and the average folk who labor away just beneath them on the hierarchy can find ways to help less well-endowed recipients at the bottom make their own contributions to the common societal project and be compensated less generously but not parsimoniously. They have to live, too. Let us not forget the equal dignity of all or that the most estimable kind of merit exists in tandem with empathy and generosity.

It goes against the American grain, especially the grain of those who have made it to or near the top, to suggest that they joined the meritocracy due to anything other than their own inner resources, some of which resources they will allow they were born with, but all of which they tend to claim credit for developing and putting to good use.

The star basketball player did not industriously self-grow to a 6'10" specimen endowed with speed, quickness, astonishing eye-hand coordination and a strong work ethic. As already mentioned, however, there is no good reason to assume that the latter qualities were any less gifted than the former. The MC, like the PSM, is a receiver of gifts rather than their initiator or creator. Although this may bruise pride in those who have hung their hats on a self-creation story, it is surely no insult and mostly an occasion for gratitude. Although the metaphoric periscope above is also not self-created, it is potentially our most bounteous aspect of selfhood, since it is the means through which we can discern, based on our entire history and who we have become, what is true, what is good, and what is worth living for as well as where to guide the boat.

If this argument is taken seriously, does it lead to egregious levelling? Does it deny merit and talent and treat people as an undifferentiated mass of mere biologically and socially conditioned robots, with never an independent or creative thought of their own? The simple answer is "No." The only levelling implied is beneficial—the relative levelling of economic disparities and pernicious hierarchies, both of which when left alone lead to dubious class distinctions and their supportive assumption that some people are inherently better than others rather than simply different. The results are maldistribution of opportunity, maldistribution of society's wealth and other rewards, and suppression by circumstance of genuine and invaluable inequalities (of talent, interests, personal qualities, aspirations) that contribute to wider diversity in forms of human expression. Impoverishment and indignity do not foster human development; straitened circumstances create straitened options for realization of individual capacities.

What the argument should lead to, I believe, is humility, a virtue greatly undervalued. We do not choose or earn our abilities but can be grateful for them and even use them as a kind of trust received from existence. If this argument leads to society's taking control of its distribution of economic rewards so that the impediments to opportunity created by the invidious suppression of some and the elevation of others—impoverished experiences on the one side facing enriched ones on the other, both owing to unmerited resource allocations—are corrected insofar as possible, then the sum total of human flourishing will have far greater space in which to blossom. The knowledge that any of us could have started and ended anywhere "but for the grace" of fate leads beyond humility and gratitude into generosity and compassion, a meritocracy of virtue, we can hope.

Of course, this aspirational denouement is hopelessly idealistic. Human frailty is widely distributed in myriad forms. One of the most enduring of these is dependence on markers of hierarchic distinction, in this case a need for excess whose possessor can use to feel above those with less and therefore superior. In a society drunk on materialism, he can use his excess to control others. There are virtually unlimited ways to express uniqueness and talent in the absence of the aforesaid resource injustices (e.g., artistry, craft, scholarship, goodness), but few seem to offer the same powerful high as material excess within a materialistic society. This could turn out to be the ultimate tragedy of humankind.

My preoccupation with these phenomena, the PSM and the meritocrat, comes from two related observations already alluded to, both of which turn the positive aura in which they are typically embroidered in a darker direction. These are the sources of merit and the consequences of its maldistribution. To clarify, I will look more closely at the ideal of meritocracy. If the gist of meritocracy is that the various realms of society—government, business, academia, and so forth—should be led by those with demonstrated merit in each realm, and the rewards distributed accordingly, then the unavoidable questions are: What are the sources of merit? How is it identified and supported? How can those who embody it find appropriate settings for it to manifest and accomplish all it is presumed to promise? Also, which areas of merit are most highly valued and rewarded? Why? Most important, how does person X come to have merit? What difference do what we might call meritorious circumstances have to do with its thriving? If merit is distributed randomly at birth, shouldn't meritocracies overall reflect this random origin if merit alone is the key variable?

The obvious first response is that individuals born with merit require circumstances that themselves have the merit of more or less equalizing each individual's prospects for joining the meritocracy. Otherwise, it can't be a true meritocracy, because the dice are loaded against some and for others. The most recent data for the United States indicate that economic mobility (and meritocracy can hardly be considered *real* meritocracy if it doesn't have cash value) has declined significantly over recent decades and that it is lower than in most other developed countries.[1] Choosing successful parents would seem to be the chief ticket to entry, the first sign of a budding meritocrat showing itself prenatally or even, if we want to get metaphysical, perhaps even prior to conception.

The truth is not that merit isn't real or the concept a confabulation. Some people are better at some things than others and improve their fields of endeavor along with themselves. If the field is socially useful, they improve society as well. They deserve credit and adequate reward. But this concept deserves more critical appraisal than ordinarily happens, because its foundation is laid on a

---

1. World Economic Forum. Global Social Mobility Index 2020: Why Economies Benefit from Fixing Inequality. January 19, 2020. https://www.weforum.org/reports/global-social-mobility-index-2020-why-economies-benefit-from-fixing-inequality

background of visible and invisible conditions for which the meritocrat can give thanks but not claim credit. "Meritocracy" can easily pass as a code word for a version of aristocracy. Although it proudly disdains the aristocrat's claims to spurious superiority based on "breeding" and such, actually it only hides the reality that preexisting conditions account for a large part of what makes the man (and woman), including the meritocrat. In short, if aristocracy is passed on by inheritance, how much less so is meritocracy?

When some start the race ahead of others—a fact cleverly described as starting out on third base while telling themselves they hit a triple—it is clearly unjust to let the "unfettered market" assign rewards to those whose rewards began with conception, rewards that pave the way forward while leaving others in the dust. One of the major problems with the idea of meritocracy is just this. Operating as it does in America, it tends to illuminate its beneficiaries while obscuring its losers, to applaud some while looking silently away from the others. Sympathetic comprehension and compassion are apparently not meritocratically relevant. Injustice is compounded.

What I have described does not constitute a revelation; it is no secret that humans are mostly made rather than arising from self-creation, just as it has never been a secret that America is and always has been a deeply bigoted country. In both cases, though, the stories we tell ourselves are very different from the reality. The PSM and the meritocrat are protagonists in some of the stories, and that is what makes them pernicious ideals. Equal chances for life, liberty, and the pursuit of happiness are not what this culture really aims for. It aims chiefly to support those who have already won various "lotteries"—genetic, environmental, circumstantial, and so on. It even may be that the ease with which we have slid into a "post-truth" environment in America is that we have been prepared for it by the multitude of stories that have been concocted to prevent our seeing our history and our present as they are. Post-truth is a sign of intellectual failure, so we need to add to it "post-honesty," since the greatest failure is moral. Lies have become well rooted in the corporate and political worlds. Apparently the infection has crossed the barrier into our brains so that millions accept being lied to with equanimity or denial. At any rate, injustice and dishonesty happen more or less as described, and their interconnection is not hard to see. Challenging our stories as they are told may be the most curative thing we can do.

AMERICA'S WAYS

The blood, the soil, the faith
These words you can't forget
Your vow, your holy place
O love, aren't you tired yet?

...

A cross on every hill
A star, a minaret
So many graves to fill
O love, aren't you tired yet?

"The Faith" by Leonard Cohen[1]

---

1. Leonard Cohen, "The Faith." (From the DVD "Dear Heather," 2004, Sony BMG Music Entertainment.)

CHAPTER 15

A Two-State Solution for the United States

AS I OBSERVE THE UNITED States fracture increasingly along multiple fault lines, more intensively over recent years, it reminds me of maps that show southern California's multiple, sometimes intersecting, earthquake zones. There's no altering the geology of those areas as they bide their time waiting for the subterranean straw that will break their stasis and set them in motion. We have, instead, to adapt or live elsewhere. People like to imagine that human behavior is more flexible than geology, but as we watch the feckless response to climate change and the endless repetition of arms races and arms uses, it is hard to be confident. The analogy between societal and geological fracturing may be more apt than we'd care to acknowledge.

American disunion is inherently alarming; it signals that our capacity for effective democratic governance has eroded below even the meager level to which it had already been brought by citizen complacency and the dominance of moneyed interests over American life and government. It is all the more problematic at present because of the fearful and nihilistic implacability on one side of the divide, a faction that has demonstrated its determination to delegitimize alternate views and unpleasant facts and its willingness to subvert democratic forms and norms whenever they interfere with its hunger for power and personal security.

Who sees any signs that this condition can be overcome, that it can be satisfactorily resolved and stable reunion accomplished? Republican officeholders and aspirants for office read the numbers—40+ percent of the electorate and 90 percent of Republicans support Donald Trump. They know their self-interest points in only one direction: placate the base, sideline the opposition, suppress certain categories of voters, use any means for the sake of the one great end—power. For a quarter century or more, the party's efforts to subvert democratic norms and processes have only grown more insidious and bold. When there are no visible prospects for reconciliation, who can doubt that we face a future of continued stasis? Or more likely, if present practices are allowed to continue, we face a drift toward minority-party, semi-authoritarian control. The pretense endures among some that citizens share basic commitments and values, ones that eventually will conduce to a greater good, but that is not possible when there is no shared view of a greater good. So how can one imagine a re-United States?

That the nation has devolved to a mere assemblage rather than a union becomes evident once we question complacent assumptions of history and habit and look at the situation objectively. With this in mind, I suggest we should dissolve the formerly *United* States and become two (or more) countries, designated here as Right-Landia and Other-Landia. Here are a few observations that confirm the fatal divergence.

First, those who are united under what may become the Right-Landia banner have forsaken commitments to the practice of true democracy; instead they traffic in an illusion of forms and engage in deceptive charade. Their antidemocratic souls manifest themselves in a multitude of ways: radical gerrymandering; establishing selective obstructions to voting by those who presumably don't support their cause; systematic lying; bigotry; refusal to consider a legitimate Supreme Court nominee put forward by the opposing party; other efforts to change the rules to tilt the table in their favor; tolerance of gross corruption among its leadership; and the practice of governing as if those not on board with their machinations do not exist. In their view, compromise equals betrayal. Winning is the only good. Failed representative government is the summit of their hopes and stasis its own form of victory.

Second, once the substance of democracy has been abandoned, the alternative is some form of poorly disguised authoritarianism. Oligarchy supported by plutocrats fits the bill to their satisfaction. Lacking a view of the common good, they believe taxes should be no higher than necessary to support an outsize military and other giant corporate ventures. Most of the remainder of society's wealth, they are certain, belongs in the banking and investment accounts—many sequestered in offshore sanctuaries—of the ruling class.

Third, these same people believe in the intrinsic goodness of corporations as mirror images of the intrinsic evil of government. Corporate excesses the opposition might object to, such as destruction of the commons, exploitation of labor, suborning of the political class, and financial chicanery, go unnoticed. The only good other than power is economic growth on their own terms.

Fourth, Right-Landians are completely convinced that everyone is fully responsible for his life situation. They hold in contempt anyone who might need compassion or merely a hand up. If, say, you cannot afford medical insurance, you will simply have to live, or die, without it; it's nobody's business but your own, the result of your own poor choices.

Fifth, Christianized white nationalism is hostile toward potential immigrants (even refugees and asylum seekers), minorities, LGBTQAs, non-Christians, and women who claim the right to make their own decisions about child-bearing. Government, in this view, can rarely if ever do anything positive but can be handy in controlling those with alternate dispositions.

Right-Landians, whose view of existence is reflected in these hierarchical convictions, can never get along with or accommodate others who do not adhere to the truth as they see it.

The time has come to face our disunited reality, to adjust to it and stop acting as if the adversaries can be made compatible. I propose that a solution won't be found within efforts to recreate unity. Rather, we must accept the radical disunity as it is and consider whether the long-ne-glected and apparently now abandoned two-state solu-tion for the Israeli-Palestinian conflict may not be put to better use at home. (Discussion will be in binary terms but there's no reason, if people wanted it, the nation couldn't break into multiple units, even dozens. Making big entities smaller ones, given the evident dangers of bigness and the concentration of power that it carries, would very likely have salutary effects not yet imagined.)

History makes clear that every political entity will tend toward domination by oligarchs of one flavor or another, or on occasion by conflict between oligarchs and the people they dominate. When the people achieve victory they even-tually become complacent, a condition not experienced by oligarchs, whose appetite for power and wealth is insa-tiable and indefatigable. So in time they resume control. Right-Landians accept this as the natural and preferred state of affairs. Other-Landians reject it, although even among them some are drawn to a sort of Oligarchy Lite, where the rich are still allowed to have more than they should but who haven't yet gone completely around the oligarchic bend. If the new nation of Other-Landia is to survive as a true alternative to Right-Landia, its citizens will have to accept the responsibilities of citizenship and put measures in place, and vigilantly monitor them, to control the inherently expansive proclivities of those afflicted by the wealth and power addictions.

The first step toward forming two new nation states should be national gatherings of self-selected Right- and Other-Landians for preparation of working documents that outline the fundamental values and vision of their future respective nations.

Next, a national plebiscite in which each of the fifty states and all cities or metropolitan areas with more than, say, a million inhabitants vote on their preferred future. Considering the division within some states, which mirrors that of the present nation, certain cities will vote to go in a different direction than the rest of their state; these will become outposts of their preferred new nation. For example, Atlanta or Seattle may become parts of Other-Landia while the remainder of Georgia and Washington join Right-Landia.

Once this is done, the proposed new nations will need to send representatives to a negotiation to determine, once the formal division occurs, how existing federal properties and responsibilities will be distributed, shared, reorganized, or abolished.

Obviously, this is a complex matter and will require a few years to finalize details. But the rewards will be worth it. No longer will Right-Landians have to endure taxes that don't support the security apparatus and instead are used to coddle slackers. After military security is amply provided for, citizens of Right-Landia can get on with the business of every man and woman for themselves. Further, after an initial election to choose it leaders, Right-Landia may decide to cancel all further elections and simply leave it to the ruling party to decide things. This is most consistent with the present political behavior of its likely future leaders and the intense desire for certainty and stability of their followers.

Other-Landia will go the way that has traditionally been identified with democracies and eschew authoritarianism and radical individualism. But it will have its own dilemmas. The rich and powerful will always be with us and can be expected to behave in their characteristic ways. Even those of them with leftward predispositions in certain areas may not be able to prevent themselves from seeking more than their fair share within the new political arrangement—which they will inevitably achieve unless their fellow citizens are more vigilant than citizens ordinarily are. In addition, whereas Other-Landians enjoy diversity and welcome refugees and immigrants, they will have to exert control over admission of disillusioned citizens of Right-Landia. Quotas and extreme vetting should help with this.

The complexities of moving forward with this proposal are considerable. Perhaps the most challenging will be the establishment of treaty-based relations between the new nations. There should be sufficient stability, trust, and respect between them—or at least a high enough wall—that each can achieve its new destiny separately and without fear of intrusion by the other. It might be that a few years under a United Nations protectorate would be necessary. But with sufficient good will and appreciation for the shared history that has finally come to closure, residents of both new countries may enjoy a peace that eluded them when they were one.

Update: I wrote "Two-State Solution" in early 2017 and it is now three years later. On November 12, 2018, an article appeared in *New York Magazine* entitled "Divided We Stand," by Sasha Issenberg. It started from the observation that "this arranged marriage [the United States] isn't really working anymore, is it?" Issenberg considered a few possible fixes, or at least ameliorations: interstate compacts, increased political localism, renewed emphasis on states' rights, new forms of federalism, and state secession movements on the model of "Calexit" and Brexit. Issenberg then asked, "If we are already living in two political geographies, why not generate a system of government to match?" He concluded his essay with an extended thought experiment on what a new form of American government might look like and how it would operate. His experimental model was a system of federations—Blue, Red, Neutral—with a much diminished government remaining in Washington, DC. He imagined a variety of scenarios and events covering a few decades, focused on the enormous difficulties of making the new arrangements work, and finished by throwing up his hands—too difficult to get from fantasy to reality, he felt sure.

Issenberg treated the question of dividing the country with seriousness, even if he ended in resignation to current realities and the hope/faith we will muddle through somehow. When I wrote three years ago, it was with tongue in cheek and frustration at the absurdity of where we have arrived as a sociopolitical entity—absurd from one perspective, perfectly coherent as seen from another. Now I think it time to approach our impasses with radical gravity. We must see our landing place for what it essentially is. Does it present irreconcilable differences for one nation to surmount in its present form? Most particularly as that nation faces, or more accurately, does not face, the apocalyptic eventuality of climate disruption? This question is based on the observation that as a fundamentally two-party political system, we no longer see a debate between Republican and Democratic ideas and policies. Instead, for three decades, more or less, the Republican Party has striven for one-party government, which necessarily would be autocratic government. As many have observed, the GOP is less like a normal, democratically committed political party and more like a radical cult.

Its decline into a desperate striving for autocratic control by what would almost certainly be oligarchic/plutocratic/kleptocratic forces is obvious in its swift obeisance before Donald Trump. It also has shrugged off legalities, Constitutional principles, democratic norms, national solidarity, truthfulness, and belief in universal suffrage, all of which rejections Trump embodies in totality. Republican leaders who, before Trump's election, spoke of him with contempt, now compete for the honor of acting as chief toady. The words "Republican," "integrity," and "honor" can no longer be spoken in the same breath with a straight face. Can anyone imagine that even a sweeping electoral victory by Democrats would alter the party when we remember its systematically obstructive actions from 2008 on, when it lost the presidency and both houses of Congress? Further, come hell or high water at least 40 percent of the country appears locked unquestioningly in its fevered embrace.

Still, as we intuitively know and as Issenberg tried to illustrate through his thought experiment, radical change would be very difficult. The only thing that might induce us to seriously consider radical options is to imagine the future *without* such change. A continuation of a status quo worsening by the day, while division deepens and the world-threatening challenges of anthropogenic climate disruption and Cold War–style nuclear weapon proliferation continue unabated, is not only intolerable but eventually lethal. So how might we get there from here?

I think it would be bracing, even sobering, to begin with the most radical prospect—a true severing of the country into two or maybe three or more units: Liberal, Republican (if it became traditionally Conservative, severing would be unnecessary), and Independent, for example. A relatively small assemblage (fewer than a hundred) of well-informed, responsible people representing views all along the spectrum of Liberal to Conservative could gather to consider the question, How can we partition the present United States so that the parts can once again function like mature polities, or at least have the preconditions for doing so? Their mandate would be to create a comprehensive document of severance and future relations for a vote by the citizenry. The point of this exercise would be to face head on what seems the only alternative to an increasingly fractured republic. Attendees might be chosen by groups such as the Niskanen Center, Public Citizen, and Common Cause—respected occupants of the "broad middle ground"—with one of the prerequisites being that no one holding office at any level of government would be invited. They would be people of unimpeachable integrity and patriotism. They might be given six months to work, with honoraria and expenses covered by a range of respected charitable foundations. Their mandate and authority would derive from a petition signed by every 501(c)(3) organization (including churches and civic groups) that supported the exercise, with no participation by economically or politically focused interest groups, for obvious reasons—their public-centeredness could never be assumed or established. To the extent possible, only individuals and groups with clear commitment to the well-being of all Americans should be affiliated with the effort.

I would expect people who fit this description would be skeptical about formally ending the United States as we have known it, but their good-faith effort to construct a plausible structural scenario would produce documents describing how it might be accomplished. The people would vote to do so in two plebiscites held a year apart to allow for thinking and rethinking about the ramifications. I assume something on the order of two or three federations of reasonably like-minded states and major urban areas would form the model, with a greatly attenuated federal government in Washington, DC left to manage the few areas requiring a national voice. But strict limitations on tenure of representatives (the Senate should probably disappear as an irrelevant relic of the nation's founding) and on lobbying would have to be in place to prevent the dominance of ideological and economic blocs such as have brought the nation to the condition now requiring this exercise in dissolution and re-formation.

I am not smart enough to know all of the areas that should be covered in the final document (called, perhaps, a Declaration of Renewal), but some would surely be: the role of the president in the shrunken federal government; shaping of systems both in Washington and the new federations that deny their executives the autonomous power to wreck things that we have seen over the last few years; legal relations among the new federated entities; the role and nature of courts and the appointment and tenure of judges; provision for universal voting under democratic safeguards. In summary, we would need attention to what has been learned about the strengths and vulnerabilities of the present Constitution and governmental structures in order to develop stabilizing replacements and protections against known fallibilities in human nature: tendencies toward authoritarianism and scapegoating, misuse of power, and uses of wealth for special interests that subvert the public interest.

The time has come, not just to strive to preserve national existence in one form or another but to preserve what makes collective existence valuable:

- The needs of every citizen receive equal consideration by a government of, by, and for the people.

- The people are motivated to fulfill their responsibilities as citizens.

- Egalitarianism, solidarity, and individualism would ensure that communities receive all the support they need to thrive.

- In contrast to our present system, the new one would value peace over militarism and economic arrangements that promote justice, restrain practices that elevate capital over communities, and that support societal well-being over wealth accumulation by a few. The present system relies on habit, fragmentation, and hope. It is not working.

Note from the future: It is now spring in 2021; we have had an election and are now over a year into a pandemic that has scythed through the country while the former President and his people worried about other things. There is nothing in any of this that leads me to question my thoughts about formally dividing the country into units in which each can operate with reasonable internal unity. Rather, the Republican response to losing the Presidency, to the pandemic, and to virtually all other issues of national interest only confirms our need for radical change. And since 47% of the electorate believed we actually need more time for Trump to practice his skills at corrupting a country for his own benefit, we should act in haste.

CHAPTER 16

THE SHUNNING OF AMERICA

ON 1 JUNE 2017, THE president of the United States announced his intention to withdraw from the 2015 Paris Climate Accord, leaving the U.S. the only officially nonparticipating country on Earth. He claimed that "The Paris accord will undermine (the U.S.) economy," and "puts (the U.S.) at a permanent disadvantage." During the presidential campaign, he had said that "...a withdrawal would help American businesses and workers..." "Trump stated that the withdrawal would be in accordance with his America First policy." (https://en.wikipedia.org/wiki/United States_withdrawal_from_the_Paris_Agreement)

Trump's rationalizations were transparently and flagrantly false and/or misguided. They merely gave the appearance of a rationally based decision while he acted out his oft-stated denials of the reality of climate change. Their objective flimsiness did not concern him, reality being optional in his strange world. What mattered to Donald Trump and the Republican Party was the simple desire to enable their patrons' unrestrained pursuit of wealth, with a hidden admixture of fear-based denial at the prospect the real world might finally burst the balloons of their duplicities, with a dose as well of refusal to imagine any problem that necessitated large scale, publicly oriented, government intervention. Their respective desires probably differed in certain respects but mostly overlapped. For Trump, pleasure and potency appear to reside in the wielding of power, and its purpose is secondary.[1] The overlap comes in their shared enthrallment to moneyed interests and to money itself, and their hatred of anything that would stand in the way— such as a healthy democratic government led by people committed to the public good. In the case of anthropogenic climate disruption (ACD), only governments could respond adequately to a threat of such magnitude and complexity. However, since it is part of extreme Republican orthodoxy that government is bad and a threat to "liberty," then no government efforts of this sort, especially successful ones, can be countenanced, regardless of the benefits to the common good. Since their capacity to deny reality and to confabulate displays itself at every turn, the disaster lurking out of immediate sight in climate change has been easily subsumed into their program and neutered.

This leaves the rest of the world facing a double challenge: First, how to prevent accelerating ACD from reaching the point where efforts to forestall it become moot, when climate disruption reaches tipping points where the Earth takes charge and drives itself over a cliff, insofar as existing life is concerned. Beyond that lies a sixth great extinction and a gravely damaged, inhospitable planet. Earth may be not altogether dissimilar to the first five extinctions, except that one species will have blindly chosen to suffer unimaginable disasters and possibly its own near extinction. Having been self-induced there is no tragedy in that, except for the nonhuman spheres of life. It will be an ironic *reap what you sow*, nicely and also biblically put as *sow the wind and reap the whirlwind*, which may be more apropos given intensified storms. Those who cause a problem and refuse to reform and fix it deserve to suffer

---

1. I don't read Trump's mind; I only interpret his psychological type and personal history. It seems clear that he lacks interest in the responsibilities of the presidency, only its perks.

the consequences. A chosen fate and the loss of so many innocents—the plants, animals, and other life, as well as those humans who took it seriously and resisted—portend grief that will circle the globe.

The second challenge is to answer a question: If the country most responsible for fostering this crisis refuses to help solve it, should all nations and peoples who are left to face it themselves agree to officially *shun* the United States? There is precedent for the practice among traditional cultures and even some religious groups. Seemingly incorrigible members of the community who are destructive of its values are, to varying degrees, ostracized. The situation regarding the United States is more complex and dire, since it involves an entire country. This one country, containing barely 5 percent of world population, is surely responsible for far more than its proportional share of the world's international problems, not merely for setting the stage for climate disasters. We also can throw in its militarism and wars of aggression; self-entitled, habitual intrusion into the affairs of other countries; and resource depletion. Just as egregious as these sins of commission is its failure also to use its wealth and power for humane purposes that could alleviate (rather than cause) great suffering, along with its refusal to roll back the dangers of nuclear holocaust and present a model of peaceful, democratic, and respectful relations that others might emulate and that could at last accurately express in real terms the presently delusional self-image that the United States tries to foster.

The reason to suggest shunning the United States is that it would be a dramatic expression of the seriousness with which the rest of the world apprehends the threats to the only Earth we have—and a damned good one it has been! It would say, "You have chosen neither to lead nor to collaborate, so get out of the way and, as you must eventually, you can follow." Delusion may yield to reality even if initially piecemeal, but who knows in this country.

Let me offer a couple of observations before we discuss what shunning would entail. First, it would be grave error to assume that in January 2021, when Trump is gone, the United States will automatically resume the more normal patterns of the ante-Trump period. Leaving aside that those patterns were none too good anyway, all things considered, remember that upwards of 40 percent of the electorate continued to "approve his performance" through bilgewater and bile, larceny, lust, and lying and 47 percent voted to keep him president.[2] He is only a garish avatar of what the Republican Party, its wealthy sponsors, and a variety of white nationalist groups have shamelessly pursued for forty years or better. The United States is a seriously fractured, troubled nation that could as easily as not swing toward infusing our present de facto oligarchic control with the elixir of full-blown autocracy. Prudence says, Be prepared for the worst until such time, if it occurs, when the Republican Party either transforms or is itself shunned while new forms of conservatism and truly democratic governance are born.

Second, as is clear, the Paris Climate Accord itself is too little and maybe too late. Apparently virtually no nation is meeting its less-than-bold aims anyway. But one hopes it can be a foundation. And as the evidence of increasingly traumatic prospects for normal Earth functions steadily accumulates, sane leaders, or at least leaders pushed by sane citizens, might be expected to act with the urgency the situation requires. One also hopes that if humanity survives more or less intact, even with many of the world's great cities largely or partially inundated and other areas parched beyond recognition and perhaps abandoned, that the people who remain will recognize how foolhardy it was to entrust so much leadership authority and control to wealthy corporations and the

---

2. To paraphrase H. L. Mencken, "Nobody ever went broke underestimating the intelligence of the American public."

U.S. oligarchy, who are preoccupied with and fully dedicated to their personal interests only. Their subversion of
truth and the political process, aided by citizen complacency and politician fecklessness and corruption, is where
one would start assigning blame. Surely not everyone is
ignorant; rather, they have consciously chosen to pursue
their own immediate good over the more remote good
of their children.

What might shunning America entail? It should begin
by stating bluntly *why*: the nature and degree of perils—the
certainties, the probabilities, and the fearsome possibilities—and what their eventuation will mean. Crisis times
demand crisis solutions; if massive socioeconomic and
political change do not occur soon, then not much else will
matter. Wake up, America!

What if the undeluded world halted all commercial
interchange with the United States? Since the U.S. is a
net importer this would hurt foreign exporters dispro-
portionately, but America would feel pain nonetheless at
the disruptions and shortages. Additionally, other countries whose leaders were prone to similar denial would be
less likely to emulate American irresponsibility; a shamed
nation is not a worthy model. And besides the shunning
per se, reduced trade between the United States and the
rest of the world would contribute to reduced fossil-fuel
use and encourage local and regional responses to citizen
needs, all of which are essential anyway for the swiftly
effective change that has become imperative. Last, the
sui generis event of shunning a nation, especially one so
powerful and arrogant, would demonstrate, as nothing
else could, just how serious the rest of the world is about
preserving a reasonably healthy Earth.

Perhaps large parts of the undeluded world would
recognize that the climate crisis is an opportunity to reconsider their material aspirations and habits, along with
industrialism itself.

They could develop low-impact, low-energy-input, more skillful, local, simple, community-oriented means of production and distribution. Considering the world conditions that industrialization, technophilia, and the redefinition of citizens as merely consumers and workers have brought, and the injustices shot through all this, the prospect of reconceptualizing good lives and societies in smaller scale, more self-reliant, and locally controlled terms has to be appealing. (In short, self-preservation can be fruitful across many dimensions.) Along with that, focusing communities and economies on happiness (in the eudaemonic sense) and satisfaction of genuine rather than contrived needs helps to present radical change as positive in its own right.

At the same time, such changes would dramatically lower greenhouse gas effusions and dramatically raise chances of preserving this good Earth and the life prospects of all its inhabitants, human and nonhuman. Wide-ranging intellectual and policy-making energy is already focusing on these prospects. For a small sample begin with www. thenextsystem.org, www.postcarbon.org, and Naomi Klein's *This Changes Everything* (along with shelves full of related books). Common themes include economic democracy, alternatives to neoliberalism and industrialism, rejection of consumerism, more equitable economic and social arrangements that foster everyone's prospects for realizing their capabilities, and transcending the ceaseless-growth orientation of world economic systems. In Klein's words: "This is a vision of the future that goes beyond just surviving or enduring climate change, beyond 'mitigating' and 'adapting' to it in the grim language of the United Nations. It is a vision in which we collectively use the crisis to leap somewhere that seems, frankly, better than where we are right now."[3]

---

3. Naomi Klein, *This Changes Everything: Capitalism vs. the Climate* (New York: Simon & Schuster, 2015), p. 7.

A second form of shunning would involve cessation of diplomatic relations and closing of embassies. The only official communication between the United States and the rest of the world would occur under UN auspices—not in the Security Council, where it enjoys excessive power, but with a representative ad hoc group in which conversations about the future would occur. A second group should be formed to help plan, coordinate, and enforce world reductions of fossil fuel use of sufficient stringency to achieve as close as possible a maximum temperature increase of 1.5° C., taking into account the U.S. continuation of its profligate, irresponsible, and possibly suicidal ways. A third group would be a center for ideas and assistance in creating what Ivan Illich called "convivial societies"—that is, societies whose goal is to set the table for enriching forms of human relatedness: to one another, to Nature, and to their god and/or their highest values, and in which economies are formed to serve such relatedness rather than to disregard such sentiments and to exclude and dominate other needs and aspirations.

It would be wildly optimistic to imagine shunning, transformation of the rest of the world into an effective force to prevent runaway climate scenarios, and rejuvenation of individual nations as a smooth process. It also would be naive to imagine that most of the rest of the world is ready, even in the face of climate cataclysm, to move in the directions suggested—not yet anyway. Change is hard and major change harder, even with disaster on the horizon. Natural human denial mechanisms arise, along with ruling-class resistance. But time is short and the goals large.

Two factors would help move things forward, one inexorable and the other a matter of choice and ingenuity. The first comes in the form of dramatically destructive weather-related events that are increasing in number and intensity and that will not abate. We must reject the silly pro forma exercises that typically follow each event in which we earnestly wonder if this flood or that wildfire or hurricane was caused by climate change. The question is anachronistic and irrelevant. In fact, the climate has changed and continues to change and weather expresses it in a variety of ways and degrees. That is the new context as predicted weather events become more extreme. As flood, fire, and famine, wind, drought, and climate refugees sweep into one's neighborhood, denial becomes less persuasive.[4]

The area of choice involves people's readiness, versatility, resilience, and creativity in devising locally appropriate new economies and communities. The reciprocal of shunning will be the emergence of convivial communities that intrinsically abate climate change and provide models to encourage others toward more satisfying forms of relatedness. And if all else fails and Earth's processes and feedback mechanisms drive us inexorably toward disaster, then such communities will provide the best imaginable forms of mutual support and coping. Whatever the outcome, we have reached a climate point where William James's "moral equivalent of war" aptly suggests what is required.

One might ask: Isn't it possible to preserve present international relations and economies while making adjustments here and there that will turn the climate apocalypse around? Is such extensive socioeconomic change really necessary?

A first response is to ask why we'd want to preserve the current economic system. Its chief claim to fame is dynamism in the generation of wealth and stuff to buy. But its monetary benefits (and the power that travels with them) mostly accrue to a few at the top, giving them influence far beyond their desert or wisdom. Nor are they able to recognize the realities of why they received while others

---

4. Speaking of refugees and their impacts, consider the numbers that have flowed into Europe over recent years as a result of wars and observe the tumultuous effects their arrival has had. Then picture them doubling, tripling, quadrupling, or more. Donald Trump's infamous and fatuous wall would not stem the tide, even if he stood atop it raving.

did not and to share appropriately. Corporations, governments, and institutions of all sorts are corrupted by this system; the Earth is suicidally ravaged and reeling; wars are commonplace; the majority of humans are pushed into the simplism of compliant worker/exuberant consumer roles and have virtually no control over the conditions of their work; and billions at the bottom still hang on by a thread. Is a new, overpriced iPhone and all that it represents really worth all this?[5]

Another reason to doubt that the present system will reform and do what's necessary—It has had forty-plus years to act, the cumulative weight of the facts is indubitable, and it has failed, the United States being only the worst and most shameful example of this. Neoliberal capitalism, the dominant economic system, is to all appearances intrinsically life denying—not surprising, since its most intense focus is on lifeless objects. It is almost as if it just can't help itself. Or, from a slightly different perspective, I wonder if its rulers imagine their wealth will shield them against even cataclysmic possibilities, while those without wealth, largely out of sight and mind, will just have to make do as best they can. Not exactly a laudable or honorable attitude, but plausible.

For a third response to the question, let's consider the fact that crisis opens possibilities for better forms of life and community. In confronting ACD we can, if we choose, simultaneously face down the challenge in radical but known ways and, as mentioned above, use this disruptive period for cultural self-examination and renewal. We can rediscover the true elements of good lives in good communities: fewer (but higher-order) needs and desires; less consumption; more local reliance; more relations of respect and care with our fellows, animals, and Nature;

---

5. This is not to say that no good has come from new knowledge, science, and technology; only that on balance, all things considered, the Earth and its progeny as a whole may suffer more than they benefit.

and other dimensions of whole and meaningful lives. An opportunity to strive against and avoid disaster would be a terrible thing to waste.

Of course, most of this essay is on the order of a thought experiment intended to provoke. Over the coming decades, our known world is going to break apart in ways predictable and unpredictable but possible and catastrophic. The relative lack of seriousness in responding says something profound about our species, and it is not positive. We might look at it as a great learning experience if the stakes were not so high.

I will close with an extension of the thought experiment. Suppose that enough people and nations wise up and act, and we avoid the worst prospects through changes like those described: fossil fuel emissions and emitters are driven into submission; the world's average temperature increase shudders to a halt before Earth reaches the point of no return; societies make major changes in their old ways that promise climate predictability, more moderate resource uses, and the subordination of the economy to cultural service rather than dominance. Economic growth is no longer the highest priority. What next?

When people once again feel secure, some will be prone to relapse. For many, industrialism is a kind of addiction that brings the money, the power, the mastery of all they behold (even though it is an oppression to others and to the natural world). Can they mature and still be economic actors without craving those highs? Can they operate within strict limits and for the public good (a superior kind of high)? Who knows? Some might retire from the calculator and the corner suite and become poets or social workers.

New forms of community with new sets of values and richer, higher types of relatedness would raise the general level of human decency and satisfaction and make for more care, security and stability. Community members would experience a wholeness and embeddedness that industrialized culture made tenuous at best. But humans are always vulnerable to egoism and the siren songs of self-aggrandizement, power over others and, to borrow a notion, the Seven Deadly Sins. Even if fossil fuels are mostly replaced and emissions of all greenhouse gases rigidly controlled—if in other words the particular dangers of ACD are safely remedied—some humans, being human, will find new or old but refurbished ways to pour sand into the gears of their and our lives. Communities will be challenged to deal with deviants and malefactors whose behavior seriously disrupts and violates community standards but not to repeat the alienating, punitive, scapegoating carceral practices of the industrial period, when life was so cheap.

It seems to me that the present crisis offers a unique chance for humanity to move up developmentally, to mature as a species and create better, though always far from perfect (whatever that would be), ways of life. Ways in which we better understand who and what we are, what we need, the ways we seriously err, and where we are and what we owe in return for being here. It offers a chance for the body-mind union that is us to become more *soulful*, a movement helped along by the awareness of how close to disaster its previous incarnations brought us.

Addendum: A few months after I finished this article, I chanced on something similar, though satirical, by John Feffer.[6] Feffer posits that the world threatens to sanction the United States after a long series of events, culminating in a UN declaration that the United States is "a rogue nation." The immediate precipitant is the continued Amer-

6. John Feffer, "World Gives America One Year to Stop Trump or Face Sanctions." Foreign Policy in Focus, April 10, 2019. https://fpif.org/world-gives-america-one-year-to-stop-trump-or-face-sanctions/

ican belligerence toward the International Criminal Court, which it had declined to join while threatening to arrest and prosecute ICC officials looking into possible U.S. war crimes in Afghanistan. Chief among international demands was that American leadership would have to be removed, preferably after arrest, trial, conviction and sentencing to community service picking up litter along major highways dressed in convict garb.

Behind the satire in this article is a recognition that American posturing, its self-justificatory lies, and the enormous damage to the world and the nation have reached a level that has been exposed by the transparent buffoonery of the Trump administration—reinforced by Republican acquiescence that had its autocratic seeds planted several decades earlier—a level that can no longer be disguised. The United States is a country run by and for its ruling class, whose self-absorbed greed has cut it loose from its moorings in the nation and its people. This momentum has combined with the much older but similarly motivated and self-absorbed aspiration to force the world to operate according to American dictates, in essence a form of colonialism. We have become a third-rate country with a first-rate military (based on expenditures, not effectiveness) but where close to 90 percent of its citizens live at or near hand-to-mouth status, or for some who do better, paycheck-to-paycheck.

I think that for many of us the recognition that, even in the extremity promised by ever-worsening anthropogenic climate disruption, an extremity in which billions of people will probably die and the world's beautiful and crucial biodiversity is being impoverished by industrial and wealth-oriented imperatives...even with this our rulers remain paralyzed in their self-centeredness. The circus rolls on, but having reached its grotesque epitome in Donald Trump, the big top is lifting to expose the shams at its heart.

Note (from 2021): Now that time has passed and taken Trump from the White House with it, it might be thought this essay has passed its "use by" date, but Feffer's satire points to a larger and longer historical picture of U.S. actions internationally that lead one to wonder about our place in the world order. For example, since WWII we have, according to Wikipedia, refused to ratify over forty treaties, many with wide support and clear value world-wide such as the Comprehensive Test Ban Treaty, the Convention on Cluster Munitions, and the Convention on the Rights of the Child. Even though we often sign these we refuse to ratify, although we tend to comply in nonenforceable ways. Opponents typically wave a banner of "sovereignty" to justify their actions but it is hard to see it as anything more than arrogance and refusal to participate in appropriate ways as a member of a world community. Which raises the question: American leaders often speak of the world's presumed need for "American leadership" on this or that matter—Does the world not grow weary of hearing this assertion and is it not more needful of our participation as one among equals working on shared concerns?

CHAPTER 17

HOW NOT TO BUILD A GOOD SOCIETY

FIRST, YOU'LL WANT TO DISREGARD human nature, chiefly those aspects of our nature that point toward fundamental and perhaps universal needs ranging from soup to soul. All living organisms seek to meet their distinctive needs. For example, the mountain lion, *Puma concolor*, depends on successfully hunting other mammals for its diet. Males cover a wide range, protect their territory from other males, and live solitarily except when it's time to mate. Interfere in any of this and you will have a disturbed mountain lion. *Homo sapiens*, too, has a genetically shaped nature and seeks appropriate need fulfillments based on what its nature calls for as well as on what its experience and capacities lead it to seek or avoid. Interrupting fulfillment of essential needs frustrates human development and life satisfactions. When community solidarity is thwarted, when basic security is structurally threatened by economic assumptions and practices, when opportunities for self-development and self-expression are impeded, when social supports are inadequate or missing, elevated levels of anxiety, stress, and social pathology will result.[1]

---

1. Most groups would not deliberately build an inferior society for themselves. However, sometimes groups will allow into leadership positions people who have generally managed to exempt them-

In lieu of genuine fulfillment of essential needs (the most important of which will be discussed below), it helps to provide substitutes if you're in control and want to preserve stability. These beliefs and gratifications don't satisfy real needs but are just good enough to give the appearance of doing so, thus holding people's attention or keeping them distracted. It is also useful to keep people busy at earning their living and dependent on less than generous remuneration. Low wages will draw people into debt to meet medical, educational, and other expenses. They will experience high stress, along with anxiety about losing their jobs and being unable to meet material needs and burdens of debt. This strategy encourages a cooperative, compliant attitude and keeps wages from getting out of hand, which would be quite aversive to those in charge.

People should be led to know that they are separate individuals, mostly alone in this world and reliant solely on their own efforts for sinking or swimming. This concept will be called individualism and given a positive façade but is actually more like atomism or separatism. Rather than seeing this atomism as a misinterpretation of their true nature, or an unfortunate aspect of present reality, or maybe even a lie—all of which are remediable—they will learn that it is actually the one true road to self-realization: the more they live and thrive, or at least survive, autonomously—the more they will recognize these very uncertainties spur their efforts and ambitions, thus contributing toward a better world for all.

selves from reliance on any particular society's norms. Such people have convinced themselves that the free-wheeling marketplace and individual self-sufficiency are ultimately in the best interests of everyone. They readily find it acceptable to override or ignore what others might regard as the general welfare for their (suitably disguised) private interests. Pulling this off requires undemocratic and deceptive means, but for those with resources, perseverance, and self-centeredness sufficient to the task, it is quite doable, as history and clear-eyed perception of the present make manifest.

Members must also understand that the presence of a small number of wealthy people at the fiscal summit of their society, who manage to harvest income and accumulate wealth at astonishing levels, is merely a sign of how good things can become for them too when they manage to become as capable and hard working as the rich. Not only that, but fabulous wealth in the hands of a few is good for those with little or no wealth because it shows that the economy is working as it should (as God intends it, perhaps), that it is dynamic and growing for everyone's ultimate benefit. Furthermore, the rich create jobs that put poorer people to work and stand serenely by as exemplars when those on the lower rungs begin to lose their grip and need inspiration to keep going.

When their essential needs are not met, organisms, including human ones, do not flourish. Many people become depressed and others actively dysfunctional, turning to drugs, alcohol, or violence to allay pain and relieve pent-up anger and frustration. People tend to accept explanations for their unhappiness that emphasize the nefarious acts of various *others* (not, to be sure, actually culpable others), acts that have deprived them of presumed rights, endangered them in some manner even if ill-defined, or victimized them as they have innocently gone about the business of being responsible citizens whose virtues are unseen and unappreciated. These scapegoats are vital for shifting attention from the real causes of distress and can provide outlets for venting and blaming. It is helpful to have means of penalizing these *others*, marginalizing them, and questioning their character, motivations, and behavior.

Lastly, to sustain just-good-enough societies, leadership steadfastly must foster and validate all of the above distractions and misdirections. They must let people know that the leaders are on their side and working diligently to right any wrongs. Since they tend not to identify the right wrongs, solutions never solve anything. However, the efforts may help expose subversive elements who, in league with the *others*, are said to be sabotaging the good citizens in some fashion and so need additional condemnation. Leaders typically are committed to protecting the privileges of the rich and powerful, the ruling class to which they themselves covertly aspire if they don't already belong. They apply their most serious diligence to promoting that class's interests while keeping the masses focused on scapegoats, the effectiveness of which is a key sign of leadership success.[2]

Eventually this system gets creaky and less effective. The leaders must magnify the distractions and perfidies of the *others*. They also must promote the need for concentrating power in themselves as the best way to finally ensure loyal citizens' protection and tranquility. Expanding the putative population of *others* and the dangers they represent justifies the authoritarian moves and citizen identification with the "strong man" excites and tranquilizes at the same time.

Those who have other aspirations, who still believe in the possibility of creating societies that serve the needs of all their members, face an uphill struggle. Considerable effort and vast amounts of money have gone into indoctrinating citizens into accepting the ideas described above. Through methodical legerdemain said citizens have come to believe that what is factually a just-good-enough society is in reality just the opposite—a very good, even exceptional, society, or at least the best possible given the obstacles. It fosters freedom, prosperity, and up-by-the-bootstraps ingenuity. Any effort to disturb its benign rhythms would be destructive to its arcane but beneficent functioning. So the story goes.

---

2. "Ruling class" may sound dissonant, since citizens have been taught that theirs is a classless society. If there are, technically, classes, they are natural and benign. Also, in a putative democracy a ruling class would not exist, so the term is disfavored except by certain *others*.

What *are* the essential needs mentioned above as fundamental aspects of human nature? I will mention only three categories: (1) basic needs for security and stability, such as adequate nutrition, decent housing, good education and health care, along with useful work fairly compensated; (2) the need for a caring community and trusting relationships within which realization of individual potential, along with fulfillment of reciprocal communitarian responsibilities, can thrive; and (3) higher-order needs for self-expression, meaning, beauty, love, and spiritual seeking.

I will refer to the first need in shorthand as the need for a Secure Foundation. The ruling-class story laid out at the beginning denies that it is society's role to ensure a Secure Foundation for its members. After all, those of their class already have one that they are sure they have earned and to which they are entitled. But research in psychology and sociology, history and neuroscience, along with reflection on one's own personal experience and observation of the experience of others who live in diverse situations all around us—all of this decisively refutes ruling-class rationalizations. Poverty does not build character, although some who are especially lucky or talented are able to surmount and learn from it. Children who are chronically hungry and sick do not typically flourish as students or in any other way. Disorder and anxiety are contraindicated if one values confidence and security in the psyches of the young (and eventually old). Jobs that are erratic, dangerous, disrespected, and poorly paid rarely contribute toward outstanding citizenship and self-advancement. Surely the need for Secure Foundations does not need to be explained and defended. And yet, in the just-good-enough society that is modern America, the lack of Secure Foundations is largely disregarded by the ruling class. Large numbers of people in all classes have learned contempt for the supposedly undeserving poor. Generation after generation repeats the cycle, whether rulers, ruled, or mere observers.

Do these words mean anything?

We hold these Truths to be self-evident, that all Men are created equal, that they are endowed by their Creator with certain unalienable Rights, that among these are Life, Liberty, and the pursuit of Happiness.— That to secure these Rights, Governments are instituted among Men, deriving their just powers from the consent of the governed.

Operationally, no, they mean nothing. This is not surprising, since they are declarations in support of Secure Foundations: what, for example, does liberty mean without a Foundation that enables one to enjoy its benefits? In a functioning democracy, if the unprivileged masses became fully aware of the false premises under which they labor, they would demand Secure Foundations. They love their children and want good lives for themselves, and they know on some level that stable lives and homes are not built on sand. Thus a rich society would be guided toward becoming also a good society.

I will refer to the second need category as Individual-in-Society (IS). In America this is a fraught area. Caring communities have certainly existed, and their lucky residents have enjoyed the benefits. But apparently they are more mythology than reality much of the time. Egalitarianism and well-distributed opportunity have actually thrived during some eras. The post–World War II period, for thirty years or so, was such an era. Small towns and city neighborhoods are objects of considerable nostalgia for many; it would not be fair to deny their occasional existence and comity. But the good that American communities have done has had serious limitations, principally of two kinds. First is the matter of inclusivity—black people and brown people; immigrants; Native Americans; women; and people who broke the norms of sexual orientation, gender iden-tification, or religious conviction—all have had and many continue to have serious difficulties with full acceptance and often even surviving violence aimed at them. As we see today, inclusion and acceptance remain a long way from where they would be in a good society.

Another limitation shows itself when aspects of insti-tutionalized communitarianism are proposed. I doubt that any legislative effort to ensure Secure Foundations for all citizens has not been fought mightily by those preaching the doctrine of atomistic individualism. The Social Progress Index illustrates how effective the atomists have been.[3] Although the richest country of all, the United States falls into the second tier of countries (twentieth from the top) as measured by provision for its citizens' well-being. It is surely no coincidence that the United States has also fallen out of the "full democracy" category into "flawed democracy" in the annual study by *The Economist* magazine.[4] Both Social Security and Medicare still, after all these years, face regu-lar political threat from right-wingers who seem unable to get comfortable with the idea that reduced suffering and enhanced security for the elderly does not threaten the nation's soul. The situation is similar with public educa-tion and support for the welfare of younger folk who find themselves poor and hungry. As mentioned above, every-one except members of the ruling class and their families is supposed to benefit from the stimulus and motivation provided by anxiety and privation—such is the implica-tion of opposition doctrine. So is the implicit assumption that adequate health care for anyone who can't afford it is sure to damage character even while mending bodies; this conviction presumably arises from the same insights into the risks to a nation striving to provide for its citizens'

3. www.socialprogressindex.com
4. "Global Democracy Has Another Bad Year." *The Economist*, January 22, 2020. https://www.economist.com/graphic-detail/2020/01/22/global-democracy-has-another-bad-year

well-being—that we would all become flaccid takers rather than tumescent makers (the contradicting experience of Scandinavians, Western Europeans, the upper class itself, and many others notwithstanding).

The third category of needs based in human nature, those of a higher order (called "being" needs in Abraham Maslow's hierarchy), depends for its fulfillment to a large extent on meeting the first two categories, for obvious reasons. Although a few people deliberately choose lives of poverty and seclusion as a route to spiritual growth, such choices are unusual and voluntary and hardly apply to the general populace. In truth, it does not appear to me that more than a relatively small proportion of Americans strive for or achieve the *goods* of this higher realm: meaning, fulfillment, comprehensively loving relations with Nature and other humans, and a vocational or other calling along with the spiritual engagement that imbues all of these. My pessimism here is based on personal impression and supported by various measures of national well-being such as the UN's annual World Happiness Report, on whose scale the United States has fallen.[5] And why wouldn't it when so many of our fellow citizens have trouble meeting both basic survival needs and those associated with participation in caring community?

These limitations suggest a population that in significant ways lives as fragmented beings within a deeply materialistic society whose prevailing ethos declares that we are responsible only for ourselves. Those who do poorly must shoulder all the blame, just as those who do well deserve all the credit. It implies that we are all equally endowed with abilities, rise to adulthood from equally propitious circumstances, and operate with utterly free will. All resulting inequalities are the natural consequence of individual virtues and vices. Of course this flies in the

---

5. World Happiness Report, https://worldhappiness.report/ed/2020/social-environments-for-world-happiness/#fn2

face of everything known about human nature and human experience and is contrary to most ethical and religious principles, but self-serving dogma among winners has amazing survivability. Unfortunately, losers often do not.

CHAPTER 18

RATIONAL PESSIMISM

I SOMETIMES WONDER HOW MUCH sustained *goodness* we humans are capable of—in any of its forms and expressions so long as they draw us to hitch to them knowingly and enduringly.[1] Since it is a general principle that *ought* implies *can*, my perplexity aims toward understanding what we should expect of ourselves and each other, and in a larger sense, what a community or society might realistically strive toward among its members, both of these based on our best understanding of human capacities.

The opposite question holds less interest, not because depravity, the various forms of moral failure, or simple *not goodness*, do not raise their own questions. We are good at *bad* in all of its expressions and appear to have been highly skilled at it since settling into incipient civilizations, if not earlier. We have bad covered from stem to stern, it often seems. Bad seems easier, as if through inattention, desire, or self-deception we might slip into it almost unconsciously, whereas goodness is more demanding. Even so, we should sometime explore how much bad can be controlled or expunged in the same light as we here consider the sustainment of good.[2]

---

1. One can wonder as well how much truth, or reality, we can manage to incorporate. We might be shocked at how much we omit, how little we make do with, but one thing at a time for now.
2. I do not hold with Hannah Arendt's notion that evil is banal,

The majority of people, it seems to me, spend most of their time in a sort of middling state between the end points, not notably bad or good, just getting along, living for whatever reasons present themselves moment to moment and day to day, eventually drifting off into nonexistence—not for lack of moral challenges but perhaps out of insouciance or complacency, lack of attention.

Sustained goodness may be the hardest challenge we face, when we face it. Not that there aren't myriad occasions where people act in remarkably virtuous ways: treating the sick and injured under dangerous conditions; sacrificing for families and communities; confronting ignorance, bigotry, tyranny, and militarism at risk to themselves; and so on. But these instances tend to be haphazard, lacking context in a larger, inclusive, and explicit vision of the good, either for the doers or the recipients of their good works. Where is there a focus on goodness on the scale of, say, commerce or war? Goodness that receives equal attention and energy and societal resources? Goodness that is taken as seriously and embraced as intentionally—that is, tracked as breathlessly—as GDP? The work of many nongovernmental organizations (NGOs) might qualify, as would various governments' social welfare programs.[3]

A couple of years ago I sat in my dentist's waiting room and saw something rarely encountered in such places: a magazine of current vintage. The cover story caught my attention. It was the January 15, 2018 edition of *Time* magazine and had the smiling handsome face of a five-year-old Ethiopian boy on the cover, a survivor of a formerly high but now shrinking infant and child mortality rate.

---

although the evildoer may often be, but I do wonder: Is evil more energetic, more driven, than goodness?

3. The United States has only pallid versions of programs common in other developed countries, and they lack a place within an explicit contextual vision. Two of the primary U.S. government versions of providing a shared good, Social Security and Medicare/Medicaid, are regularly eyeballed by a certain variety of today's conservatives much in the manner of a pathologist seeking to expunge pathogens.

He symbolized one of the reasons for the theme of this issue, "The Optimists," which was edited by Bill Gates and included a host of well-known contributors (e.g., Warren Buffett, Trevor Noah, Bono). My first thought was that the jury for the thematic state of mind might be biased and the dice loaded—the affluent and successful may find optimism easier to achieve under most circumstances than the rest of us. Money does not buy happiness, but it probably makes it easier to be optimistic about one's prospects. Why were no hotel housekeepers, fast-food workers, or recent military veterans invited to contribute?

Those who were included spoke about their personal commitments and interests, which were all genuinely laudable. But I wanted to know the source of their upbeat judgment about the bigger picture, one which these days I find difficult to share. There were about twenty pages of positivity and a similar number of contributors. I acknowledge that they did not deny, their optimism notwithstanding, that dark shadows still lurk. And it wasn't always clear in the reports how much of what they feel is more akin to hopefulness than optimism, which are quite different attitudes. Nor to what extent they may share the late John Lewis's comment: "You have to be optimistic. If not, you will get lost in despair." That sounds to me more desperate than optimistic, but you be the judge.

Here is a synoptic excursion through their thinking. Many of the stories relied on data, since many objectively measurable improvements have occurred around the world, as in children's health, extreme poverty rates, human rights, and educational attainment. To the surprise, I am sure, of most other contemporary observers, Warren Buffett announced that "most American children are going to live far better than their parents did" and that "large gains in the living standards of Americans will continue for many generations to come." Although I respect Buffett for usually breaking the plutocratic mold as to lifestyle and personal authenticity, this seems more delusional than optimistic as a fact-based observation of at least half of American households. There is a similar disjunction in his observation that today only two percent of workers are needed to produce agricultural products, whereas the figure was once eighty percent. I recall that a few decades ago this was considered a victory. It is not so much today, in light of small farms' replacement by "agribusiness," with its large-scale, industrial, high-energy and chemical inputs; eroded and sterilized monocultural farmscapes; and lost values and lifeways of small-scale farming and the communities that served it. Still, Buffett realizes that mushrooming economic inequality is a growing problem; he is optimistic we will ameliorate it, but does not say how or when. It would have been most interesting to learn his thoughts about this situation, since economic inequality is a primary saboteur of the optimism that would flow within a society of sharing and caring based on fairer distribution of its resources.

Last, I couldn't help noticing his blasé attitude about the disrupted lives and careers that have resulted from America's heedless rush toward ever more wealth (a view seemingly shared by Bill Gates as he discusses the effects of AI on people's jobs). If more workers had anticipated the coming upheavals, they might have opposed change. This might have, in Buffett's words, "doomed innovation," which apparently would have been a tragedy of operatic proportions. Since America does almost nothing to soften the blows to the millions who are often innovated into unemployment and eventually lower wages, it seems to me that these human effects of economic "progress" deserve more weight in these equations. Nor would it hurt to ask about the benefits and beneficiaries of innovation, maybe even what innovation really amounts to in the scale of human welfare, and why it is lauded so uncritically.

Next, Laurene Jobs manages optimism toward immigration, even under Trumpian assault, and seems sure that *e pluribus unum* will eventually return to the land. Trevor Noah, speaking on behalf of millennials, is optimistic that the world is getting better "because we have access to information on how bad the world actually is" (a plausible irony and surely a necessary beginning). He is sure that energetic, optimistic millennials like him will use this information "to create change." Malala Yousafzai is committed to girls' education in places where it is generally frowned on. She sees change happening, but her optimism is paired with a plea: "We must invest in girls today," which suggests a large component of wan hope as yet unfulfilled more than genuine optimism.

Lili Cheng is optimistic about what AI will offer and believes it will be "profoundly transformational," which it no doubt will be, just as the innovations Buffett cited were and with similar effect. Samantha Budd Haeberlein is on track toward a cure for Alzheimer's disease with an optimism "rooted in the science." Steven Pinker looks on "The Bright Side," as does Bill Gates, who announces "The Good News": the data tell them that every day in every way, almost, the world gets better and better. Many of us, he says, don't see that, owing to "irrational pessimism." (It seems that with his most recent writing, Pinker may have achieved the status of the publishing and academic world's most optimistic man.)

And so on. These people and others in the magazine see a glass half full and heading up toward the brim. They believe in progress. And it would be unfair, even wrong, to deny that within their spheres of attention there are good things to see. Even today's world is not unrelievedly grim. But I can't help noticing, as mentioned, that much of what's called optimism is really only hopefulness, and that the signs of betterment are generally technological, material, and quantitative—as if those kinds of change equated with true human progress. Certainly, more girls educated and more diseases treated are valuable in their own right. Suffering relieved and capacities expanded are "hallelu-jah" material. But this picture is far from complete. The omissions could push the stuff of optimism into the back-ground and in certain scenarios into irrelevance. It strikes me as significant that none of the optimists cited work to protect the natural world and its climate or to confront the dangers of war and nuclear disaster.

To illustrate my meaning, I will focus on the United States. I know it more intimately, and in many respects it is a worst case example of reasons for rational pessimism. Those commentators featured in the optimist section of *Time* presumably agree with Gates and notice that bad things are happening (hurricanes, mass shootings, war, the prospect of annihilation by nuclear explosions, etc.). As Gates said, "But these events—as awful as they are—have happened in the context of a bigger, positive trend. On the whole the world is getting better." From my perspective, Gates has it backward. Consider the meta-phoric forest and trees: in certain places, trees of some species still flourish. But a view from above, taking in the whole forest and its place within the surrounding ecosys-tems, sees massive clear-cuts, wildfire devastation, and large stretches of dying forest succumbing to drought, heat stress, and devouring insects. The forest is quieter and less diverse, as vast numbers of birds and other wild-life have perished in recent decades and have not been replaced (half within the last fifty years or so alone, biol-ogists say). Nature shrinks under assault from economic development impingements on behalf of industrial farm-ing and urban spread.

The pessimist has even more to chew on. It is no secret to anyone who examines the reality behind deceptive curtains of words that moneyed special interests dominate the political process. Data that even Gates and Pinker must acknowledge demonstrate that whenever those interests speak, they carry the day in Washington, even when a constituent majority wants something else. A party that represents fewer than half of voters denies legitimacy to the other party, reliably serves the oligarchy, and acts as if facts and truth do not matter except when they accidentally coincide with fact-oblivious predetermined positions. This party controls most of government from state to federal, including judicial.

War is the most serious business a nation can conduct abroad, but after seventeen years of futility and death since 9/11, where is the democratic debate? Nor is it hysterical to notice that besides wars and other conflict in the Middle East, Central Asia, and Africa, we have been baiting North Korea and Iran toward more of the same. The prospect of nuclear annihilation receives relatively little attention considering the risk. How much of this kind of thing can U.S. citizens endure before rousing from their post-democratic stupor? How many millions more refugees will be set in motion by our bombs and foreign policies, and eventually extreme climate disruptions?

What about the trillion-dollar-plus annual cost of "national security" operations? The intrinsically most secure nation on Earth spends more than the next eight or nine countries combined on "defense," but who could show a correlation between cost and benefit? Who even asks? Who evaluates the blowback? Who measures the extra defense costs that arise from violent reactions to policies and interventions funded by the initial defense costs? The only discussion is how much to raise the Pentagon budget. What are the opportunity costs of pouring such largesse into the latrine every year?

Radical gerrymandering, voter suppression, changing the rules as they go along—to whom does this resemble democracy? Of course, many of the magazine's reasons and reasoners for optimism may be unaffected as the system drifts downward into thoroughgoing crony capitalist oligarchic rule, but still....

Even pessimists would be challenged to reconsider if we saw a society learn from its mistakes and do better in the next go-round. But the United States, which endured nearly fifty years of the Cold War and an arms race fueled by profligacy and waste and irrational in its extremity, has now launched a new one, already committing yet another couple of trillion dollars for "modernization" of its nuclear arsenal. Certain high-level voices even want to modernize the weapons into usability and seemingly are searching hard to find new reasons for hostilities and preparation for conflict. Is recognizing mistakes and learning from them unacceptable in this country?

The answer seems to be "yes," which raises the question of whether America knows how to do peace—to pursue it directly, intentionally, and intently, rather than as the supposed product of conflict after conflict.[4] Is it possible to imagine a commitment to peace promotion and humility, or that we might abandon the urge to dominate others at whatever costs to the others' lives (and ours)? Might we accept how much we do not know about them and their needs and be more respectful of their autonomy?

A few more words about the American attitude toward the military and its uses: I've just seen a remarkable graph in Wikipedia that tracks the course of the defense budget since 1900. It is quite low until WWI when it rises sharply but falls back at the war's end, not quite as low as

---

4. As I wrote this, it was a few days after the announcement that President Trump and the North Korean leader Kim Jong-un agreed to meet and negotiate some sort of agreement to control North Korea's nuclear weapons and avoid war. Accounts in major newspapers were to me surprisingly nervous in their responses: from the *New York Times*, "a breathtaking gamble," "risky and seemingly far-fetched," "doubts persist"; and from the *Los Angeles Times*, "Trump Already Hands Kim a Victory," a headline about the mere agreement to meet. These are representative responses of reporters and pundits, most of whom seem distressed and disbelieving that peace might break out. Of course, the prospect of Trump's negotiating anything this serious was far-fetched itself, but that's another issue.

before but still low until WWII when it shoots up again and much farther than before. After the war it declines but still remains high in historical terms, and the trend ever since has been upward, ever upward. The base budget is now about $700 billion ($700,000,000,000) and the total is close to $900 billion when other defense-related items are included; some calculations put it over a trillion. In the immortal words of the late Senator Everett Dirksen, "a billion here, a billion there..." (he may have concluded the sentence with "and pretty soon it adds up to real money.") Although the largest budget item except for Social Security, national security seems to be the only item that is rarely questioned in any serious way by Congress, and it is never subject to the assaults faced by programs that directly support citizen well-being and about which Congress-persons are prone to worrying over affordability. (I still remember the whimsical observation from the Vietnam War era that "When the Pentagon has to hold bake sales to fund its wars..." but that day has yet to dawn.)

Apropos of this breathtaking spending, I once read the *Summary of the 2018 National Defense Strategy*, prepared by the Department of Defense. Among other purposes, this document is clearly intended to justify the mind-blowing budget numbers noted above. The strategy is written in a military-bureaucratic language that tends to be obscure when not incoherent. For example:

> Without sustained and predictable investment to restore readiness and modernize our military to make it fit for our time, we will rapidly lose our military advantage, resulting in a Joint Force that has legacy systems irrelevant to the defense of our people. (p. 1)

> We face an ever more lethal and disruptive battle-field, combined across domains, and conducted at increasing speed and reach—from close combat,

throughout overseas theaters, and reaching to our homeland. (p. 3)[5]

Challenging as this document is to interpret, it has evident themes. First, international differences ineluctably imply conflicts, for which we must spend large amounts of money in preparation. Second, war, planning for war, the prospect of war, the apparent inevitability of war—these are always with us and always need more and more money. Third, "defense" is a euphemism; we are militarily present in a majority of the world's countries every year (around 150 according to many sources, including CNN, *Forbes,* and Wikipedia) and apparently must be ready to stay there even though the "defense" rationale is at best weak and often unsubstantiated and questionable. Fourth, we must be number one in all "domains," in all "theaters," in all ways, for all time ("Full Spectrum Dominance" forevermore). Fifth, neither the actual costs nor the opportunity costs of this largesse merit discussion: "[W]hile this strategy will require sustained investment by the American people, we recall past generations who made harsher sacrifices so that we might enjoy our way of life today." (p. 11) In other words, only an ingrate or wimp would question the costs. "A dominant Joint Force will protect the security of our nation, increase U.S. influence, preserve access to markets that will improve our standard of living, and strengthen cohesion among allies and partners." (p. 11) So get aboard; our standard of living depends on it.

I suppose my pessimism had not had enough fodder for its dark muse when I finished reading this National Defense Strategy, so I then turned to the *Nuclear Posture Review February 2018* for satiation. It seems to have been composed by the same mind. As above, and as has been common among national defense and foreign policy

---

5. U.S. Department of Defense, *Summary of the 2018 National Defense Strategy,* https://dod.defense.gov/Portals/1/Documents/pubs/2018-National-Defense-Strategy-Summary.pdf

specialists since the end of World War II, magnification of threats, or "threat inflation," lumbers forward unabated: "North Korea's nuclear provocations," "Iran's nuclear ambitions," "the threats we face and the uncertainties," "global threat conditions have worsened markedly," "a more diverse and advanced nuclear-threat environment," "an unprecedented range and mix of threats," "rapid deterioration of the threat environment," and so on.[6] And this was just the first five pages. Lest anyone quail at the anticipated cost of surmounting these horrors, "Given the criticality of effective U.S. nuclear deterrence to the safety of the American people, allies and partners there is no doubt that the sustainment and replacement program should be regarded as both necessary and affordable." (p. IX) This is no doubt true in some quarters, the military-industrial complex most of all.

Both of these documents are relentlessly bellicose and seem to suggest that the trillions upon trillions of dollars that have already been sucked into this black hole were actually not sufficient. Sadly they note that we must now spend more to compensate for earlier deficiencies. Both state explicitly that hegemony is our only acceptable posture, and both are obviously oblivious that other countries may not agree.[7] One of the most perduring American traits in our relations with potential adversaries (and would-be, could-be, or soon-to-be adversaries) has been the inability to see ourselves as others see us. Worse, we always assume a stance of unblemished righteousness in the face of nefarious enemies and act as if their resistance and response to our actions is without basis or under-

6. U.S. Department of Defense, *Nuclear Posture Review February 2018*, https://media.defense.gov/2018/Feb/02/2001872886/-1/-1/1/2018-NUCLEAR-POSTURE-REVIEW-FINAL-REPORT.PDF

7. For example, it is a sign of China's growing aggressiveness, says the report, that the Chinese "are challenging traditional U.S. military superiority in the Western Pacific," which is to say off their shores. The report doesn't mention how we'd respond if the Chinese wanted to establish military superiority in the eastern Pacific, which is to say off *our* shores.

standing in the record of our earlier behavior toward them. We are merely innocents standing up for goodness and virtue while batting down gratuitous "threats." ("They hate our freedom," said George W. Bush after 9/11 to explain the attack.) We know no road to peace, apparently, that doesn't run through combat zones. We don't understand that peace is not just an absence of overt conflict but that real peace is built on a foundation of peacefulness, the eschewing of incessant warlikeness.

And climate change? The U.S. is withdrawing at Trump's direction from the Paris climate accords, which are too timid in conception anyway but the only organized game in town. When a society prioritizes economic ends and values above those that affirm life and justice and the Earth's health, it will be an unhappy one that is bound to decay. It does not need external enemies to bring it down; rather, enemies, endless enemies, endless potential battle-fields (i.e., nations) will distract citizens from the essentials and further feed the warrior beast. All while the climate moves along inexorably toward an unavoidable reckoning, the price we all will pay for allowing our societies to be led by people who do not actually care about them except as instruments for their own self-blinding desires.

The optimists' positives are real, but they happen in the shadow of events that can swiftly make them minor in the bigger picture of potential destruction. This coun-try—its citizens and representatives—sits on its hands and keeps its mouth closed while bonfire material piles high. Nuclear weapons must either go away or in time they will go off like a string of otherworldly firecrack-ers, taking large portions of life with them. Continued excretion of fossil fuel by-products into the atmosphere and oceans will eventually cause billions of dead and displaced humans to take their place alongside Nature's other anthropogenic catastrophes.

I intend no denigration of the optimists. Most are doing

laudable work, fueled by compassion and their own view of the good of society. If worse does not come to worst, if neither of our looming apocalyptic probabilities is allowed to fulfill the deep darkness that defines the essence of their being and of those who are the enablers...if this, then the optimists will be a large source of the redemptive energy that could shape a better period ahead for life, human and nonhuman. But for now, it is as if they were all on a great ship heaving its way through a storm and laboring below deck to make the conditions there and the crew and passengers happier, healthier, and more fully realized. All can see progress. But up on deck, knowable but unperceived, the ship's captain and officers have been bribed and intimidated by unsavory elements who see profit (for themselves) in turning the ship into the riskiest of waters. They believe they are invulnerable and care not for the ship or for those below deck who are in fact better people than they, and who could, if roused, take control of the ship, but for unfathomable reasons do not.

A large spiritual element to this pessimism is available for those who revere *being* and the great mystery of existence and who see what they love desecrated and squandered for superfluous wealth and trivial acquisitions. In places, Nature chokes and staggers and slowly blinks out under assault by ignorant greed and quotidian *making a living* and *building wealth and prosperity*. But with unmitigated climate change, Earth prepares retaliation. She suffers massive losses but after ultimate disaster will come back over a few million years to a renewed condition of health with new species players and renewed plenitude. Her response to nuclear suicide would presumably follow a similar course of resurrection. She will come back. She has before. Ultimately she is wiser and more powerful than we. But as perpetrators of this disaster, we cannot but ask if it would be good that humans came back with her. On the basis of our record, the answer can only be No. On balance,

Earth and her other inhabitants are far better off without the human element, which will have forgotten its place sufficiently to have destroyed it. How many other species, plant or animal, have ever shown themselves so ill-suited for life in harmony with the whole? Some people propose colonies on other planets, where a small portion of humanity (the wealthiest, assuredly) could survive Earth's demise, as a hospitable place for humans. But why bother? Humans would be there. It wouldn't endure.

Is this attitude toward one's own species misanthropic? No, it is ecophilic, reverential toward the whole of being, within which *Homo sapiens* is but one among many and the only one who could countenance destruction of the commons, the community of life toward which we owe moral sensitivity and restraint, respect and love. Beauty will exist without humans to perceive it. Goodness thrive without human agency. Truth abides beyond our knowing. Value will survive our absence.

I search for an embracing vision of a good society that will incorporate the optimists' inventory of the cheerful and hopeful and that could also respond to a pessimist's doleful perceptions. Simply more good occurrences and fewer bad ones is insufficient. My dark view of American society sums as this: it displays a profound disrespect for life and so naturally lacks compassion and deep-seated community spirit. What is more essential to the moral quality of a culture than its fundamental attitude toward life? And what can we surmise about that attitude in a country that still has not come to a reckoning with its genocidal and enslaving origins, its militaristic rampaging around the world for the last hundred-plus years, its rampant domestic violence, its gun fetish, its rate of incarceration, its indifference to the health and well-being of children, its manifest injustices, its abuses of animals and Nature? This country obliviously accepts the Damoclean perils that we are responsible for engendering and aggravating—degradation of the Earth's gifts through both today's systematic aggressions against climate stability and tomorrow's flirtation with the nuclear precipice.

I wondered at the beginning how much goodness humans were capable of sustaining. I still wonder, but I think I know a few things about human needs and how we work. Raising them high in our awareness would go a long way toward building a lasting foundation for optimism. We seek meaning, even if only unconsciously. We are fundamentally social creatures, depending on each other in more ways than most will acknowledge and finding value in giving and receiving. We are born of Nature and suffer from alienated attitudes toward it just as we do when separated from our human family networks. We enjoy the competence of doing good work well. We long for commitments to goods beyond ourselves. We want to be real.

Well-founded optimism about the human condition and the human trajectory will arise on its own when we can share and embrace a vision that builds on a fundamental respect for life, what I have spoken of elsewhere as a *reverence for existence*. We can realize that our world is imbued with intrinsic goodness around which, in multiple dimensions and different fashions, each person can shape a life that reflects and promotes their own distinctive elements of goodness, taking account of the human characteristics whose truth I have asserted above. As shared vision happens, one could begin to feel the great value of lives and of the natural and social/cultural worlds where they are lived. One would want to share this goodness and protect those who are deprived or oppressed.

As a political program, optimism would ensure that no one suffered unnecessarily and that everyone had equal access to necessities and equal opportunity to build autonomous but linked and responsible lives in community. It could not avoid facing the fact that in every group there will always be a few who want more than their fair share of its resources, principally money and power. If they are not restrained by the community, they will find ways not merely to get their unfair share but use it to defeat restraints and foster magnification of their share. They are unrelenting, so restraints must always be reinforced. (For evidence I refer you to daily doings in DC and other centers of political and economic power.) What Iris Murdoch identified several decades ago as the primary impediment to morality, the "fat, relentless ego," continues its predictably gluttonous ways, its girth ever expanding.

I doubt it's possible for even the most confirmed optimist to imagine that remedies for what ails this country will begin at the federal or even state levels. I once heard an expression, in Spanish, that wryly described the circumstance of Mexico: "Poor Mexico. So far from God and so near the United States." Government today is largely toothless in relation to the common welfare—"So far from its constituents and so near the lobbyists." If it can possibly come, optimism will grow as change emerges from communities of people who know, or know about, and care for each other. They will have their own visions. They will value life and communal connectedness of the sort where you feel that if one suffers, we all suffer. They will recognize the proper place and nature of work and the kinds of rewards that make it valuable. That the natural world is home and not mere resource and relate to it accordingly. That the world is fuller with meaning than anyone knows. And that peace and justice arise and flourish from peaceful and just people acting peacefully and justly. Optimism will be validated when citizens demand that the twin threats to Earth and life be confronted and removed. Nothing less will do if the work of *Time*'s optimists is to receive the support it needs to flourish and not sink with the ship.

CHAPTER 19

PICKING ONE'S POISON

ANYONE WHO'S PAID SERIOUS ATTENTION to information and discussion about anthropogenic climate disruption (ACD) realizes how serious a situation we face. How can so many of our fellow citizens remain unconcerned? Some have been convinced to doubt the reality, even though it has repeatedly and with increasing urgency been affirmed by almost all climate scientists—97 percent at last count.[1] Among these scientists there is no doubt about where we are headed, despite less certainty about the speed and particular pathways by which we can expect disasters to strike. Some of our fellow citizens agree that it's happening but feel helpless and so turn to other matters. Many seemingly don't think much about it, out of either ignorance or *la belle indifference*. And others, I venture, are vaguely aware of the prospects and choose not to have an opinion of their own. They accept the word of the deniers, who, they assume, are more knowledgeable because they are rich, prominent, and apparently filled with certainty—forgetting to wonder about their values, judgment, and character. After all, how could a denier become head of a major corporation or president or senator if he didn't have good sense?

---

1. NASA, Do Scientists Agree on Climate Change? N.d. https://climate.nasa.gov/faq/17/do-scientists-agree-on-climate-change/

The most usual explanation points to the hugeness of the issue, the complexity, the remoteness, the unbelievability of such a radical upsetting of the way things have always been. Furthermore, trust in expert opinion is at low ebb and is manipulated to remain so, the prospect of world-altering ACD has been made to seem controversial when it isn't in reality, and it's been turned into a partisan issue alongside so many others—it's just more than most people want to deal with. All of this is plausible.

But I can't help thinking about another factor that hasn't been much talked about. For almost eighty years we have lived under the shadow of nuclear apocalypse. When I was a child, we had drills where we dove under our desks to protect ourselves against a Soviet warhead that might be coming our way. When I was in high school and the Cuban missile crisis arose, we considered that each day might be our last, desk or no desk. Now we hardly think about it. It's become part of the background of life. For those who might occasionally feel concerned, there's always access to versions of the avoidance that works so well with ACD. The danger has become so normalized, so drained of blood-chilling, end-of-the-world angst by habituation. The knowledge that due to accident, error, or human incompetence or misjudgment, our days may well be numbered doesn't set nerves on end as one might expect. We could all be dead in thirty minutes, or well on our painful way, and all that we've known and cared about shattered. How can we whistle past this particular graveyard?

I don't know how, but we do. Probably because it would be just too emotionally depleting to attentively stare it in the face, especially since there doesn't seem anything we can do about it. The Washington foreign policy establishment not only doesn't bother to debate better solutions to internationally based anxieties for which nuclear weapons are considered by them the sedative, not only doesn't seriously consider abolition, not only fails to cringe at the waste and excess and gratuitous danger that were wrapped into our nuclear weapons fixation over the decades following Hiroshima and Nagasaki, not only all this—but it has now thrown itself wholeheartedly and with looks of solemn necessity into "modernizing" the whole shebang. A few trillion dollars more for unnecessary weapons never to be used and if, oops they are, they will have sponsored the potential death of our civilization for...some reason or another.

So, with that, what's a little bit of less apocalyptic global warming to worry about? All of the psychological defenses and other means of dealing with the nuclear threat that never arrived are familiar and comfortable and ready to hand. We've dodged that bullet so far, so who would be such a naysayer as to think we couldn't also dodge this one? Fewer and fewer of us are old enough to remember the movies and books and international conflicts that spoke of the likely consequences of failure to control the means of our end. It's all background into which this new potential disaster can readily be shoved, since the foreground lacks space.

If there's much truth to these thoughts, we face the most ironic of situations. Having survived a heart attack and its wrenching anxieties and yet still afflicted with heart disease, we don't feel much inclination to worry about our cancer, or perhaps lack the emotional energy ("apocalypse fatigue," someone calls it). Although the nuclear danger has not passed, it is passé. Having so far survived this particular means of hurling humanity into eternity, we may not have the psychic wherewithal left to face our other self-inflicted crisis. If people cannot feel two sources of pain at the same time, does it follow that they cannot face two invitations to catastrophe simultaneously? And if not, what can we look forward to?

Chapter 20

The Day After

THE ELECTION IS SORT OF over, thank the gods...

As I switched off the computer this Wednesday morning, the fourth of November, 2020, the last headline I saw was this: "Presidential Race Too Close to Call." I mulled this for an hour, then the hidden clarity in this announcement, its essential meaning, swept over me physically, leaving a smile. It is unusual for revelation to confirm itself in this perceptible way. A burden was lifted, and I felt relief. No more would I harbor hopes for positive change in my lifetime for the land of my birth; no more disappointment as they are dashed. No more thoughts that if this or that occurred, perhaps a page would turn on all the nonviral afflictions of this virus-ravaged land. What other conclusion was there when four years' experience such as we have passed through led not to repudiation but to a race too close to call? Stoic wisdom means accepting what appears inevitable or beyond your control. In relinquishing futile hope, I found peace.

My relief would not be affected by who won after the votes were counted or after the lawyers reconnoitered and marched through courthouse doors protected by armed guards. The incumbent's tweets moved into newly scurrilous territory, if any is left. I prefer Biden, because he will block some of the more egregious assaults on Nature—long live the Tongass ecosystem!

He will promote scientific approaches to the coronavirus—the absence of which amounts to a president's culpable negligence measured by the body count. He will support measures to mitigate climate change—before it's too late to matter, I hope, which is sooner than most people think. And more of course, and most would be good as I see it—at least whatever initiatives are allowed to happen in the face of Republican obstructionism, also culpable.

The relief I speak of is based on the clarity of that morning moment when I accepted the hopelessness of our situation (not with satisfaction). It has much to do with this: no matter the victor, the vote totals show that the American peoples—we no longer can accurately be spoken of as *a* people—are nearly evenly divided, and not over mere policy preferences. Identities, fundamental anxieties, antipathies, fears, and more drive the Republican mass (the infamous "base"). Liberals of all stripes have been unable to turn any tides or even to grasp fully how deep runs the abyssal divide and propose a convincing course correction. Not that liberals are without guilt for our degraded society and politics, but in comparison: it is the difference between one night's infidelity and a libertine career, between a cocktail and a binge.

For people like me, who wonder how any citizen who has been present for these four years of the Trump Show and witnessed its calamities and corruptions, deceptions and destructions, and not fled the theater—who wonder how anyone could ask for four more years of the same but worse—whatever the reasons, they appear to be people with a single focus. They were not slumbering; they just do not care about the costs so long as their single-mindedness offers the security of holding on to power, which they believe will protect them. Obviously, this belief paves the road toward authoritarianism, but they do not object.

Those numbers, those numbers, so nearly equal; think what they mean. How can anyone imagine climbing out of that abyss? Can we understand how deeply alienated those people are, how the country has failed them, how they have failed the country as they flee into false security, all else be damned? How long can we tolerate this impasse before the ship of state founders and society divides irremediably—if it hasn't already?

Do I exaggerate? Is reconciliation more likely or more possible than I realize? I doubt it. The only idea I have heard that offers a chance to avoid our apparently suicidal plunge into societal collapse, our movement into a First World version of Third World autocracy—midwifed in my view by Banana Republic-ans—points to versions of local communitarianism. Initiatives like those reported by James and Deb Fallows in *Our Towns*, those associated with Weave: The Social Fabric Project, and the Communitarian Network portray versions of reconciliation arising through pursuit of shared goals, from collaborative actions and their results, and the experience of spending time and working with fellow collaborators who would otherwise be strangers and often presumptively despised. People find that they can care for their community, including members not from the same party or perspectives; that difference is not threatening; that negotiation and compromise are possible; that solidarity creates its own rewards and meanings. These efforts of course stand in stark contrast to what we see in the political realm. One hopes that in time they would lead to demanding the same accountability from town councils, county commissioners, members of Congress, and so forth, as local collaborators expect of each other.

Without accountability (measured out in "eternal vigilance" as the price of liberty), human nature is such that greed, fecklessness, and power lust, unrelenting as they are, will always seek control.

This is an appealing and probably well-founded picture of human possibilities actuated by a central aspect of human nature—our need for the security and satisfactions of sociality, mutual care, and liberty bound solidly to responsibility (all of which appear to have found spurious substitutes in Trumpism). Can it happen soon enough and with a broad enough base? Can it neutralize the dividers and egoists? Consider a few of the threats it faces:

- Climate change: Credible voices backed by considerable data portraying plausible scenarios tell us that without substantial action within this decade followed by further decisive action in the next, the trajectory of human-caused climate disruptions may spin beyond our control. We are already facing more weather catastrophes, more wildfires, more drought, heat, and flood, leading toward shortages of food and clean water, famine and disease, and mass migrations of desperate people looking for relief. Once the worst becomes commonplace, political and cultural divisions may not matter; survival would be paramount, and in the American case it would be each for himself.

- The COVID-19 pandemic: Having seen how climate disruptions, whose casualties are less visible and identifiable, and whose causative forces are more readily ignored, especially with the malign complicity of those with corporate or political desires to satisfy—having seen this, how can we imagine a different response to a deadly viral pandemic to be any different? The fight against COVID has been politicized and degraded; the consequent piling up of casualties has had no effect on the deniers and perpetrators of false narratives. Like climate change, COVID is a transformative threat in itself, revealing an American society that lacks the will and intelligence to take care of itself.

- Political dynamics: The Republican Party has demonstrated that it operates without moral compunction. Over recent decades, it has focused relentlessly on securing and protecting power by any means it considers necessary, with pervasive mendacity its necessary enabler. For example, it passes tax cuts for the rich while calling them cuts for the middle and lower classes. It works assiduously to undercut medical care while claiming the reverse. It politicizes shamelessly while blaming the opposition. It suppresses voting. It works to overthrow legitimate electoral outcomes, as we see right now. And so on ad nauseam. And plus or minus 47 percent of the electorate wants more of the same. Eternal vigilance? Occasional unfettered consciousness would be an improvement.

• Rot at the top: Two days after the presidential election a *Washington Post* headline reported: "Wall Street Rallies as Investors Believe Washington Gridlock Is Good for Business." Several other publications reported the same trend and reached the same conclusion. Congressional gridlock implies no new taxes or regulations, even when reason and the common good require them. Investors salivate and count their blessings. A nation that increasingly reveals it was built on sand; a disordered climate that will provide the forces to further undermine that sandy foundation; a deadly caste system that persists and moves now past its five hundredth year; pernicious and growing economic injustice—all this makes investors happy. Gridlock will not threaten to solve any of these problems, thus relieving investors of imposed responsibilities and releasing them to make hay while the sun shines hotter and hotter.

• Inertia, habit, propaganda: Human nature is still incompletely understood. From my perspective, it is the only animal nature that seems, at least in the forms it has taken in historical time, almost constantly at odds with itself; confused about why it is here and what it should do; prone to self-sabotage, projection, and aggression. When fearful, it tends toward gullibility. Always it is bound by habit and the momentum of the known. America is one of the few countries, and the only "advanced" one, whose government has gone laissez faire in its response to COVID-19 and refuses to see what that has wrought and adjust course.

As I write, we're at nine days after. On day five Biden was declared the winner. As expected Trump cried foul, fraud, and conspiracy, claiming he was robbed of his rightful victory. That was the only way he could appear to have lost, which he is sure he did not do since he never loses. Only losers lose, and he is not a loser. So he moved onward, unleashing the lawyers, who have tried valiantly to support his calumnies but face the embarrassing hurdle that no evidence has been found to support the charges. To a layperson, it sometimes appears that the lawyers themselves make fraudulent claims in the courtrooms, but I may miss the subtlety of their arguments. Even so, they lost every suit. Other lawyers and a few judges assert that Trump's team had better watch themselves, since there are professional ethical and legal prohibitions against frivolous lawsuits containing seriously bent versions of truth and known reality.

So it was no surprise that Trump reacted as he has—he has mastered the art of victimhood. It probably should be no surprise that Republicans, including party leadership, uniformly either supported his claims or kept quiet. Nevertheless, it seems to me remarkable that a Grand Old Party that goes back as far as this one does is so ready to forgo even the appearance of integrity and love of country with so flimsy an effort that has so little chance of accomplishing anything other than self-debasement and further national decline. I know they mostly don't expect to prevail and do this with other motivations having to do with the Senatorial run-offs in Georgia, fear of Trump even as a loser, and the unwholesome notion that this is a good way to keep their legions fired up. In short, though more extreme, this gambit comes from the same manual the Republican Party has been using for close to five decades, which resembles a magician's trick: The hand juggling the fears, bigotries, and deceptions that work so well with a certain portion of the electorate holds its attention, while the other hand is behind the Party's back feeding the plutocracy. Along with holding power (to enable the feeding), this is their real goal. It's a simple means-ends calculation. It may seem like playing with fire and with the country's future, but what else can they do when all their other matches are wet and it remains effective. They don't care about side effects— when your end justifies any and all means that's where you're left.

But party malfeasance is not what interests me; it was predictable. It is the followers who mystify me. By now it may be questionable who is leading whom. The masses have become a runaway horse and leaders just hold on for dear life and political hegemony. The margin is now so narrow between those who yearn for more robust democracy and those who seek one-party minority rule that the latter is conceivable and may even be in sight. The United States could easily undergo a Hungarian- or Polish-style transition from fair and square (more or less) electoral victory to permanent rule built on destruction of the formerly democratic systems that set the rules and were thought to prevent shenanigans like this. Regardless, my curiosity at what makes people, the Republican masses, act as they have is intense. How could 47 percent of the electorate have witnessed what they have over these four years and want more? Clearly they no longer believe in accountability and public morality, but how did they get there? It is as if a sick man visited a clinic but found that the doctor had gone for the day and left incompetents in charge. They lied about the doctor's absence and offered bogus treatments that made the patient sicker. Nevertheless, the patient cheerfully pays his bill and makes another appointment. Who cares so little about their health and how they are treated? Do they not notice the progression of their disease?

Since I was young I have wondered how humans work as biological, mental, and emotional beings. What makes us think and feel and do as we do? A large part of the answer lies in the outer world, or rather in the interaction between inner and outer worlds. The outer world has the initiative, owing to our early helplessness. Every form of life—plant, animal (humans included), fungus, bacteria, others—depends utterly on suitable conditions for beings of their kind to live and, they hope, flourish. Cholla cactus does fine at particular elevations with the right measure of rain, the right temperature range, and suitable soil. Alter these even slightly, as is happening in certain deserts now—add heat, subtract from the meager supply of moisture—and the cholla withers and fails to reproduce. Similarly, the pika enjoys life at preferred montane elevations with a fitting supply of warmth and other essential goods, but raise the temperature and they head upslope until they reach the top—and then what, as the heat also climbs? Humans aim to finesse the imperatives of Nature but we, too, have our basic circumstantial needs; because human nature is more open than the nature of others, it may also be more vulnerable to surrounding influences, innate vulnerabilities, and its own misjudgments about what's good for it.

People don't do well under persistent conditions of excess insecurity: insufficient nutrition and health care; instability of family and community; uncertainty about work, wages, and housing; a threatened sense of identity and place in the world; unsafe environments; navigating the burdens of caste distinctions and bigotry. Poverty, for example, may be thought of as a disease as well as a social condition. Both disable their victims, sicken body and mind, lead to uneven and unequal life courses, and add burdens to the life journey. And yet, except for hard-earned exceptions, American society considers itself *as a society* unaccountable for basic security among its citizens. This has serious consequences for citizens and nation— and not those trumpeted by the disingenuous adherents of "personal responsibility." This concept so commodious and adaptable that former Vice President Pence recently explained, during a campaign debate, that because of his and the president's trust in every American's assumption of personal responsibility, the administration didn't need to assume a leadership role in fighting the pandemic. In other words, national problems don't really require a national response. Americans could be trusted to take care of themselves, contagion be damned. Given the unique characteristics of the present viral pandemic, this particular instance of the personal responsibility rationalization means that hundreds of thousands of our fellow citizens will have gone to their graves prematurely before it is all over, graves dug by malfeasance. In addition to the prospect of early death, existential insecurities piled atop each other lead to other serious damage: anger, scapegoating, vulnerability to demagogic appeals, and hatred and violence against purported sources of the unspoken anxieties. They also make for a fragmented and unhappy country.

American society does not believe in looking at itself as an entity that can be made better through assuming more concern for its cultural quality and social conditions. These are left for personal responsibility to take care of; society says this even to the sick and hungry two-year-old: every person should pull themselves up by their boot-straps, even when they have no boots. Meritocracy does not notice that its winners mostly start on second or third base, whereas others can hardly get a hit, their bats are broken, and their gloves are secondhand and worn out.

Add to the insecurities built into our social fabric another one—the cultivation of fear, a regular part of the national diet. Much, perhaps most, American international aggression has been based on fear-related rationales, with greed and the dominator impulse hovering more discreetly in the background. Native American genocide, the Monroe Doctrine and Latin American interventions from Veracruz to Honduras, the unrelenting hostility to Cuba that still beats in the hearts of some even after sixty years, and the establishment and maintenance of the American caste system are examples. Other expressions: overthrown governments in Iran in 1953, Nicaragua in 1954, and Chile in 1973 were explained as anti-Communist, as was the Vietnam debacle. After World War I and especially since World War II the always exaggerated "Communist threat" has been the carrier of American fear, heavily promoted among the citizenry. As others have said, we appear to thrive on "endless enemies," countries and forces that might keep us awake at night but for the shield of national defenders and homeland securitors. The nation's reflexive fight response eventually goes slack when fear is omnipresent; I suspect it mostly falls unconscious but always is subject to manipulated arousal that is bound to leave the fearful vulnerable to demagogic promises.

It is paradoxical that millions of immigrants and refugees found homes here, even as fear of outsiders has always flowed steadily beneath and sometimes on the surface. Even more paradoxical is that the land of freedom and equality accepted slavery, followed by the steady, vicious drumbeat of racist terrorism and Jim Crow oppression. It seems to me that fear promotion has been a long-running drama in this country, with a rotating cast of communism, the Cold War, the prospect of nuclear holocaust, ubiquitous threats conjured by the "defense" establishment, and terrorists. Is it surprising that persistent fear mongering at the macro level, accompanied by genuine anxieties and fears owing to the structures and values of our society at the micro level, would create the conditions for what we see happening now under Republican sponsorship?

So my hypothesis about why almost half the electorate continues to support Trump—a support that requires the suspension of moral judgment, reality testing, and love of genuine freedom—builds on the previous observation that we are fundamentally a fearful, insecure people. And it concludes with the observation that unreasoning fear of various others and unreasoning hope that a nationalistic/white supremacist/oligarchic president and party will protect them against existential identity anxiety, which is linked manipulatively to fear and hatred of liberals and most lower-than-whites-of-any-class caste members. As is obvious from their own words, theirs is a culture of victimization and resentment. All it takes to harness that for political purposes is the right demagogy, which now has arrived.

I must add another factor that motivates support for Trump, one that has nothing to do with social and psychological threats. In addition to seeking harbor in a changing world—the unsettling world of difference, novelty, and new ideas—many Americans may share his views and appreciate his permission to be open about it. The coarseness, indifference to self-respect and morality, the meanness and selfishness, the bigotry—for those who previously might have been embarrassed to feel, let alone express these things, seeing someone at the top not only feeling them but making no effort to hide it, even parading it openly, a voice for the unspoken...this would provide a new kind of comfort. If this is how a large part of the country actually feels but didn't consider it quite respectable before 2016, they now have a person and political party to call home.

If Trump had not been so personally repugnant even to many sympathizers and fellow travelers, had there been a hundred or so thousand fewer Covid-19 deaths (readily manageable by a less inert, ignorant, and self-centered president), I suspect that one-party, autocratic government would have won the election. Angst and alienation will do that to people. We appear to have built a society that is good for business (owners primarily) but bad for the people living and working here. Its ideology: Economy first! and happiness, community, confidence that basic needs will be met, national solidarity...all the amenities, quiet satisfactions, and expansive opportunities of a humane, egalitarian democratic system come last.

How can such fear and hostility toward scapegoats, well nourished by the very groups scapegoaters look to for safety, be overcome—if it can? It may well be that the only alternative to impasse or autocracy would be dividing the country up into as many self-governing units as are desired, linked perhaps, if even this could be managed, in a sort of overarching federation around clearly shared interests, national defense, for instance. (That little corner of Georgia that has just elected a Q-Anon congresswoman might want to become its own independent fantasy land.) Pandemics, of which there will of course be more, and climate disruption logically would fall into this category. Division even by choice would not be easy. But at least the parts would be severed politically and culturally and could choose their own paths—until major calamity brings them together in a shared and final closure.

In order to flourish, humans require alleviated fear and anxiety and social and psychological security—an alternative to our present culture of atomized pseudo-individualism and you're-on-your-own-ism. Personal responsibility as a healthy reality rather than a cop-out depends on having as many of the right supplies and early and continuing forms of security for most of those who undertake the journey to have a good chance to succeed. As far as I can tell, the most likely source for this happy situation lies within caring families and communities, as I said earlier. The mutualities, the supports appropriate to individual development and needs, the pleasures of giving and receiving care: these are among the attitudes and practices whereby people can see themselves as members of a nourishing whole, a place with binding relationships. Relatively small, voluntary, mutually respectful, beneficial, and responsive...such a place used to be described as one where people looked out for each other, where eccentricities and myriad beliefs were tolerated and sometimes enjoyed. If Trumpism constitutes a distorted and hollow simulacrum of genuine communal solidarity, then perhaps real community would be welcomed by some of its members.

If it is true that fear and insecurity, nourished by greed and power hunger, are the primary source of America's tilt toward division and autocracy, then I don't know where else to look for a solution than resurrection of communities where fear can be alleviated and security ensured. They might eventually turn things in a different direction. In the meantime, and even if they do not, they provide satisfying sanctuary from and alternatives to our failing society.

CHAPTER 21

WAR & TRUTH,
CULTURE & FUTURE

IN THIS FINAL CHAPTER I point back to the beginning. One of the fruits of writing with an emphasis on self within the political context has been a heightened awareness of how formative American militarism was during my youth; I do not doubt I would have turned out different had I lived in a more peaceful culture, so I wanted to understand the interwoven histories of this country and myself. It was during the 1960s that their intersection assumed its most visible, conscious, and problematic character. Vietnam and the draft were determinative experiences, especially for the soldiers who fought in it and the resisters, among whom I am proud to count myself, who fought against it. The war is considered by most who have studied the period a societal and moral debacle, and I emphatically agree.

Those who became soldiers in the 1960s were often forced into it by the draft. Many of them submitted against their better judgment and under duress, whereas those serving today are, theoretically, volunteers. The draftees were sometimes treated shabbily on their return and may in part have felt they deserved it— they knew what had happened over there. The reward for many of them was profound *moral injury*, which washed over society as well, albeit without the average citizen's awareness—an injury to the soul rather than the body, one that left the moral structure and compass damaged. Participants in today's volunteer army, on the other hand, are lionized as "heroes" and "warriors," even though the necessity and justice of their wars is no more apparent than that of their draftee predecessors'. The fact is that neither Vietnam nor today's wars were or are rational as national defense or moral endeavors. All have been fought mostly by the lower and middle classes and have resulted in millions of foreign casualties along with tens of thousands of our own, without even taking account of the damage to society's moral fabric. A wiser, more ethical foreign policy would have avoided vast suffering and death because it avoided gratuitous war-making. It may be that unconscious recognition of these factors has resulted in compensatory laudation—shallow though it is—of today's soldiers. Vietnam vets were not honored (until later) because the country knew their sacrifices had been wasted and preferred to look away rather than face that tragedy. Today people may suspect the same thing is happening once again. Rather than either face it or look away, the soldiers' fellow citizens pretend the risks and sacrifices are necessary "to keep us safe," a phrase whose wide currency suggests societal infantilization and delusion. "Thanks for your service" and all the other pseudo-patriotic hoopla nicely mask the facts. I saw a good example of this phenomenon on a recent trip as I drove through Oregon, where I discovered roads memorialized as "Fallen Hero Highway" followed by the name of a dead soldier who presumably had lived in the area. How much compensation, I wonder, do dead soldiers' families feel as they drive along the namesake memorials?

My undergraduate degree was in political science and economics; my deep interest in American foreign policy was influenced by Vietnam and didn't cease when the war ended (for the United States in 1973 and for the abandoned,

hapless South Vietnamese in 1975). My transition into pacifism, precipitated by the forced choice of submitting to the
draft or forming a conscience that rejected violence, was
genuine and has never abated. Not extreme pacifism but
on the continuum I sit comfortably at 9 on a range between
utter militarism at 1 and absolute pacifism at 10. Given the
American proclivity toward violence, which has characterized the country from its beginnings, and overt militarism,
which seems to have effloresced since World War II (but
was by no means absent before then), I've never lacked
grist for the mill. Aggressive American foreign relations
have been a continual presence in my life and rarely absent
from my adult consciousness.[1] I always suspected that
healthy societies don't accept so much violence whether
against other societies or among their own people.

It turns out that pacifism in contemporary America is
an absent issue, as is ignoring the war question more or
less completely. With no draft there's no compulsion into
military service, no draft board to face, no reason to pay
much attention (other than the hypothetical, relatively
flaccid, ambiguous, and nowadays apparently optional
requirements of good citizenship). Vigorous debate about
our wars has gone dormant, missing in action. Furthermore, we are at war somewhere more often than not, in
wars that quickly lose their luster and reveal their irrationality. Nevertheless, no one, including Congress, who lacks
a friend or loved one whose life is risked in these ventures
has reason to think about them. Rather than raising taxes
to pay the bills, Congress and Presidents simply borrow
the money, which removes the last reason average citizens might have to think about our theaters of imperialist
power projection. I suspect that a pay-as-we-go policy, one
that mandated tax increases to pay for our interventive

---

1. Maybe even my childhood consciousness: I've earlier mentioned the
memory of myself as a seven- or eight-year-old during the Korean War
and someone's informing me that wars never end. Whoever that was
knew what he was talking about.

enthusiasms, would alter Americans' complacency. Since Republicans despise taxes (even to support new wars) but not debt, borrowing offers a double benefit for them, and Democrats have been complicit.

I have heard it said that "peaceniks," draft resisters, and the like were no more uniquely conscientious about the wrongs represented by Vietnam, were no more morally aware by nature, than young people at other times who were or are quiescent in the face of wars concurrent with their youth. The assertion was that the draft threatened our freedom and therefore demanded we pay attention to the violence into which we could well be thrown regardless of our political views or moral make-up. I do not doubt this played a part, although the spirit of the time was one that provoked awareness of peace and justice issues on their own merits. One didn't have to be Black to reject racism or female to reject sexism: they were simply wrong. It seemed morally irresponsible to many of us not to face these facts, just as we chose to face the irrationality, the political and historical ignorance, and the manifest wickedness of initiating, continuing, and escalating that war in Vietnam well after its absurdity and destructiveness and needlessness became evident. The times, the issues, the culture—they conspired to engender awareness and response within those who paid attention and were not self-absorbed.

I now realize what I did not then: the draft can be part of equalizing a social structure, one that prevents people from retreating into absorption with only their own interests. As one option within mandated universal service, for example, it would contribute to a situation where all young citizens could contemplate bigger picture values while postponing preoccupation with smaller personal interests. While serving their country for a year in a role chosen by themselves, they could mature and perhaps become better persons. It seemed logical at the time that without a draft to force citizens into the military they would opt out, making wars harder to prosecute. ("What if they gave a war and nobody came?" as we used to say.) But now we know that enough true believers will always show up whenever the flags fly, the drums beat, and large enlistment bonuses are waved at them; people facing economic or other hardships can be recruited on that basis alone. Also, some are attracted to the military life. There is never a shortage of bodies to throw into the war machine. As I said, if we required that taxes rise in union with the costs of war to preclude wars being fought on the installment plan, that might influence public consciousness as the draft did. Then everyone would have "skin in the game," you might say. One might even surmise that the political class has removed the impositions of war from the masses (via ending the draft); sheltered the majority from the preparations, costs, and consequences (via secrecy and credit-card war making); and shifted the discomforts to volunteers with a purpose: It helps to avoid protest and leaves the war makers free to act, untroubled by a disturbed and attentive citizenry.

To some extent, one's relation to one's country and the concurrent historical period is analogous to that of children and parents: a large part of their personal and relational evolution includes accepting the disappointment that no one turned out quite as hoped but that it could have been worse and is not altogether bad. At the same time, though, one never understands oneself without understanding the forces that built and tilted one in certain directions and assessing both the forces and one's responses. Acceptance does not preclude inquiry and, sometimes, severe criticism.

I came of age in the 1960s, which were tumultuous times. I was not a mere bystander, owing to internal ethical impulses and external impositions that affected how I lived and grew, what I believed, and choices I made. My life has been a series of answers to questions and demands: How are you going to live in light of here-and-now events and dilemmas, moral and otherwise? Because of these factors, I took the major contemporary sociopolitical conflicts of the 1960s seriously, and for those more current, I still do, although I am less preoccupied by them now. Still, I want to talk critically about some of those events, because in many ways they are still alive within me as well as within the nation. Not all history is just history, as we see with the centuries-long racism of a country birthed in the extremities of genocide and slavery.

America's persistent and ubiquitous war-making stands out as one of its defining characteristics. One of the few things our largely polarized country, its government, and its DC foreign-policy establishment share is a strong predisposition toward aggression and domination. We strive to impose our will and tell other people how to conduct themselves—at least until the preliminaries end and a quagmire of futility and destruction reveals itself. According to the Congressional Research Service, as reported at nationalinterest.org in December 2017, there were 111 American military interventions between 1950 and 1999, and 126 between 2000 and 2017—astounding figures that are accelerating: 2.2 per year from 1950 to 1999 and 7 per year from 2000 to 2017. Mostly these were not massive interventions but numerous they obviously were. The thinking seems to be that the nation's security is unremittingly threatened by hostility from endless enemies before whom we tremble with anxiety that can be soothed only by demonstrating our toughness and stamping out divergence from the Great American Way.[2] The congruence between aggressive behavior, empire building, and cancer-like expansion of the infamous military-industrial complex is a coincidence that receives too little attention from the citizenry.

---

2. In dogs, this is called fear-based aggression. Much of the verbiage coming out of the political and foreign policy establishments sounds consistent with this syndrome but with an admixture of old-fashioned imperialism—the urge to dominate, set the rules, realize economic benefit.

I do not think the fearfulness that leads to national "defense" and other so-called security operations and bureaucracies is necessarily insincere, even if self-centered and misguided. However, their budgets, compared with those in the rest of the world, are astonishing and growing, and they lack evident objective need and discernible positive achievements. It seems pathological and inscrutable in its origins, at least to me. Is it as simple as intoxication with power? The national character? Are we simply a people prone to fearfulness, international ambitions, and violence? Our concomitant efforts to control the world, set its rules, and achieve the "full-spectrum dominance" (most recently referred to as "overmatching") that is supposed to support that project have the happy effect, for those making their home in the M-I complex, of assuaging fear, raising profitability, justifying an overgrown military establishment, and enabling imperialism. And equally, it impoverishes such efforts as there are or might be to take better care of the "homeland" and its citizenry—enabling people to go to college affordably, maintaining our infrastructure, ensuring adequate health care and living conditions for everyone, and investing more in our parks, schools, and libraries, our arts and sciences. The human and monetary costs of our endless wars are immense—since 9/11, Afghans, Iraqis, and others in the Middle East have endured well over a million casualties. The monetary costs incurred to date for the United States alone are projected to exceed $6 trillion before all the debts are paid (according to Brown University's Cost of War Project).

The depth of this "defense" mania is shown, among other instances, in the claims made in 2019 that we had to escalate the Pentagon budget by tens of billions of borrowed dollars owing to our having *neglected* our military, words that were spoken and received with straight faces rather than the appropriate scorn. The money was shoveled toward the Pentagon with hardly a question and despite the Pentagon's inability to pass a financial audit and to account for tens of billions of dollars that were trustingly sent its way over recent years. The mindless juggernaut of militarism always has fuel for just about any trip it wants to take, one of which stops at the nuclear depot to enact a near $2,000,000,000,000 (yup, two trillion dollars) "modernization" over the coming years of our ability to incinerate people and Earth, and I suppose for some to feel secure or potent and others to become richer.

It is hard to talk about this without anger and perplexity. What does the nation really care about? What is its *soul* made of? Within what moral, cultural, or political framework does this pattern fit? What the heck is going on here? When did leadership lose its mind and citizens their critical judgment? Are bankruptcy or destruction the only outcomes that can end this? I recently read several books on prospects for thermonuclear war, including Daniel Ellsberg's *The Doomsday Machine*, his personalized history of the U.S. nuclear weapons complex, where he worked for many of its early years and about which he has many instructive things to say. The doctrine of mutual assured destruction, which incomprehensibly remains our peace-protection policy, is the culmination of what I would call a somewhat novel way of imagining national security. It seems to boil down to, "We will be secure until such time as the policy fails through accident, madness, or misjudgment, and then we die along with much life of all kinds in all places." I suspect that a few reasonably intelligent civilian amateurs could put their heads together and come up with a better policy, since few of us are likely to consider millions of deaths acceptable for any purpose whatever. Any who think I exaggerate the madness in the assumptions and risks incurred within this bizarre realm are urged to read Ellsberg and related literature.

Does no one believe any longer that—morally, strategically, pragmatically—war should be *a last resort* conducted with the least destruction necessary to achieve vital, legitimate aims (such as self-defense) not otherwise procurable and with conscientious rigor to avoid civilian deaths? How has this perpetual, potential violence affected us as a people and why have we accepted it so placidly. I see no way to trust the judgment and intentions of those who maintain the country on a permanent war footing, one that has us fighting somewhere the majority of the time, that thinks we need hundreds of bases large and small (about 800 at last count) scattered across over roughly 150 countries, and that keeps our Special Forces active in over a hundred countries annually. According to the Centre for Research on Globalization, the United States has fought somebody somewhere during 222 out of the 239 years after 1776.[3] Isn't that enough? Isn't it time to give peace a chance? This record may be good for the military-industrial complex, but it is not good for this country or its values and most of all not good for the human and nonhuman bodies that are slain or maimed.

Speaking as one of those civilian amateurs, I set aside critique for a moment and suggest alternatives. I begin by noting that we are a very powerful and rich country, uniquely located, with oceans to east and west and friendly countries to north and south, albeit often uneasy countries owing to the American domination complex. Thus, we have always had less to be afraid of and faced fewer real threats to national security than most other countries. We can relax a bit, take risks, extend helpful hands. An analogy from ecology comes to mind: humans are fundamentally members of the vast life community, not separate, not its owners, not elevated above its natural limits. So, too, the United States is a member of the community of nations, to which our resources may allow us to offer leadership from time to time but that we have no need or right to dominate and bend to

3. "America Has Been at War 93% of the Time—222 Out of 239 Years—Since 1776." Washington's Blog and Global Research, January 20, 2019. https://www.globalresearch.ca/america-has-been-at-war-93-of-the-time-222-out-of-239-years-since-1776/5565946

our will. We can collaborate on behalf of shared interests. We can seek peace peacefully, negotiate, compromise. We can help those who need help and will use it wisely. We can be a model of tending to our own knitting while caring about the community of nations and participating in respectful and appropriate ways. We can mind our own business (which is not the same as "America First") except when circumstances invite us to step peacefully forward and cooperate with others on shared goals. We can maintain a military *sufficient for national defense* but not for running the world. We must eschew the possession and use of excess power; too much power is as toxic to a nation as it is to individuals and groups. We can define our interests more narrowly and our threats more discerningly.

We can be strong, firm, and decisive without bullying. As for mutual assured destruction, we can reject the notion on the grounds of reason and morality, sign on to the UN Treaty on the Prohibition of Nuclear Weapons, and show by action and words our intent to join others in fully complying. It would be a multiyear process of change, but as a sign of sincerity and to encourage cooperation we can begin dismantling weapons unilaterally and divert that two-trillion-dollar "nuclear modernization" boondoggle toward benefiting people rather than preparing to kill them. We must stop the arms race that is beginning to re-erupt and remind ourselves and others about the waste, expense, danger, and futility of the decades-long race that followed World War II and of the need to prevent a recurrence while rolling back existing weaponry.

A large part of who I have become was forged in rejection of Vietnam and subsequent war-making. The folly of militarism would not leave my mind. Therefore I could not escape developing a worldview and values that took it into account. My social ethic as a whole was shaped by it, and I even suspect that other commitments not obviously related, such as my ecocentrism and sense of occupying

a sacred reality, are infused with that early intense staring into the darkness that power, fear, and violence are
prone to put before us. I know how the persistent violence
has affected me, and I wonder how much of our national
callousness is fostered and exacerbated by it. The Buddha
knew about the human suffering brought by ignorance,
desire, and fear. I have been made to feel a version of this,
too, indelibly, along with the rest of the country, although
most may not recognize where it comes from.

We cannot talk about this without remembering 9/11
and the disasters that followed (and follow still), which
were brought on by our knee-jerk violence, our vengeful-
ness, the desire of leaders to use the tragedy for their own
aggressive purposes, and the complacent citizenry that
accepted all this on the grounds that a violent slap to America's face was the equivalent of sacrilege. We forgot how
many foreign faces we had previously slapped with impu-
nity, or so we imagined. Since ours is a putative democracy, we-the-people are accountable for everything done
in the country's name. It can hardly surprise anyone when
some of those who are as violent as we consider all of us
fitting targets, a practice we have indulged toward others
for many years. This is not to defend or exonerate adversaries but to admonish ourselves for failures of empathy and responsible democratic citizenship. How do we
not see that a response to 9/11, even if it had to be briefly
violent, could have been launched and finished by the end
of 2001 or shortly after? We continue making and supporting wars over at least a half dozen countries in the Middle
East, Central Asia, and Northern Africa—including of all
places Afghanistan, *still!*—with little debate or even awareness around the country. We stand at attention, unroll
gargantuan flags to cover football fields, march the color
guard, do the flyover, say "Thank you for your service," and
then sit down with beer-and-burger, or stare into our little
screens, and forget all about it. But the bombed school

buses, hospitals, and wedding parties, the rubbled cities, the errant missiles... Others cannot so easily forget, and in their not forgetting may lie the seeds for 9/11 sequels.

This casual violence can hardly not make you angry, but more than that, what do we learn about the American political process through this and Americans' way of being democratic citizens? How much alienation, how much self-centeredness, how much lost compassion, and how much willingness to have given free rein to a blatantly incompetent and corrupt narcissist as president who claimed he had the answers—How much can we lay at the feet of our militarism and the oligarchy that feeds off it or averts their eyes, as long as their looting of the nation's wealth is allowed to continue? Actions have consequences. I venture to suggest that permitting a ruling class to act as ours does was bound to hurt the nation while alienating people who once admired what it claimed to stand for, many of whom appear to have now pledged their eternal troth to a demagogue and the Party that enables him.

More to the point, though, I write about this not just for polemical reasons or because it has occupied so much of my mind for so long. I want to understand why U.S. policy makers have been allowed to follow this violent path and how it has fit in the psychic worlds of my countrymen and me, how it has shaped our inner and outer experiences. This may put me in the land of the chicken and egg: has our leadership's proclivity for violent means toward its ends been essentially consistent with the public's already existent violent tendency? Or did the militarism appear for some other reason and proceed to shape our nature toward our characteristic acceptance of violence? Option one strikes me as the obvious answer for several reasons. First, America's origins in the early seventeenth century were steeped in violence toward the indigenous peoples, which in cooperation with imported disease had genocidal effects, which were more often welcomed or seen as signs of God's providence than not. Second, we have only to look at the easy fit of slavery, also present from the early 1600s, eventuating in a bloody civil war, followed by decades of post-Reconstruction racially discriminatory laws and law enforcement ("Jim Crow") and lynchings of African-Americans. Third, consider the history of war-making and interventionism discussed above. Fourth, having just read a history of California, a land and eventual state (1850) far removed from the contiguous United States to its east but settled and dominated by immigrant Americans, I learn that a similar pattern in the treatment of nonwhites occurred there: brutality toward Native Americans (whose population declined by over 90 percent), Latinos, Chinese, and when the occasion arose, toward each other. Fifth, the American attitude toward guns, unyielding despite the casualties. Last, consider our relation to the natural world and wildlife, factory-farmed animals and landscapes, water and air—all ravaged and brutalized. We lament today the divisions between red states and blue states, but they are uniformly stained red with the blood of humans, not to mention other animals such as bison, beavers, passenger pigeons, wolves. . .

As for the effects of this brutality on me, clearly it pushed me toward nonviolence. I am grateful to have arrived there, but the violence has been a concerning presence in my consciousness throughout adulthood, which I would have preferred to furnish with items more pleasant. It surely had a seriously alienating effect on the bond I want to feel with my home country. As for American citizens, whose violence toward one another exceeds that of any other advanced nation and of most that aren't, I can only surmise that violence sponsored by this country toward others has left us all either fatalistic or more callous in what may be thought of as simply *the way things are and will always be* in America. I won't try to inventory a lengthy list of symptoms, but just consider our complacency over the millions of casualties since 9/11 in our so-called war on terror; carceral policies that put more people behind bars for longer sentences, more cruelly imposed, than any other country; and our practice during the Trump years of forcibly separating young children from their would-be refugee and immigrant parents at the Mexican border. Chronic war-making abroad has consequences at home. I assume the reverse is true as well, that American violence toward one another helps build a mutually reinforcing process in which we are also readily violent to non-Americans.

I consider my evolution toward pacifism has been for the good. My feeling for others who become victims of our nation's policies is highly sensitized, and my bullshit meter for the claims of our policy promulgators is finely tuned. Advocating peace in all dimensions is one of my central values. I may be alienated from the violent aspects of American culture but not from the human and nonhuman beings who struggle to survive its values and practices.

I became a student at a state university two months before President Kennedy's assassination, which surely goes down as one of the more jarring introductions to the larger world for a very green eighteen-year-old. I still recall heading toward class, learning that the president had been shot, wondering what that meant (the possible assassination of an American president was not yet part of my mental contents), observing how the streets seemed depopulated, finding no one in my or any other classroom, and finally realizing that something extraordinary really had happened. I do not imagine that many late adolescents today consider the shooting of anybody especially remarkable—it is so common—but it was then.

This was followed by President Johnson's important legislative work for civil rights, Medicare, and related social welfare initiatives that was soon and sadly eclipsed by his descent into the mendacity and depravity of Vietnam. Then came the Whitman University of Texas Tower shootings, graduation and facing the military draft, and additional assassinations, which led me to wonder just where and how these things would end, and finally, Nixon's continuation of Johnson's mendacity and war. As I think about this period, I'm surprised to realize that, critical as I've been about many of the ways American society has developed since the 1960s, it has only been in recent years that the directions it has taken finally brought me to what now appears obvious: just as *Homo sapiens* is a flawed species, so too is America a deeply flawed society and not one I can imagine transforming into anything much better within the foreseeable future. [This was written while D. Trump was still in office; it is now a half year since the election. I offer that interim as partial proof of my dismal prophecy.] In all likelihood, its flaws will worsen since the pendulum shows no signs of swinging in the opposite direction. How could it when so many prefer to deny that anything seriously symptomatic is going on or that we must reckon with our national history if we are ever to be free of its pathological aspects?

What does it mean to speak of *Homo sapiens* as flawed? Aren't we obviously the crown of creation? Well, no, that has always been a fatuous and self-serving prejudice; as far as I can tell, creation has no crown. It is one great web of life, arranged in several taxonomical kingdoms, spread out over the Earth—from the depths of the Mariana Trench to the top of Mount Everest, from desert to rainforest, from pole to pole, from subsurface to ethereal stratosphere. It is vibrantly, diversely, and often surprisingly alive, as well as functioning in many ways like a self-regulating organism. The ancient Stoics spoke of Earth and Nature as aspects of *universal nature*, but only aspects; universal nature was commodious and included gods and sources of guidance and meaning. They believed it a rational and providential setting in which the human role was to discern what it wanted of us (rather than what we wanted of it) and to live accordingly. I've always admired that vision. The essential species flaw, particularly evident over the relatively recent millennia, seems to me the ease with which we fall out of congruence, out of coherence, within ourselves and outwardly in relation to existence. When I observe other animals, I notice how naturally they appear to fit with one another and the ecosystems in which they reside, not in a harmony uninterrupted, say, by predation and population expansions and collapses, but in what I can only speak of as the *rightness of their place*, a place that accepts predation and transience as Nature's infallible script; like good Stoics, they live in accordance with it, accepting reality and, I venture, finding it good.

Human intelligence was once spoken of by a famous biologist as a possibly "mutant variation." Did evolution stumble and forget itself, combining great capacity with unlimited ways of screwing up? We carom unendingly along the continua of being: individualism versus community, spirit versus matter, sufficiency versus gluttony, adaptation versus transformation, love versus hate, and so forth, all coinciding with and fostering anxieties and uncertainties that typically we act out harmfully. To paraphrase Pascal, the flaw of falling out of congruence may preclude a human ability *to sit quietly alone in a room*, an inability that he considered the chief source of human sorrow; instead, we smash through the doors and windows and wander blindly, staring at the sun. The generalized spread of inner peace and the solidarity it would allow escapes us.

The American instantiation of falling out of congruence takes it whole cloth and turns it against the Earth and its inherent values, the goods implicit in existence—for example, natural beauty and healthy ecosystems and the lives participant in them—exploiting and replacing their gifts with grifting and grabbing, ego-centered desires and commodified satisfactions. We see the results.

Through the last quarter of the twentieth century, before I fully appreciated the existence and ramifications of our flawed condition, I assumed the possibility of a turn toward a more humane, communitarian, and peaceful nation, but if this potential existed, it did not materialize. The toxic seeds of American history appear to be germinating. Without a well-developed capacity for detachment, one might despair. Among the most visible signs of what I am referring to are these:

- the decline of the public sphere, the common good, and the lost solidarity that typically accompanies a vibrant civic life

- the amassing of vast national wealth diverted to a fraction of the population, further starving the public sphere, depriving the lower classes, and feeding cynicism among all classes and delusory entitlement and cupidity in the privileged realms

- the decline of government as a democratic equalizing force and its transformation into an enabler of plutocracy

- the acceptance by a large proportion of the population of being methodically and persistently lied to and the rejection of information discordant with preferred belief and of anything approaching an objective view of the world

- the dissolution of ethics and accountability within a large swath of the ruling sectors

- the genuine possibility of this country's easing into a form of soft authoritarianism and one-party minority rule in the near future, a prospect once so inconceivable that most people don't seem to notice

One question sums it all up: at the national level, where can one find a single, widely supported, uplifting initiative or vision that attracts enthusiasm and conviction that a cohesive, caring nation could be born—a nation committed to the welfare of all citizens equally? If a vision of this sort dared to emerge, how many would get behind it? How could it be achieved?

As I look back I acknowledge naiveté, especially in my largely unconscious confidence that in considering sociopolitical and related issues most people would think things through, discern facts, form different but informed opinions, and approach fellow citizens in a spirit of fair debate, goodwill, and trust in democratic consensus.[4] I suppose there have been periods in American history when that was somewhat true, but the present is certainly not one of them. Merely writing the words reveals how far we are from that ideal, one that we can never fully accomplish but that we set aside at our peril. Trust and mutual respect are far more easily broken than restored.

It's impossible to paint a picture of such apparent cultural malaise without asking how it came to be that way. Much of it has worsened coincidental with my lifetime (not to suggest it sprang forth ex nihilo), so I'm naturally curious and must consider how much I've done, in any small way, to affect the process, for better or worse. And posing that question leads to another: what does this decline mean for the lives led in its midst? I believe that the anciently described highest values of truth, goodness, and beauty, which may sound abstract but that refer to real presences and absences with ethical force, are so entwined that when one of them suffers the others hurt as well. When I speak of cultural decline I refer to these values and the forms of their expression, values that permeate the measures of decline listed above. These are difficult issues to comprehend,

---

4. This was a mistake I believe President Obama made and couldn't seem to get past, which made his administration a disappointment.

bound to compose a tapestry of many threads and colors when sorted and fathomed. One marker of the transit from youth into adulthood is said to be movement away from idealism toward "realism," but really, now, would anybody consider the described changes normal or predicted or even "real" in any genuine sense of the word? It isn't, for example, that mendacity hasn't always had a secure place in our political and economic life—Vietnam plus big tobacco and the petrochemical industry's eagerness to trade lives for profit and other follies are exemplars. But just as there's a significant difference between tippling and binging, there's also a difference between even the grave lies of Vietnam, Philip Morris, and ExxonMobil and the full-bodied, bald-faced, shameless deceptions that have become our regular fare today.

No, I'm wrong about that; the political and corporate lies were equally serious and perhaps were the early flames that burst into our contemporary conflagrations. Before the Bush administration official who famously spoke disdainfully of the "reality-based community" in contrast to the world he imagined he occupied, where true reality was generated, I don't recall anyone who denied the very existence of facts and evidence. The fall has been precipitous, downward into the darkness, and we are still falling. Some would have us accept the situation as simply alternative facts or viewpoints, or perhaps a new form of language—Confabulated Esperanto for Dummies, it might be called. But that won't wash for anyone who knows we suffer a malignancy in the sabotage of truth and the promotion of lies. This is only one dimension of our loss, but a particularly serious one owing to its ramifications: the effects on discourse, the subversion of trust, the rejection of moral norms. Truthlessness is ugly and does not reflect well on those who tolerate being lied to. It has also, I believe, meant less satisfactory lives for the majority of us, the citizenry. Most (I hope) would prefer solidarity, but we are divided. We would like to think the system is fair, but we see that it tilts radically toward the greater benefit of a few. It would take some getting used to among Americans, but I expect most would prefer peace to war and to hearing the unending reasons the foreign-policy establishment concocts to keep the wars going. We want our children to have bright futures in more than material dimensions, but it is doubtful now they will have such futures in any dimension. People would enjoy the basic security that a rich society could provide all of us but instead inhabit a society where basic needs are left to chance and egalitarian sharing depicted in the frightful aura of dreaded socialism. The majority, according to polls, live from paycheck to paycheck in constant economic anxiety; sad to say, large numbers have been convinced that that's really the best kind of society, since people are said to get what they deserve and always have the free will to choose to do better.

I was gifted with curiosity and a desire to know the truth, so if I am told anything that seems at all questionable, I seek other information sources for validation or invalidation. But what are the effects of all this deception and balderdash on the mental lives of those not sufficiently curious or too trusting about what to support and what to reject? What to furnish their interior landscapes with? I lay the primary blame at the feet of materialism (money-mind and will to power) and egoism, which have supplanted the lost values of spirit and community. I blame capitalistic excess and the wealth-power nexus it leads to and unceasingly promotes, to the elevation of matter over spirit. As I look back forty years, more or less, the signs are apparent that those having or seeking wealth-power were already shifting into gear and doing all they could to disguise their intentions, which were to promote the maldistribution of society's wealth and to disable a corrective government response. They have succeeded, and society has metastasized into the garish extremes of economic inequality that face us today, the highest in the Western world. "Devil take the hindmost" for those who don't do so well in this merciless business; "to the victor belong the spoils" for the others. My egalitarian, communitarian spirit recoils.

If patriotism means love of country, what happens when that love is unrequited or when it is betrayed by an adulterous, so to speak, government? Love of country, like love of spouse or team, must be earned—it is the result of a respectful, mutually beneficial relationship. This is why the manipulation of ersatz patriotism that has become common at athletic contests is offensive and irrelevant to true, well-founded patriotism. It is a thinly disguised advertisement for the military and its endless wars.[5]

I acknowledge that I no longer *love* America. I love large chunks of its landscape beyond words. And yet, they struggle to survive in this commodity-driven culture. I love the people who see the falsities and actively resist them. I love humane, democratic, egalitarian, nonviolent, communitarian, peace-seeking values and could love a country and government that strove to embody them. Some parents have to watch helplessly as a grown child slips farther and farther into failure and degradation, but they continue to love the connection they have had and the potential they want to believe is still there. In that sense, one might love America, but hope is hard to hold on to.

If there are such things as nearly sacred human endeavors, one of them should be public service, along, in less formalized ways, with any efforts expended for the good of others rather than self. Having worked my entire career in private nonprofit organizations, I include these within public service. It's fair to say that many of those who work in the nonprofit realm feel that nonprofits

5. The cooked-up controversy over football players' taking a knee during the national anthem as a reminder that the nation does not serve all citizens equally and serves some hardly at all or even, instead, violently—the Trumped-up falsity and pretense that patriotic honor was besmirched—is just another instance of disingenuous imagery in the name of distraction.

carry special responsibilities both because of their organizational missions and because they generally owe their
existence to donations, to people believing in their work
enough to share their resources of time (as volunteers) and
money. Governmental work—the public sector's public
service—ought also to be considered a sort of sacred trust.
It is conceived not as work for profit but for community
and national well-being. I've met countless civil servants
who feel this way about the work they do. But then there's
the political sphere of the public sector. One might expect
politicians to feel even more deeply the values implicit in
having been chosen by constituents in trust that the public
good will guide their behavior and who swear an oath to
that effect.

I believe these values are intrinsic to government
and private nonprofit work. However much the specifically political component may betray these values and
however resigned the public becomes to their failure (and
shares responsibility for its continuance through failing to
enforce accountability), I retain my belief, but certainly no
longer the expectation or even the hope. Only during this
century has the full force of my disillusionment come home
to me, but it makes sense that the seeds of realization
began to take form during those earlier years of Vietnam
and its sequels. People speak of the events of 9/11 having
"changed everything," but I believe those changes have
been largely manipulated, artificial ones contrived to suit
powerful political interests that have carried along much
of the trusting citizenry while gathering a momentum that
few seem to question and fewer challenge. In short, 9/11
changed nothing fundamental in this country's operations.
The "war on terror" has been a war on rationality and truth.
The Vietnam War's depravity brought changes that were
organic and that have infused society ever since; this latest
iteration—in Afghanistan, Iraq, northern Africa, and in
military intrusions all around the Earth—follows the same

path. The shame that should be felt has been avoided so far, but the broken trust persists.

Four generations have been born in the time since World War II ended, mine followed by three others.[6] It has become clear to me as I've thought more intensely about those years that we have all lived in the presence of two stories about the kind of people we are and the sort of country of which we are citizens. The first, intended for public consumption, issues mostly from the "ruling class"—a great term the story tells us not to use but that is wonderfully descriptive and evocative—and is suffused with nostalgic pabulum. According to this story, which far too many have swallowed mostly whole, America is a great democracy, an exceptional country, a place of freedom and equality where anyone with gumption can get ahead. As a nation we stride the world, cloaked in righteous altruism, wanting the best for everyone and intervening in others' affairs only to help set things right, which should be obvious to any of them who have clarity of understanding. Sometimes we declare the intervention necessary for our own national security, but few on the other end suffer who do not deserve to suffer. Whether at home or abroad, our leaders assure American citizens that they always act with our welfare uppermost through established democratic processes. It's a great country despite occasional miscues—honest mistakes, really, failures of good intention; it's all for one and one for all, and we're damned lucky to live here, where free-market democracy ensures the best for everyone, or at least the best they have earned.

The other story is reality, the real world that, thanks to a national proclivity toward self-satisfying delusions, is unnoticed by the majority and accepted with fatalistic

---

6. Generations X, Y, Z, and whatever else isn't my interest; I speak of generations as traditionally demarcated, roughly twenty-five years each, which naturally wraps in all those end-of-the-alphabet cohorts.

resignation by others. In this story—not much spoken of but that sits in the room like an elephant that we've learned to look past—culture and social welfare have been cannibalized by the economy. Nothing is allowed to disturb the economy in its beneficent dynamism (except for its occasional breakdowns). It is a powerful wealth generator but bad for individuals and communities. Unending militarism and interventionism are disguised as national defense. Our caste system tries to hide itself or deny its very existence. The public realm, the realm of schools, parks, roads, libraries—all those places and programs that benefit everyone who needs or uses them equally—shrinks and degrades as resources are concentrated among a small segment of the very wealthy. And so on… This reality has made for lesser lives than could have been lived due to the opportunity costs of too-low taxes on the wealthy, distorted priorities, and a culture of fear and social fragmentation. The disingenuous bromides issuing from story #1 have obscured the national leadership's betrayal of the common good. And these leaders have told that story so convincingly that people still accept much of it as true, more or less.[7] So the responsibility is both ours as complacent, trusting citizens and the ruling class's for its propagation of story #1 while merrily scooping up as much of the system's spoils for themselves as they could get away with. The ruling class has squandered possible goods, existential as well as material, of the country while driving a failed political system toward one-party rule built on a hollowed-out simulacrum of democracy. Our national

---

7. In fairness, much of Trump's appeal to his "base" was his dishonest claim to recognize national failure in this respect and to be the one man who could fix it. Unfortunately, the Trump "cure" has only added pathogens to the bloodstream of the body politic; it was merely a continuation of story #1 in a new, demagogic guise. The Trumpian vision of victimization, his and theirs, is a curious add-on. Parenthetically, I must add that I used "Big Lie" (below) before it came to describe the Republican denial of Biden's victory; it fits for both uses.

reality, the disregarded story #2, will not be confronted until such time, if it could possibly happen, when a new story, a new vision, arises among the people. But that is unlikely to happen until ordinary individuals comprehend the Big Lie under which they have lived and that has treated them as mere resources, as workers and consumers, as serf-like cogs. Militarism, violence, and other societal ills can be seen as expressions of the dire situation that causes our plight—that is, a situation of deception by governing oligarchs and plutocrats preserving their privilege by suppressing citizen yearning for a common good in any way necessary.

There are many measures of societies' health these days. You can find independent reports, based on international studies, that identify our flawed democracy, the extent of loneliness, the decline of happiness, and probably more if you have the spirit to pursue it. It can hardly be denied that the United States is a culture and society in decline with mounting casualties; the evidence shows up in the measures of all these reports. I have presented my version of the indictment. Others can present their own. Each will emphasize one factor over another, but collectively I have not found much divergence except from those who benefit from the present situation or those who either have come to accept it as normal or who are in denial. My critique arises during the last chapter of my life. It does not sit beside a perception of an earlier golden age, for I have experienced none. I am pleased to say, though, that my gloomy picture of contemporary America does not dim my satisfaction at having lived a good life anyway; it simply adds sadness and disappointment to the picture. I discovered in that good life the sacredness implicit in *being* and the astonishing opportunity I had to experience and be grateful for it. This is the note I choose to end on, except for one last observation. I write now over a year into the Covid-19 pandemic and the cracks, failures, and defects of the American Way have shown themselves graphically and in numerical measures of infection and death. Myths collapse, reality hits us in the face. Our house is built on sand. Who will lead the response to the cultural crisis and in what direction?

Made in the USA
Middletown, DE
03 December 2022

16808501R00222